The Unbound Organisation

Building Cultures of Connection, Courage, and Compassion

Dr John McSwiney

https://www.timetotransform.world

McSwiney, John (author)

Title: *The Unbound Organisation: Building Cultures of Connection, Courage and Compassion* / Dr John McSwiney, author.

Illustrations: Canva

ISBN: 978-1-7643962-1-9

Leadership Transformation
Organisational Wellbeing
Emotional Intelligence
Workplace Culture
Heart-Centred Leadership
Corporate Renewal
Mindful Management

DEDICATION

To every leader who dares to pause. To every team member who chooses heart over haste. To every organisation brave enough to ask, *"What if we led differently?"* This book is for those who know that progress without purpose is hollow, and that the real future of work is not built in spreadsheets, it is grown in the human spirit.

To the quiet changemakers, who listen more than they speak, who lift others without needing credit, who choose integrity when it is inconvenient, you are the pulse of the Unbound movement.

To those standing at the edge of transformation, ready to let go of what no longer serves, may these pages remind you that it is not too late to return to what matters most, to your people, your purpose, and your heart.

For those who lead not just with strategy, but with soul, this is your invitation to become Unbound.

FRONT COVER

The Living System – A Visual Invitation to the Unbound Way

The cover of *The Unbound Organisation* was designed with intention, not as decoration, but as a visual embodiment of the philosophy within these pages. It features an **aqua-blue river** dividing into two branches, framed by **rock and forest**, enclosed in a **gold frame**, set against a **royal navy-blue background**. Every element carries meaning, mirroring the journey of transformation this book invites you to take.

The River – Flow, Connection, and Renewal

The river represents the living energy of an organisation, fluid, adaptive, and interdependent. Its movement symbolises the constant flow of creativity, trust, and communication that keeps a system alive. The river does not resist the terrain; it shapes and is shaped by it. In this way, it reflects an Unbound Organisation's capacity to move with change rather than against it, finding strength in responsiveness instead of rigidity. The **split in the river** speaks to adaptability, the capacity to evolve in multiple directions while remaining connected to a shared source. It reminds you that coherence, not control, is what holds people and purpose together.

The Shoreline and Forest – Structure and Humanity

The **rocky shoreline** represents the structures and systems that give an organisation its form. They are not barriers but boundaries, the edges that guide the flow of energy. The **forest**, lush and alive, symbolises the people within the organisation, diverse, dynamic, and growing toward light. It reminds every reader that organisations thrive not through procedures alone, but through the wellbeing, creativity, and heart of their people. Together, the river and forest create balance: systems and souls, process and purpose, the harmony at the heart of being Unbound.

The Gold Frame – Conscious Structure

The **gold frame** surrounding the image conveys value, illumination, and wisdom. It represents conscious structure, frameworks that support life without suffocating it. Gold also carries spiritual resonance: it is the colour of awakening, reminding leaders that integrity, compassion, and self-awareness are the true measures of success. The frame does not confine the river; it honours it, reflecting the idea that effective leadership provides clarity and focus, not limitation.

The Royal Navy Blue – Depth, Presence, and Calm Authority

The **royal navy-blue background** gives the design depth and presence. Blue is the colour of trust, stability, and reflection. It evokes the night sky and the deep ocean, places of stillness and expansion. For readers, this tone sets the emotional stage: stepping into *The Unbound Organisation* is like entering calm water after a long swim against the current. It signals that this book is not about working harder, but about leading from stillness and presence.

The Tagline – Building Cultures of Connection, Courage, and Compassion

This tagline embodies the heartbeat of the book. It speaks to the kind of workplaces and leaders the world now needs, those who build trust before performance, lead with empathy before authority, and prioritise courage over compliance.

1. **Connection** reminds us that every organisation thrives through relationships, between people, purpose, and shared values.

2. **Courage** acknowledges that transformation requires honesty, vulnerability, and the bravery to question old systems that no longer serve.

3. **Compassion** represents the humanity at the centre of all sustainable progress, the understanding that people, not policies, are what make organisations truly exceptional.

Together, these three forces form a new kind of organisational intelligence: one that balances wellbeing and performance, structure and soul, growth and grace. In Essence *The Unbound Organisation* calls leaders, teams, and organisations to reimagine what it means to lead, to belong, and to build. It reminds us that the future of work depends not on control, but on coherence, not on speed, but on presence. Building Cultures of Connection, Courage, and Compassion is not just a tagline. It is a declaration. A living invitation to create workplaces that breathe, people who feel seen, and systems that grow, unbound, authentic, and alive.

Why the Cover Matters

This cover is not simply a visual, it is an invitation. It invites you to reimagine what an organisation can be: not a machine to maintain, but a living system to nurture. It reminds you that beauty and purpose are not luxuries in leadership, they are the foundation of meaning, belonging, and sustainable success. The river, forest, and frame together form a meditation on the central truth of this book: **that when people and purpose flow together, organisations come alive.**

The cover of The Unbound Organisation is more than an image, it is the first reflection in the mirror of your own leadership. A reminder that every system, like every river, becomes clearer when it is allowed to flow from the heart.

ACKNOWLEDGMENTS

This book was not written alone. It is the result of countless conversations, collaborations, and quiet moments shared with people who have lived, led, and believed in the possibility of something more human, an organisation with a heart. To every leader, colleague, and student who has allowed me to witness their journey of transformation, thank you. Your courage to question, to grow, and to reconnect with what truly matters has been the living proof that the Unbound way is not a theory, but a practice. To the extraordinary people I have worked alongside across education, government, business, and community, your stories, insights, and authenticity have shaped every module of this work. You reminded me that leadership is not about titles, but tone; not about control, but connection.

Finally, to every reader who dares to pause, reflect, and begin again, this book is yours. May it remind you that the future of leadership will not be built through force, but through flow, and may you always remember that the most powerful organisations, like the most powerful people, are those that lead from the heart. With gratitude, respect, and quiet hope, may you continue the journey of becoming Unbound.

Personal Message

PERSONAL MESSAGE FROM DR JOHN

When I began writing *The Unbound Organisation*, I was not trying to design a new model for business, I was trying to understand why so many good people were losing themselves inside systems that once inspired them. I have sat in boardrooms, classrooms, and community halls across the world, and no matter where I go, the story is the same. People want to contribute. They want to care. They want their work to matter, but somewhere between the metrics and the meetings, something essential, something human, gets lost. This book was born from that longing to remember. To remember that leadership is a human art. That wellbeing and performance are not opposites but partners. That organisations, like people, are living systems, capable of renewal, compassion, and growth. *The Unbound Organisation* is an invitation, not to work harder, but to work more consciously. It is about finding flow again: between purpose and profit, structure and spirit, the head and the heart. It asks you to see your organisation as alive, not mechanical; as relational, not transactional; as a space where people can breathe, belong, and become. If there is one message I hope you carry from these pages, it is this: **the health of any system begins in the heart of its people.** May you lead with calm, create with courage, and remember that the most powerful transformations begin quietly, in awareness, in presence, in the simple act of being human together.

With gratitude for every person who chooses to lead with heart, this book is for you.

WHAT IS AN UNBOUND ORGANISATION?

A Living System of Heart, Humanity, and High Performance

There comes a moment in the life of every organisation when it must pause and ask, *Who are we becoming?* Are we merely operating efficiently, or are we evolving consciously? Are we managing systems, or are we nurturing souls? An **Unbound Organisation** is not defined by its size, sector, or structure, it is defined by its state of being. It is an organisation that has remembered its humanity. It functions not as a machine to be driven but as a living ecosystem to be cultivated, one that breathes, adapts, and evolves in rhythm with its people and purpose.

From Bound to Unbound

Bound organisations operate through control, compliance, and convention. They rely on rigid hierarchies, fear-based motivation, and performance measured only by metrics. While efficient, they often become brittle, unable to adapt, innovate, or truly engage the human heart. Unbound organisations, by contrast, are fluid, conscious, and heart-led. They value alignment over adherence, creativity over compliance, and connection over command. They understand that emotional intelligence is not a soft skill, it is the bloodstream of sustainable success. To be Unbound is to lead from trust, not tension. It is to build frameworks that liberate potential rather than confine it. It is to create cultures where wellbeing, belonging, and purpose are not programs, but daily practices. *An Unbound Organisation does not just meet objectives, it awakens potential.*

The Four Dimensions of the Unbound Organisation

1. **Heart-Led Leadership**: In Unbound Organisations, leadership is not a title, it is a tone. You lead through presence, through listening, through

the courage to be authentic. Leaders cultivate emotional literacy, humility, and trust, recognising that people follow not power, but sincerity.

2. **Human-Centred Culture**: The Unbound Organisation builds culture around care, not control. Wellbeing, inclusion, and psychological safety become operational imperatives, not optional extras. People feel seen, valued, and empowered to bring their full selves to work, because that is where innovation lives.

3. **Purpose in Motion**: Purpose in an Unbound Organisation is not a statement on a wall; it is a pulse that moves through every decision. When teams align their daily actions to a shared "why," energy replaces exhaustion. The organisation shifts from reactive to regenerative.

4. **Ecosystem Intelligence**: Unbound Organisations see themselves as part of a wider system, communities, environments, industries, and act with awareness of their impact. They collaborate rather than compete, contribute rather than consume. Their growth is not extractive but expansive, enriching both people and planet.

The Evidence Behind the Unbound Way

The Unbound model integrates leading research from organisational psychology, neuroscience, and leadership science. It draws upon emotional regulation, psychological safety, positive organisational scholarship, and the biology of trust, the evidence that proves heart-based cultures outperform transactional ones in every measurable domain: engagement, retention, creativity, and innovation, but beyond the data lies something deeper, a knowing. You feel it when you walk into an Unbound Organisation. There is a calm energy, a sense of shared purpose, a quiet confidence that people are not surviving work, they are growing through it.

The Journey of Becoming

Becoming Unbound is not a change initiative, it is a transformation journey. It starts with individuals reclaiming self-awareness and ripples outward until it reshapes the entire organisational field. It requires courage, to question, to unlearn, to forgive outdated patterns. It requires humility, to listen deeply, to experiment, to hold space for uncertainty, and it requires heart, the willingness to lead with empathy, integrity, and vision, even when the path ahead is not linear.

The Unbound Organisation is not built, it is grown.

A Reflection for Leaders

Ask yourself:

1. Are we creating a culture that people have to recover from, or one that helps them recover?

2. Do we measure what matters most, or only what is easiest to count?

3. Are we inspiring compliance, or awakening contribution?

If you find yourself asking these questions, you are already on the path, because awareness is where transformation begins.

To lead an Unbound Organisation is to lead a living conversation, between purpose and people, between performance and presence, between what is and what is possible.

The Unbound Series

Oath

YOUR UNBOUND ORGANISATION OATH

The choice of an oath, rather than a policy, declaration, or leadership code, is intentional. An oath reaches deeper than compliance, it speaks to conscience. It cannot be mandated or measured; it must be lived. This version (like all the Unbound Series Oaths) preserves the sacred tone of personal accountability but extends it into the collective context of organisational life, honouring leadership, wellbeing, and shared humanity. It recognises that transformation begins not in systems or structures, but in the integrity of those who lead and serve within them. By taking this oath, you acknowledge that the health of an organisation is inseparable from the health of its people, and that culture is not crafted through words alone but through presence, example, and care. You understand that your leadership, whatever form it takes, is an act of stewardship, a commitment to nurture safety, inclusion, and possibility for all who share this space with you. This oath is both personal and collective. It is your individual promise to live with awareness, and your shared pledge to help create workplaces that breathe, cultures that empower growth, compassion, and authentic human connection. It is a reminder that being "Unbound" is not about breaking rules; it is about freeing potential, yours and others'. When you speak these words, you stand alongside a growing community of Unbound Leaders, individuals who believe that organisations can be both productive and peaceful, ambitious and kind, structured and soulful. Together, you form the living heart of The Unbound Organisation, one that leads with humanity, coherence, and courage.

Your Oath

I, [Your Name], on this [Date], choose to lead and live as part of **The Unbound Organisation - [Name]**.

1. **I commit** to leading with presence, to breathe before I act, to listen before I speak, and to honour the humanity within every interaction.

2. **I promise** to nurture cultures of safety, inclusion, and respect, where people feel seen, heard, and valued for who they are.

3. **I vow** to balance performance with wellbeing, recognising that true excellence flows from a calm, connected, and compassionate heart.

4. **I choose** to challenge what no longer serves, systems, beliefs, or behaviours, and to create space for renewal, creativity, and truth.

5. **I commit** to self-reflection and growth, holding the mirror to my own assumptions, biases, and blind spots with humility and care.

6. **I promise** to practise forgiveness, to repair relationships with grace, and to cultivate trust through empathy, accountability, and consistency.

7. **I vow** to lead with kindness and compassion, knowing that leadership without love is motion without meaning.

8. **I choose** to live and lead Unbound, free from fear, open to growth, and guided always by integrity, curiosity, and heart.

This is my **Unbound Organisation Oath**, a sacred promise to lead consciously, connect authentically, and help shape a world of work where wellbeing and purpose move in rhythm, and humanity becomes our greatest measure of success.

HOW TO USE THIS BOOK

A Guide for Leaders, Teams, and Cultures Ready to Evolve

This book is not a manual to be followed; it is a living framework to be felt, explored, and applied. *The Unbound Organisation* is designed to meet you, and your workplace, exactly where you are. It invites reflection, conversation, and transformation, not just in the systems you lead but in the way you show up within them. Each section has been carefully structured to support both personal growth and collective renewal. Whether you're a senior leader, a manager, or a team member seeking a deeper sense of meaning and connection at work, you will find practices and perspectives here that can be integrated immediately into your daily rhythm. This is not about adding more tasks to your list. It is about bringing greater awareness, heart, and humanity to the work you already do.

1. Read with Presence, Not Pressure

Move slowly. Let each idea breathe. You do not need to finish this book in a single reading, in fact, you are encouraged not to. The Unbound approach is cyclical, not linear. Read one section, reflect on it, and observe how it shows up in your workplace or leadership. Use pauses as practice. After each module, take a moment to journal, discuss, or simply notice how your body and emotions respond. Transformation begins not when you finish reading, but when the message begins to live through you.

2. Engage with the Practices

Throughout the book, you will find Modules with **guided reflections, heart-based exercises**, and **evidence-informed frameworks** drawn from organisational psychology, emotional intelligence, and leadership science, as outlined and presented in the Book – *Time to Transfortm: Living Unbound.*

These practices are designed for real-world application, in meetings, strategy sessions, mentoring conversations, or moments of quiet self-inquiry. You can work through them yourself, within teams, or as part of an organisational development program. Where appropriate, you will also see connections to national and professional standards, including the **Australian Qualifications Framework (AQF)**, **ASQA**, **NSQHS**, and the **APS Capability Framework**, ensuring your journey is recognised not only personally but professionally.

3. Reflect, Integrate, and Share

At the end of each section, take time to reflect using the **"Unbound Reflections"** prompts. These questions are not tests; they are invitations. They help you uncover insights, explore resistance, and translate awareness into action. You may choose to bring these reflections into team meetings, wellbeing workshops, or leadership retreats. When discussed openly, they become catalysts for deeper trust and authenticity within your organisational culture.

4. Apply Through Conversation, Not Compliance

This is not a book of rules. It is a book of reconnection. You are encouraged to use the language, practices, and frameworks here as starting points for dialogue, not directives. Change unfolds through conversation: between leaders and teams, colleagues and clients, humans and their own hearts. Use this book to open those conversations, with curiosity, compassion, and courage.

5. Make It Your Own

Every organisation is unique, and every leader brings their own rhythm. You may wish to read this book from start to finish or focus on one part that resonates most deeply:

- **Part 1: Workplace Wellbeing Reset** - restoring calm and clarity.
- **Part 2: Diversity & Inclusion through the Heart** - building belonging and compassion.
- **Part 3: The Corporate Reset** - releasing, renewing, and realigning purpose.

Whichever path you choose, remember: there is no single right way to lead Unbound. There is only your way, guided by awareness, anchored in integrity, and expressed through action.

6. Return Often

This book is meant to be revisited. Each time you return to it, you will meet it from a deeper level of awareness. What felt abstract will become practical. What once seemed simple will feel profound. Keep it close, on your desk, in your boardroom, or beside your morning coffee. Let it be a reminder that the true measure of leadership is not how much you control, but how deeply you connect.

A Final Word

You hold in your hands more than a leadership book. You hold an invitation to transform the way you and your organisation breathe, grow, and belong. Approach this work with openness. Bring your full humanity. The Unbound Organisation is not something you build it is something you become.

Read slowly. Reflect deeply. Lead with heart.

THE PROFESSIONAL ASSURANCE BEHIND THE UNBOUND SERIES

When you hold a book from the *Unbound Series* in your hands, you are not holding another self-development text, you are engaging with a nationally aligned, evidence-informed framework for transformation. Each page, principle, reflection, and capability within these works has been consciously mapped to Australia's highest learning and leadership standards: the **Australian Qualifications Framework (AQF)**, the **Australian Skills Quality Authority (ASQA)**, the **National Safety and Quality Health Service (NSQHS)** Standards, and the **Australian Public Sector (APS) Integrated Leadership System (ILS)**.

This alignment ensures that the Unbound journey, whether personal, professional, or organisational, is **legitimate, measurable, and transferable**. It means the growth you experience through these pages is not abstract or anecdotal, but grounded in the same principles of quality, rigour, and ethical practice that guide the nation's most trusted education, health, and leadership systems. The *Unbound* methodology stands apart because it bridges **heart and evidence**, translating emotional intelligence, compassion, and authenticity into assessable professional capabilities. Each program is built on decades of applied experience across education, health, governance, and corporate leadership, ensuring that transformation is not just inspired, but **validated, replicable, and sustainable**.

At the centre of this assurance sits *Time to Transform: Living Unbound – The Evidence Companion*, the scholarly and scientific foundation that underpins the entire *Unbound* ecosystem. Developed from a 30-module emotional-intelligence and wellbeing program (2024–2025), the *Evidence Companion* provides the **academic architecture and evaluation framework** that legitimises the Unbound practices for both professional and peer-reviewed application. Where the *Unbound* books invite transformation, the *Evidence Companion* provides the proof. It houses thirty analytical essays, one per *Living Unbound* practice, each combining theory, neuroscience, and practical application. Together, they:

- Map emotional and leadership competencies to national frameworks (AQF, ASQA, NSQHS, APS ILS).

- Integrate insights from neuroscience, psychology, and leadership studies into applied, evidence-based practice.

- Offer implementation tools, fidelity checklists, and psychometric measures (WHO-5, PANAS, PSS-10, optional HRV).

- Provide logic models, data rubrics, and reporting templates to ensure every Unbound program can be delivered with transparency, accountability, and measurable impact.

This alignment does not imply endorsement, it ensures **professional legitimacy**. It confirms that Unbound learning outcomes mirror the competencies sought in today's most capable leaders, educators, carers, and changemakers. Every *Unbound* title, from *Heart Unbound* to *The Unbound Organisation*, is both **mirror and manual**: a bridge between reflection and application, between emotional depth and operational excellence. Whether you are leading teams, teaching students, healing others, or rediscovering yourself, you will find tools that are **recognised, credible, and human-centred**.

By choosing this path, you affirm your commitment to lead, live, and serve not only with intellect and skill, but with integrity and heart. This is transformation with structure, soul with standards. It is nationally benchmarked, globally relevant, and deeply human. Welcome to the *Unbound Series*, a continuum of evidence-based, heart-led transformation where growth is recognised, wisdom is measurable, and your evolution truly matters.

INTRODUCTION

A New Way of Seeing Work, Leadership, and Yourself

There comes a moment in every organisation and within every leader when something no longer feels right. The meetings still happen, the goals are met, the metrics move, and yet, beneath the rhythm of achievement, something deeper begins to stir. You feel it, that quiet sense of misalignment. You are working harder than ever, yet feeling less alive.Maybe you have seen it in your team's eyes too, the fatigue behind the focus, the stillness behind the smiles. It is what happens when people spend too long surviving systems that were built for speed but not for soul. When we measure success by productivity alone, we begin to lose sight of the human pulse that makes it all possible. *The Unbound Organisation* invites you to pause. To breathe. To see that burnout, disconnection, and exhaustion are not personal failures, they are feedback. They are signals that the system itself is ready to evolve, that you are ready to lead and live differently.

Why You Are Here

You are here because something in you already knows there is another way. You know that leadership doesn't have to mean pressure without presence, and that progress doesn't have to come at the cost of peace. This book exists to remind you of what you already sense: that work can be alive again. That people, including you, can feel valued, inspired, and connected through purpose. For decades, organisations have been engineered for efficiency, but you are not an engine. You are a living system, intelligent, adaptive, relational, emotional. You thrive through coherence, not chaos. Through trust, not tension. Through heart, not haste. The Unbound Organisation is not a framework you impose, it is a way of being you remember. It begins inside you, then ripples outward into the culture, the team, and the systems you touch.

Your Journey in These Pages

Across the modules ahead, you will explore how to bring balance, presence, and humanity back into your organisation, and into yourself. You will see how emotional intelligence, compassion, and wellbeing are not soft skills, but the foundations of sustainable leadership and collective excellence. The journey unfolds through three dimensions of renewal:

- **The Workplace Wellbeing Reset** – where you learn to restore calm, clarity, and energy in a world that never stops moving.

- **Diversity & Inclusion through the Heart** – where inclusion becomes something lived, not legislated.

- **The Corporate Reset** – where you release what no longer serves and make space for what truly matters.

Each part is both personal and practical. Together, they form the rhythm of a new kind of organisation, one that breathes, grows, and leads with heart.

Becoming Unbound

To be Unbound is to let go of old ways of working, the ones that equate worth with output and leadership with control. It is to remember that the future of work is not about speed; itis about awareness. That the most courageous leaders are not those who push hardest, but those who pause long enough to reconnect with what is real. An Unbound Organisation does not reject structure; it realigns it. It does not slow progress; it makes it sustainable. It does not weaken performance; it restores purpose. When you lead Unbound, you discover that calm is not the opposite of action, it is the foundation of it. That trust is not earned through control, but through presence, and that the true power of leadership comes from coherence, when your values, your people, and your vision begin to move as one. *To lead Unbound is to remember that every system, like every heart, beats strongest when it is free to breathe.*

Your Invitation

As you step into this book, give yourself permission to slow down. Read not as an academic exercise, but as a reflection. This is not a book about management, it is about meaning. It is not about changing everything overnight, it is about returning to what truly matters. You do not need to start over. You simply need to start awake. Ask yourself:

1. What would it look like if our workplace became a space for humanity to flourish?

2. What if leadership was less about control and more about connection?

3. What if success felt like alignment, not exhaustion?

This is where your journey begins. Not with a new strategy, but with a single breath, because the health of your organisation, like the health of your heart, begins with awareness. *The Unbound Organisation begins wherever you choose to lead differently, with heart, with honesty, and with hope.*

PART 1 - WORKPLACE WELLBEING RESET

Cultivating Calm, Clarity, and Presence in the Heart of Work

(Time to Transform: Living Unbound - Chapters — 1-Breathing • 8-Nutrition • 21-Relaxation • 11-Grounding)

The Pulse of the Modern Organisation

Every organisation beats with the rhythm of its people, with your rhythm. The pulse of performance is not found in spreadsheets or profit margins, but in your capacity to stay well, clear, and connected. You are the system's breath, its intelligence, its heart. When your rhythm becomes strained, when exhaustion replaces engagement, when tension replaces trust, and when disconnection seeps into the spaces between colleagues, the organisation weakens. The numbers may still move, but meaning fades quietly from the work. What once felt purposeful becomes mechanical. Productivity turns into motion without intention. Creativity narrows into repetition, and slowly, you withdraw behind screens, tasks, and silence. This is the hidden cost of modern work: the erosion of inner equilibrium. You live in a world that rewards speed over stillness and output over awareness. Yet beneath the surface of all that striving lies a truth too easily forgotten, you are not a machine. You are a rhythmic, emotional, relational being. Your ability to perform depends on your ability to pause, to restore, and to reconnect. For too long, workplaces have treated wellbeing as a bonus, a seminar, a token initiative, or a policy on paper, but true organisational health is not achieved through programs alone. It is cultivated through culture, through a shared permission that says, *"It is safe to breathe here. It is safe to rest. It is safe to be human."*

The Unbound Organisation begins with that truth: the health of your organisation is inseparable from your own. When you learn to manage your

22

energy, regulate your emotions, and align your actions with shared purpose, you contribute to a culture that thrives, one heartbeat at a time. This is not about slowing down for the sake of stillness; it is about restoring coherence, between your body and mind, your purpose and practice, your leadership and life. When you return to breath, balance, and being, you do not lose momentum, you rediscover it. You find that calm is not the opposite of action but the source of it. From this space, creativity reawakens, relationships strengthen, and your organisation begins to move in rhythm again, steady, human, alive. The **Workplace Wellbeing Reset** invites you to begin there, not with another strategy or system, but with the most powerful instrument of renewal you already possess: **your breath.**

A Moment of Realisation

Somewhere between the meetings, the inbox, and the quiet hum of busyness, you start to feel it, that subtle sense that the way you have been working is not the same as truly living. You are productive, yes, but the peace that used to follow achievement feels distant. You are connected to everyone, yet somehow disconnected from yourself. You take deep breaths between deadlines, but never quite feel restored. If you are honest, there is a part of you that wonders whether the pace of modern work has outgrown the pace of what makes you human. The long hours, the constant connectivity, the drive to do more, they have built success, but at a cost that's harder to measure. Your focus fragments. Your energy wanes. Your clarity dulls around the edges. Welcome to the modern workplace: a world that celebrates motion but rarely makes space for meaning. A culture that prizes performance yet quietly starves the very qualities that make work worth doing, presence, perspective, and purpose, and yet, something inside you knows there's another way. You sense that real leadership does not come from pushing harder, but from returning home, to calm, to clarity, to a rhythm that feels sustainable. This is where your reset begins. This is where you pause long enough to feel the rhythm beneath the rush, to remember that wellbeing is not indulgence, but intelligence. It is not an escape from performance; it is the foundation of it, because the truth is simple: the health of your organisation begins with the health of its people, and that includes you.

Breathe. Notice this moment. You do not have to run faster. You simply have to come back to yourself.

Why Wellbeing Matters

You have probably heard it before, *take care of your people, and the rest will follow,* but in the rush to meet targets, deliver outcomes, and stay ahead, that truth can start to feel like a slogan instead of a strategy. The reality is this: wellbeing is not a bonus. It is the baseline of every sustainable, high-performing organisation. When you are calm, centred, and clear, you think more deeply. You make better decisions. You create space for others to do the same, but when stress becomes the default setting, even the most capable teams start to fracture. Think about it. You've seen it happen, brilliant people burning out, culture turning brittle, creativity shrinking under the weight of constant urgency. Work becomes mechanical. Communication loses warmth. The spark that makes collaboration thrive begins to fade. This is not about weakness. It is about biology. Your body and mind are not separate tools; they are one integrated system. When you are overloaded, your nervous system tightens. Cortisol rises. Focus narrows. Empathy declines, but when you breathe deeply, move intentionally, nourish well, and allow moments of rest, something shifts. Your body softens. Your thinking expands. You remember how to connect. That's what wellbeing really is, a return to coherence. A recalibration of the human system. It's what allows you to show up with clarity rather than chaos, with compassion rather than control, and when you do, the ripple is immediate. A calm leader builds calm teams. A regulated individual creates a safer meeting room. A single mindful pause can turn a reactive workplace into a reflective one. So, why does wellbeing matter? Because without it, performance becomes pressure. With it, performance becomes presence. This part of your journey invites you to reimagine leadership, not as something you do from exhaustion, but something you embody from equilibrium. It is about creating cultures where people can breathe, think, and belong. Cultures that understand that success and stillness are not opposites, they are partners.

You lead best when you are well. You create most when you are calm. You inspire most when you are real.

The Four Pillars of Wellbeing

Wellbeing is not a single act; it is a rhythm, one that you relearn through daily practice. There are four pillars to that rhythm: **Breathing, Nutrition, Grounding, and Relaxation.** Each one is simple, but together they form the quiet architecture of balance, for you, your team, and your organisation.

1. Breathing – The Art of Returning Home

Everything begins with your breath. It is the first thing you do when you arrive in this world, and the last thing you do when you leave. Yet somewhere between those moments, you forget how powerful it is. When you breathe consciously, you regulate your body's stress response. You steady your heart rate, quiet your mind, and bring yourself back to the present. This is more than mindfulness; it s physiology. The breath slows cortisol, restores clarity to your prefrontal cortex, and gives you the space to choose your response rather than react. In the middle of a difficult conversation, one deep breath can change the tone. Before a meeting, a single exhale can reset your focus. In a world that moves fast, breathing reminds you that presence is your most profound form of productivity.

When you return to your breath, you return to yourself.

2. Nutrition – Energy as Leadership

What you feed yourself is how you lead yourself.Your energy is not infinite; it is a resource that needs nourishment, not punishment. Food is more than fuel, it is information for your body, chemistry for your mind, and clarity for your heart. When you nourish yourself well, you support concentration, emotional steadiness, and creativity. You become the kind of leader who makes decisions from balance, not burnout. Modern workplaces often equate long hours with loyalty, but true leadership begins with self-respect. To eat mindfully, to pause for a meal, to choose water over adrenaline, these are acts of wisdom. They are how you teach your nervous system that you value sustainability over sacrifice.

You cannot lead from depletion. You lead best when you are nourished, in body, in energy, and in purpose.

3. Grounding – Standing Still to Move Well

Grounding is your anchor in uncertain times. It is how you remind yourself, *"I am here."* When you ground, physically, emotionally, and mentally you reconnect with stability. It may be as simple as placing your feet firmly on the floor, feeling the weight of your body supported by the earth, and allowing your breath to deepen. From this small act, your perspective widens. Stress loses its grip. Focus sharpens. A grounded workplace is one where people feel safe to speak, to pause, and to recover. It is where calm replaces chaos, and where purpose guides action instead of pressure. As you learn to ground yourself, you help ground those around you, creating a culture that moves from steadiness, not fear.

You do not have to stand still to be grounded, you just have to stand in truth.

4. Relaxation – The Courage to Reset

Relaxation is often mistaken for laziness, but it takes great courage to rest in a world that never stops. To relax is to reset. It is a conscious choice to step out of constant doing and allow your body and mind to recover. Rest is where integration happens, ideas connect, creativity returns, and solutions surface that you could not see when you were exhausted. Without rest, even purpose turns heavy. As a leader or team member, giving yourself permission to rest gives others permission too. It signals that humanity, not hyperactivity, is what sustains excellence. The best ideas, the kindest actions, and the wisest decisions all come from a rested state.

Rest is not what you earn after working hard, it is what allows you to work wisely.

Together, these four practices are not about changing who you are, they are about remembering what is already within you: calm, strength, and presence. They are not one more thing to do; they are a way of being that restores balance where imbalance has quietly taken root. When you breathe, nourish, ground, and rest, you create not just a better day, but a better way.

The Synergy of the Four Pillars

Each of the four pillars, Breathing, Nutrition, Grounding, and Relaxation, supports you in a different way, but together, they create something far more powerful than balance. They create **coherence**, that deep inner alignment where body, mind, and purpose move as one. When you breathe consciously, you invite calm. When you nourish yourself well, you sustain energy. When you ground yourself, you stabilise. When you rest, you restore. This is not theory; it is lived truth. You have felt it before, those moments when everything seems to flow, when clarity arrives without strain, when ideas feel effortless, and connection feels natural. That is coherence. It is not luck; it is alignment. In a workplace that moves quickly, coherence becomes your quiet advantage. It allows you to be present without being pulled in a hundred directions. It gives you the steadiness to lead with empathy and the energy to show up fully. When teams begin to embody these rhythms collectively, culture changes. Meetings soften. Communication deepens. Decisions slow just enough for wisdom to enter. The organisation starts to breathe again, and so do the people within it.

The wellbeing of the whole begins with the coherence of each part. You are one of those parts. You matter more than you know.

A Closing Reflection

Take a moment. Let your shoulders drop. Feel the weight of the day leave your body. Breathe slowly, just once, all the way in, and let it go. Notice what happens in that small pause. That is the space where transformation begins, not in grand gestures, but in these quiet moments of awareness. You do not have to do everything differently tomorrow. You just need to begin differently, a slower breath before a meeting, a meal eaten without rush, a moment to stand barefoot in the grass, or a few minutes to close your eyes and simply be. As you begin to live these small resets, you will notice something shift. The same work feels lighter. The same people feel easier to connect with. The same challenges feel more manageable. You will find that calm is not the end of action, it is the start of real impact.

Stillness is not your escape from the world; it's how you stay connected to it.

A Heart Invitation

As you step forward from this first part of *The Unbound Organisation*, let it be with gentleness. You do not need to fix yourself, only to remember yourself. When the world tells you to hurry, pause. When stress tightens your chest, breathe. When fatigue whispers that you have nothing left, rest. When the noise gets too loud, ground. When doubt creeps in, nourish yourself and return to what you value most. Your wellbeing is not separate from your leadership; it is the heart of it. The way you care for yourself teaches everyone around you what care looks like, and that is where transformation begins, one breath, one act of awareness, one moment of returning home at a time.

You are not here to survive your work; you are here to bring it to life, calmly, clearly, and from the heart.

MODULE 1 - BREATHING

Your Opening Reflection

An Invitation to Breathe - Before you move forward, allow yourself this simple gift: pause, soften, and breathe. Your breath is not just air, it is life moving through you, a gentle reminder that you are here, alive, and connected. Let each inhale welcome you home to your heart, and let each exhale release what no longer serves you. With every breath, you are reminded that presence, peace, and renewal are always within reach.

- "What does your breath feel like in this moment, tight, shallow, soft, steady?"

- "When you pause to breathe deeply, what changes within you, even slightly?"

- "What single word or phrase describes your relationship with your breath today?"

- "How does your body respond when you bring awareness to your heart as you breathe?"

- "What would it feel like to let your breath be your guide, instead of your mind?"

Let these questions open the doorway into presence. Every answer you give, whether in words, sensations, or silence, is a bridge between where you are and where you are going.

Learning Objectives

The learning objectives are included here to give you a clear focus for this module, ensuring that each practice you explore moves you closer to mastering the skills, insights, and heart-led awareness that will enrich your life well beyond the program. By the end of this module, you will:

- Understand the role of breath in emotional regulation and self-awareness.

- Practice deep, heart-centred breathing techniques.

- Identify physical and emotional shifts that result from conscious breathwork.

- Connect with your heart space to access intuitive and emotional guidance.

- Develop a sustainable self-regulation practice anchored in conscious breathing.

Core Emotional Domains

The core emotional intelligence domains covered here are essential because they form the foundation for lasting heart connection, guiding you to deepen self-awareness, regulate emotions, build resilience, and strengthen the mind-body bond throughout your *Unbound* journey.

- **Self-Awareness:** Breath draws your attention inward, helping you notice your thoughts, feelings, and physical state.

- **Self-Regulation:** Conscious breathing soothes the nervous system and helps you respond rather than react.

- **Emotional Healing and Resilience:** Breath anchors you through emotional waves, creating space for release, reflection, and recovery.

- **Mind-Body Connection:** Breathing links your physical body with emotional presence, grounding you in calm awareness.

"Breathing – The Bridge Between Your Mind, Body And Heart"

The Science and Soul of Breathing

Breath is a bridge between your mind, body, and heart. Ancient traditions and neuroscience agree: breath regulates the nervous system, releases stress, and activates inner peace. Ancient traditions and modern neuroscience come together to affirm a timeless and powerful truth: your breath is one of the most effective regulators of your nervous system. Across thousands of years, wisdom traditions such as yoga, meditation, tai chi, and pranayama have harnessed the breath to still the mind, release stored tension, and open the doorway to inner peace. In these traditions, breath has never been only a biological function, it has been a sacred bridge between your body, your mind, and your spirit. Today, the precision of neuroscience confirms what those ancient practices have always known. Conscious breathing, especially slow, deep, and rhythmic breathing, activates your parasympathetic nervous system, signaling safety and calm to every cell in your body. It reduces the production of cortisol, the primary stress hormone, and restores balance in moments when life feels overwhelming. It creates a physiological shift away from the hyper-vigilance of fight-or-flight and into the grounded steadiness of rest-and-digest. When you choose to slow down and breathe with intention, you are giving your body a clear message: *It is safe to let go*. This simple act changes your chemistry, softens the constant activity of your mind, and allows your awareness to expand. You step out of survival mode and into a deeper state of presence, one where you can think clearly, feel deeply, and respond rather than react. In this space, peace stops being a fleeting visitor and begins to feel like your natural state of being. Your breath is both an ancient ally and a scientifically validated tool, always within reach, waiting to guide you back to balance, clarity, and connection. It is the one practice that unites the wisdom of the past with the breakthroughs of the present, a living bridge between who you are now and the grounded, heart-led life you are capable of living.

Conscious Breathing Helps Detoxify The Body, Increase Energy, Support Digestion, And Calm Emotional Responses

When you breathe deeply and with full awareness, you awaken and activate your body's natural systems for healing, balance, and restoration. Each slow, intentional breath draws more oxygen into your lungs, delivering fresh life to your cells. This increase in oxygen flow helps to flush out toxins, revitalise your tissues, and renew your energy from the inside out. As you consciously breathe, you gently stimulate your parasympathetic nervous system, your body's *"rest and digest"* mode. This shifts you away from stress-driven states and into calm, steady balance. Your digestion improves, nutrient absorption is enhanced, and your entire internal system begins to function with greater ease and harmony. On an emotional level, each conscious breath is a reset button. It calms heightened stress responses, softens anxious thoughts, and clears mental fog. You create space between what you feel and how you respond, giving yourself the power to choose presence over reactivity. In this grounded state, you move from reacting impulsively to responding with clarity and intention. Your breath becomes more than an automatic process, it becomes your anchor, a reliable and profound tool that can realign your body, settle your mind, and harmonise your emotions in any moment you choose. It is always with you, ready to guide you back to balance whenever you need it most.

The Role Of The Vagus Nerve In Emotional Regulation

Your vagus nerve is one of the most vital yet often overlooked components of your emotional wellbeing. As the longest cranial nerve in your body, it acts as a major communication highway between your brain and vital organs, especially the heart, lungs, and digestive system, but beyond its physical functions, your vagus nerve plays a central role in your capacity to regulate emotions, connect with others, and return to calm after stress.

1. Your Built-In Reset Button

When you are overwhelmed or anxious, your sympathetic nervous system kicks in, this is the "*fight, flight, or freeze*" response. The vagus nerve is the primary activator of your parasympathetic nervous system, your body's "*rest and digest*" or "*tend and befriend*" mode. When stimulated, it sends signals that slow your heart rate, lower your blood pressure, deepen your breath, and signal safety to your brain. In essence, it tells your entire system: *It is okay. You are safe now.*

2. Your Vagus Nerve and the Emotion-Body Connection

Your emotions are not just "*in your head*", they are experienced throughout your body. The vagus nerve helps regulate this experience by transmitting information from the gut and heart to the brain and vice versa. This bidirectional communication helps shape how you feel and how quickly you recover from emotional upsets. A well-toned vagus nerve supports quicker emotional recovery, greater resilience, and an increased ability to stay grounded during stress.

3. Vagal Tone and Resilience

Vagal tone refers to how efficiently your vagus nerve performs. High vagal tone is associated with emotional flexibility, stronger relationships, better heart rate variability (HRV), and increased capacity for compassion and empathy. It means you can shift more easily from stress back to calm, think clearly under pressure, and respond instead of react. Low vagal tone, on the other hand, is often linked to anxiety, depression, digestive issues, and emotional dysregulation.

4. Practices That Activate your Vagus Nerve

You can tone and strengthen your vagus nerve with intentional daily practices:

- Deep diaphragmatic breathing (especially with longer exhales)

- Humming, chanting, or singing (activates the vocal cords connected to the vagus nerve)

- Cold exposure (e.g., splashing your face with cold water)

- Gentle yoga, grounding, or tai chi

- Loving-kindness meditation and connection with safe people

- Mindful touch or placing your hand on your heart

These practices are simple yet powerful ways to train your body to return to emotional balance more quickly and naturally.

5. Your Vagus Nerve and Heart Intelligence

Your vagus nerve also plays a critical role in what some call "*heart-brain coherence.*" When your breath, emotions, and nervous system are regulated, your heart rhythm becomes smooth and coherent. This coherence sends signals to your brain that create calm, clear thinking, and prosocial emotions such as gratitude, compassion, and love. It is through this heart-vagus-brain connection that you experience emotional intelligence at its most embodied level. In essence, your vagus nerve is a bridge between your body and your emotions, between survival and thriving. Learning to activate and care for this vital nerve is not just a wellness trend, it is a deep act of self-connection. When you tune into your vagus nerve, you reclaim your power to self-soothe, relate, and live from a grounded and open heart.

The Difference Between Shallow And Deep Breathing

Breathing is the most constant and essential act of your life, but not all breaths are created equal. How you breathe can profoundly affect your nervous system, emotional state, energy levels, and overall wellbeing. Understanding the difference between shallow and deep breathing gives you the power to regulate stress, improve focus, and connect more deeply with your body and heart.

Shallow Breathing: The Breath of Stress and Survival

Shallow breathing, also known as chest or thoracic breathing, is when you take quick, short breaths that primarily fill only the upper part of your lungs. It often goes unnoticed, yet it is common in daily life, especially when you are under pressure, anxious, or distracted.

Effects of Shallow Breathing:

- Activates your sympathetic nervous system (fight, flight, or freeze)

- Increases your heart rate and blood pressure

- Reduces oxygen exchange, which can cause fatigue, fogginess, or dizziness

- Restricts your diaphragm, your body's natural breathing muscle

- Can create a feedback loop of anxiety, where poor breathing fuels more tension

You might not even realise you are breathing shallowly, it has become a norm in high-stress, fast-paced environments. Over time, habitual shallow breathing can contribute to chronic stress, emotional imbalance, and disconnection from your body.

Deep Breathing: The Breath of Presence and Calm

Deep breathing, sometimes called diaphragmatic or belly breathing, involves drawing air deep into the lungs so the diaphragm expands downward, allowing your belly to rise gently. This type of breath is slower, fuller, and more nourishing, both physiologically and emotionally.

Benefits of Deep Breathing:

- Activates your parasympathetic nervous system (rest and digest)

- Lowers your cortisol and stress levels

- Improves oxygen flow, energy, and cellular health

- Calms your mind and relaxes your body

- Enhances heart-brain coherence and emotional regulation

Deep breathing is a direct and accessible way to ground yourself in the present moment. It creates space between stimulus and response, allowing you to feel more centred and make wiser choices.

Breath as a Bridge Between Mind and Body

Your breath is one of the few functions in your body that is both automatic and under your conscious control. This makes it a powerful tool for regulating your nervous system, mood, and mental state. Shallow breathing often reflects a state of unconscious reactivity, while deep breathing invites mindful awareness and heart connection.

Try This: Shift from Shallow to Deep

1. Place one hand on your chest and one on your belly.

2. Notice which one rises when you breathe.

3. Now, slow down your inhale and gently breathe into your belly.

4. Let your exhale be just a little longer than your inhale.

5. Repeat for a few minutes, staying present with each breath.

Summary

Shallow breathing is a signal of survival. Deep breathing is a practice of self-awareness and presence. When you choose to breathe deeply, you return to your body, regulate your emotions, and cultivate calm from the inside out. It is not just a technique, it is a form of self-kindness and emotional intelligence.

Why Breath Awareness Equals Emotional Awareness

Your breath is more than just a physiological process, it is an intimate reflection of your emotional state. Every emotion you feel subtly changes the rhythm, depth, and pace of your breath. In the same way, bringing conscious awareness to your breath becomes a powerful gateway into emotional awareness, regulation, and healing.

The Breath-Emotion Connection

When you feel anxious, your breath becomes short and rapid. When you are sad, it may be slow and heavy. Joy may bring a light, expansive breath. Anger can make your breathing sharp and fast. Even without thinking, your body responds to emotion through breath. This connection is not symbolic, it is neurological, hormonal, and physiological. Your breath and your emotions are intimately wired through the autonomic nervous system, particularly through the **vagus nerve**, which links your brain, heart, lungs, and gut. This means that by tuning into your breath, you are actually tuning into how your entire emotional system is operating in real time.

What Happens When You Pay Attention to Your Breath?

1. **You Notice Subtle Shifts:** Breath awareness brings you into the present moment, where you can begin to *feel* what is really happening inside,

sometimes before the mind can label it.

2. **You start noticing when you are tense**: When you are holding your breath, or when you are breathing too fast. These are cues that something emotional is arising.

3. **You Interrupt Autopilot Reactions**: Without awareness, emotions often run unconsciously, leading to impulsive reactions, but when you are aware of your breath, you create a pause. In that pause, you find choice. You find space. You begin to respond, not react.

4. **You Regulate Your Nervous System**: When you observe your breath and intentionally slow it down, you stimulate the **parasympathetic nervous system** (rest and digest), which helps regulate cortisol and reduce emotional overwhelm. This in turn makes you more resilient and clear-headed.

Breath as an Emotional Mirror

Think of your breath as a *mirror* for your emotional landscape:

- Shallow breath = fear or stress

- Uneven breath = anxiety or agitation

- Held breath = suppression or shock

- Deep, flowing breath = calm, grounded presence

Learning to read your breath is like learning a language your body has always spoken, but you may not have listened to.

From Awareness to Compassion

Breath awareness is not about control, it is about curiosity and compassion. It invites you to meet yourself where you are, without judgment. To notice your trembling breath in sadness. Your held breath in tension. The flutter in excitement, and by bringing love and presence to your breath, you offer love and presence to the emotion beneath it.

A Simple Practice: Breath Check-In

Take a moment, wherever you are. Close your eyes if you wish.

- Notice your breath.

- Is it deep or shallow? Fast or slow?

- What might your breath be telling you right now?

- Can you soften it... just a little?

Summary

Breath awareness is emotional awareness. Your breath is your body's emotional compass, always guiding you inward, offering insight, balance, and peace. When you listen to your breath, you are not just breathing, you are *feeling*, *understanding*, and *healing*. Breath is the language of your heart.

Exercise: 3 Minute Detox & Reset Breath

Purpose: To experience how conscious breathing supports detoxification, boosts your energy, aids digestion, and calms emotions.

1. Sit or stand comfortably. Close your eyes if you feel safe to do so.

2. Inhale deeply through your nose for a count of 4, feel your belly expand.

3. Hold the breath gently for 4 seconds - allow oxygen to circulate.

4. Exhale slowly through your mouth for a count of 6, release tension and toxins.

5. Repeat for 3 minutes, staying present with each breath.

Reflection Prompts:

1. How do you feel physically and emotionally after this practice?

2. Where might you be holding tension or resistance in your life?

Case Study Discussion: Caitlyn's Journey

Caitlyn once described herself as an anxious, restless, and highly energetic woman, always in motion yet feeling strangely absent from her own life. For as long as she could remember, she had felt disconnected from her body, a separation born from the emotional wounds and traumas she had endured over the years. She never felt truly safe expressing her feelings or emotions, and so, without even realising it, she had built walls around her inner world, cutting herself off from her own heart as a means of self-protection. When we began practising balanced heart breathing, Caitlyn admitted that the process felt both strange and deeply uncomfortable. It was confrontational, not because the technique was difficult, but because for the first time in decades she was allowing herself to pause, to be fully present, and to listen to the quiet truth of her heart. The stillness brought her face-to-face with emotions she had long buried.

We often returned to the old saying, *"What you resist will persist."* The more she resisted facing these emotions, the more they silently shaped her life. Yet, with each deep, conscious breath, Caitlyn began to shift. She found moments of peace she had not known in years. She felt balanced, grounded, and connected to herself in a way that was entirely new. The practice unlocked suppressed feelings, but instead of being overwhelmed, she began to meet them with compassion. Over time, the balanced heart breathing became her anchor. She opened up in ways she never imagined possible, and in doing so, she began to heal, to learn, and to grow. She found forgiveness, for herself, and for others, and she discovered a deep well of self-love she had never touched before. Today, Caitlyn's transformation is profound. She now teaches deep breathwork as part of her yoga practice, guiding others to find the same peace, connection, and inner freedom that reshaped her life. Her journey is living proof that the simple act of breathing with awareness can open the door to a life of balance, wholeness, and love.

Reflective Exercise: Caitlyn's Journey

Here are four profound and reflective questions inspired by Caitlyn's story:

1. In what ways might you be unconsciously disconnecting from your own emotions or body as a form of protection?

2. How do you typically respond when asked to slow down and be fully present, do you resist it, avoid it, or embrace it?

3. What emotions or memories arise when you begin to breathe deeply and consciously? How do you usually respond to them?

4. What would it mean for you to create a safe space, within yourself, to feel, release, and heal long-held emotions?

Heart Whisper Affirmations For Integration

Affirmations have the power to quiet the noise of doubt, open the doorway to self-trust, and draw you back into the wisdom of your heart. When practised daily, they nurture an inner dialogue based in love and truth, helping you live each day more aligned with who you truly are. I invite you to repeat silently or write:

- I feel centred and calm when I focus on my breath.

- I am able to quiet my mind through deep breathing.

- Breathing deeply helps me to release tension in my body.

- I find peace in the rhythm of my breath.

- My breath is a reminder to stay present in the moment.

- Through conscious breathing, I nurture inner harmony.

- Each breath I take fills me with clarity and light.

- With every exhale, I release what no longer serves me.

- My breath connects me to my heart and to the present moment.

- Breathing with awareness helps me move through life with ease and grace.

- My breath is my constant companion, guiding me back to peace.

Application Exercise: In-the-Moment Breathing Anchor

Purpose: To centre yourself, regulate your nervous system, and reconnect with your heart's wisdom during moments of stress, anxiety, or emotional overload.

Step-by-Step Practice:

1. Pause and Become Aware: Gently stop what you are doing, and acknowledge what you are feeling without judgment. Name it if you can: *"I feel anxious, overwhelmed, tense…"*

2. Place Your Hand on Your Heart: This simple gesture activates oxytocin (the calming hormone) and helps your body feel safe. Feel the warmth and weight of your hand. Let it be an anchor to the present moment.

3. Begin Balanced Heart Breathing (3 Rounds): Inhale slowly through your nose for **4 seconds**. Exhale gently through your mouth for **6 seconds**. Repeat **3 times**, focusing on softening your shoulders and relaxing your jaw

4. Ask Your Heart:: *"What do I need in this moment?"* Be still and listen, your heart may answer with a word, a feeling, or a sense of direction (e.g., *rest, space, support, courage, nothing at all*) Trust whatever comes up, even if it is silence.

Close with Compassion

Affirm: *"I honour how I feel, and I give myself what I need."* Gently return to your day with renewed presence.

Closing Reflection

Breath is more than survival, it is a sacred rhythm, a quiet guide, and a constant companion. Today, you have taken your first step into reconnecting with your breath not just as a function, but as a bridge to your heart. With each conscious inhale and exhale, you create space for clarity, healing, and grounded presence. In slowing down, you have begun to listen, not just to your breath, but to the quiet wisdom within you. This is more than a practice; it is a return. A return to yourself. Trust that your breath will meet you in every moment, and guide you gently, truthfully, toward peace and emotional wholeness.

The Path Opens Further

You have taken a step. The next step is waiting. Every book in the Unbound Series widens the path, deeper into your story, sharper into your strengths, and closer to the life you were meant to live. When you are ready, turn the page into the next Unbound journey – www.timetotransform.world

MODULE 2 - NUTRITION

Your Opening Reflection

An Invitation to Nourish Yourself - As you enter this module, remember that every bite you take is a form of self-communication. Food is not only fuel; it is a way of honouring your body, your energy, and your heart. Let this be a moment to approach nourishment with love rather than judgment, with mindfulness rather than habit. Each choice can be a quiet act of self-care, reminding you that you are worthy of feeling strong, balanced, and alive.

- "What is one way I have nurtured or neglected my body this week?"

- "How do the foods I choose each day make me feel physically and emotionally?"

- "Am I eating out of hunger, habit, or emotion?"

- "What is one small change I could make to nourish my body better?"

- "Do I listen to my body's signals of hunger and fullness?"

- "How can I make eating a more mindful and enjoyable experience?"

Let these questions open the doorway into presence. Every answer you give, whether in words, sensations, or silence, is a bridge between where you are and where you are going.

Learning Objectives

The learning objectives are included here to give you a clear focus for this module, ensuring that each practice you explore moves you closer to mastering the skills, insights, and heart-led awareness that will enrich your life well beyond the program. By the end of this module, you will:

- Understand the relationship between nutrition and emotional intelligence.

- Identify foods and habits that support physical, emotional, and heart-centred wellbeing.

- Develop self-awareness through mindful eating practices.

- Reflect on how diet influences mental clarity, mood, and heart connection.

- Commit to simple, sustainable nutrition strategies that nourish both body and soul.

Core Emotional Domains

The core emotional intelligence domains covered here are essential because they form the foundation for lasting heart connection, guiding you to deepen self-awareness, regulate emotions, build resilience, and strengthen the mind-body bond throughout your *Unbound* journey.

- **Self-Awareness:** You tune into your body's unique needs, recognising how different foods affect your energy, emotions, and overall wellbeing.

- **Self-Regulation:** You make more mindful, intentional choices about what and how you nourish yourself, rather than reacting to impulse or habit.

- **Motivation:** You are inspired to care for your body with consistency, aligning your eating patterns with your deeper desire to feel vibrant, grounded, and well.

- **Empathy (toward self and others):** You cultivate compassion through sustainable and ethical food choices, nourishing your own body while honouring the earth and its communities.

"Nutrition – Nourishing Your Body With Love"

Proper nutrition is not just a physical requirement, it is a form of communication with your entire being. Every bite, every sip, is a message you send to yourself: *I care. I am listening. I am worthy of thriving.* Too often, food is treated as an afterthought, rushed, numbed, used for escape or control, but when you slow down and connect with the deeper meaning of nourishment, it becomes a powerful emotional and spiritual practice. It becomes heart work.

Self-awareness invites you to notice how food influences your emotions, thoughts, and physical state. What nourishes not only your stomach, but also your sense of calm, vitality, and presence? You begin to realise that hunger is not always about food, it can be a hunger for grounding, love, creativity, or rest.

Self-regulation allows you to make choices from a place of balance, not habit or emotional impulse. You become more conscious of why you are reaching for something, whether it is to soothe, to celebrate, to avoid, or to fuel. Through this awareness, you cultivate kindness, not judgment. You become your own safe place at the table.

Motivation comes not from guilt or perfectionism, but from a desire to honour your body as a sacred vessel of life. You begin to nourish yourself because it feels good, not just because it is *"healthy."* You realise that true wellness is not a punishment; it is a path of joy, clarity, and strength.

Empathy, especially toward yourself, emerges as you stop waging war on your body. You begin to listen with tenderness. To notice what foods energise you.

To respect your hunger, your fullness, your preferences, and your boundaries, and as your relationship with food softens, so does your relationship with yourself. Gratitude for food and where it comes from deepens your sense of interconnectedness. You become more aware of the environment, the hands that grew and prepared your meals, and the impact of your choices. Nourishment becomes not just personal, it becomes relational, ethical, and spiritual. This is the heart of nourishment:

- A return to wholeness.

- A remembering that eating is not just survival, it is sacred.

- It is one of the most ancient forms of prayer and self-love.

- You do not have to get it *"perfect."*

You only need to begin again, one breath, one bite, one moment of presence at a time.

The History Of Nutrition As Heart-Centred Medicine: From Hippocrates To Ayurveda

Long before modern nutritional science emerged, cultures around the world understood that food was more than sustenance, it was medicine, energy, and sacred ritual. From the wisdom of the ancient Greeks to the holistic teachings of Ayurveda, nutrition was seen not just as fuel for the body but as nourishment for your heart, mind, and spirit.

Hippocrates and Ancient Greece: "Let food be thy medicine"

The basis of Western nutritional thought trace back to Hippocrates (c. 460–370 BCE), often called the *"Father of Medicine."* He believed that health was a state of balance within the body, and that imbalance could often be restored through diet and lifestyle before turning to harsher remedies. His famous guidance, *"Let food be thy medicine and medicine be thy food,"* was not a metaphor, it was a clinical principle. Hippocrates viewed digestion, environment, and emotion as interwoven. He believed that the quality, seasonality, and simplicity of food mattered, and that eating should be done with awareness. In this view, nourishment was not mechanical, it was intuitive and relational. Meals were meant to bring harmony, not only to your body, but to your entire inner ecosystem.

Ayurveda: The Sacred Science of Life

In India, the ancient system of **Ayurveda** *("the science of life")* developed over 3,000 years ago, offering one of the most comprehensive nutritional philosophies in human history. Ayurveda teaches that food carries a life force (*prana*) and that each person has a unique constitution (*dosha*) that determines which foods are most supportive for their wellbeing. Nutrition in Ayurveda is not just about nutrients or calories, it is about how food feels in your body, how it is prepared, and how it is eaten. Food is chosen according to qualities such as warming or cooling, grounding or stimulating, moistening or drying. Each meal is an act of alignment, a chance to restore balance, cleanse the system, and calm the mind. Importantly, Ayurveda recognises that emotions and digestion are deeply linked. A meal eaten in stress, anger, or distraction is thought to leave *"mental residue"* that can disrupt the body and spirit. Gratitude, intention, and presence are part of the nourishment.

Nutrition as Medicine for the Heart

Both traditions, Hippocratic and Ayurvedic, saw food as an intimate bridge between the outer world and the inner life. They believed what you eat shapes how you feel, how you think, and how you connect with others. Food was never isolated from the emotional or spiritual dimensions of living, it was woven into them. In this light, the act of eating becomes more than biological necessity. It becomes an opportunity to:

- Centre yourself in compassion

- Honour your body's signals

- Respond to your emotional needs without judgment

- Strengthen your connection to the Earth and to others

Returning to this heart-centred understanding of nutrition is not a regression, it is a remembering. In a world often dominated by speed, fad diets, and disconnection, these ancient teachings gently remind you: *True nourishment is never just about food, it is about how you live, how you feel, and how you love yourself through each choice.*

The Biochemical Effects Of Food On Mood, Energy, And Emotion

How what you eat shapes how you feel, physically, emotionally, and mentally.

You may often think of food as fuel, but it is far more dynamic than that. Every bite you take initiates a cascade of biochemical reactions that affect your brain chemistry, hormonal balance, energy levels, and emotional state. The connection between nutrition and mood is now well, documented in both neuroscience and integrative medicine. Your food choices are not just shaping your waistline, they are shaping your mind, mood, and moment-to-moment wellbeing. Below are key ways food influences how you feel:

1. Omega-3 Fatty Acids - Feeding Your Emotional Brain

Omega-3s, especially EPA and DHA found in fatty fish like salmon, sardines, and mackerel, are essential fats that support brain health, emotional regulation, and cognitive function.

- How they help: Omega-3s improve neuronal communication and reduce inflammation in the brain. They are linked to lower rates of depression, anxiety, and brain fog.

- The science: Studies show individuals with low omega-3 intake have a higher risk of mood disorders, while supplementation may ease depressive symptoms and increase emotional resilience.

Foods to focus on: Fatty fish, flaxseeds, chia seeds, walnuts, algae oil.

2. Sugar - The Mood Spike and Crash

Refined sugar and high-glycemic carbohydrates cause rapid blood sugar spikes followed by sharp drops, which can wreak havoc on emotional stability and energy levels.

- How it affects you: After a sugar high, insulin surges to bring blood glucose down, which can lead to a crash in energy, irritability, brain fog, and even feelings of anxiety or sadness.

- The emotional cycle: This crash often triggers more sugar cravings, creating a loop of emotional instability that mimics the effects of stress.

Mindful tip: Pair natural carbs with protein or healthy fats to reduce blood sugar volatility and promote steadier mood and focus.

3. Hydration - The Often-Ignored Mood Regulator

Dehydration, even at a mild level, can significantly impair your mood, focus, and cognitive performance.

- The brain & water: Your brain is about 75% water. Even slight dehydration can cause fatigue, low mood, headaches, and difficulty concentrating.

- Hormonal balance: Hydration supports the regulation of cortisol (your stress hormone) and helps maintain the fluid balance needed for efficient neurotransmitter function.

Daily reminder: Drinking enough water is one of the simplest and most powerful ways to improve your emotional baseline. Aim for regular sips throughout the day, not just when thirsty.

4. Micronutrients - Small Nutrients, Big Impact

Deficiencies in key vitamins and minerals can directly affect your mood and mental health.

- B Vitamins: Support energy production and neurotransmitter synthesis. Low levels (especially B6, B9, and B12) are associated with fatigue, irritability, and depression.

- Magnesium: Calms the nervous system and supports sleep. Deficiency is linked to anxiety and restlessness.

- Zinc & Iron: Essential for mood balance and cognitive clarity; deficits are associated with low energy and depression.

Focus foods: Leafy greens, legumes, seeds, nuts, eggs, and whole grains.

5. Gut Health - Your Third Brain

The gut microbiome is now understood to play a critical role in emotional regulation. Why? Because the gut produces about 90% of your serotonin, the neurotransmitter most associated with happiness and emotional balance.

- The gut-brain axis: A thriving gut microbiome communicates with the brain via the vagus nerve, sending signals that can either enhance or disrupt your mood.

- Fermented & fiber-rich foods: These feed beneficial gut bacteria and support healthy digestion and mood stability.

Mood-boosting foods: Yogurt, kefir, sauerkraut, kimchi, legumes, oats, bananas, and prebiotic fibers (like garlic and onions).

You Are What You Digest (Not Just What You Eat)

When you begin listening to your body, you notice what brings lightness, clarity, and joy, and what dims your energy or disconnects you from your heart. This is emotional intelligence through food. Not about restriction or rules, this is about reverence. It is about aligning your choices with how you want to feel. So today, when you eat, ask yourself:

1. *"Will this nourish me?"*

2. *"Will this support my clarity, calm, and connection?"*

Let your meals become a daily act of love.

Let food be your reminder: *you are worthy of feeling well.*

Food As A Daily Emotional Practice

When you begin to eat with awareness, not with perfection or pressure, you discover something profound: food is not just physical. It is emotional. It is energetic. It is deeply personal. You start to notice how certain foods make you feel grounded, light, clear, or calm. A warm meal can soothe your nervous system. A crisp piece of fruit can awaken your senses. Sometimes, certain foods, especially when eaten in haste or stress, can leave you feeling heavy, scattered, or disconnected from yourself. This noticing is not about judging your choices. It is about gently listening. Tuning in. Honouring what your body and heart are trying to tell you. When you feel tired, are you dehydrated? When you crave sugar, are you actually needing rest, comfort, or connection? In this space of awareness, you begin to make different decisions, not from willpower, but from wisdom. Not from control, but from care. You realise that food is not the enemy, and it is not just fuel. It is a relationship. One that reflects how you care for yourself moment to moment. You stop obsessing over being *"good"* and instead ask yourself more loving questions:

1. *"Does this nourish me?"*

2. *"Does this align with who I want to be today?"*

3. *"What am I truly hungry for?"*

Through this lens, nourishment becomes an act of emotional intelligence. It is how you build trust with your body. It is how you self-regulate. It is how you honour your internal rhythms and meet your emotional needs without shame. It is no longer about rules or rigid plans. It becomes a conversation between your biology, your history, and your heart. Each meal becomes a mirror. Each bite, a choice. Each day, a chance to come back home to yourself. You are not just feeding your body. You are feeding your clarity, your presence, your peace. This is food as a daily emotional practice, and when done with love, it becomes a form of healing, one you carry with you, one bite at a time.

Nutrition As A Form Of Self-Love And Empowerment

The way you nourish yourself is one of the most consistent and powerful expressions of self-love. Every time you choose to feed your body with intention, you are not just making a nutritional decision, you are making a statement: *"I matter. My wellbeing is worth the effort. I am worthy of feeling good."* So often, eating is tied to guilt, control, shame, or neglect. You may have been taught to see food as something to manage, restrict, or use to soothe pain, but when you shift the narrative, nutrition becomes something sacred, an act of care rather than control. Choosing to nourish yourself well is not about perfection. It is about compassion. It is the daily decision to honour your body as a partner, not a project. To eat not just for appearance or performance, but for how you want to feel in your skin, your mind, and your life. When you eat with presence, you reclaim your power.

- You take ownership of your energy, your emotions, and your choices.

- You tune in instead of numbing out.

- You listen to your body's wisdom, instead of overriding it with outside opinions or old habits.

Food becomes a form of emotional intelligence. You start to recognise how certain meals fuel your clarity and calm. You notice what drains you, what lifts you, and what truly supports you in being the person you want to be.

That awareness empowers you. You are no longer ruled by impulse or shame. You begin to feel strong from the inside out, and with that strength, you begin to rise, not because you followed a diet plan, but because you remembered how to love yourself with every bite. When you nourish yourself in this way, you send a ripple effect through every part of your life.

- You sleep better.

- You think more clearly.

- You move with more confidence.

- You show up more fully in relationships, work, and purpose.

Because true nourishment is not just about food. It is about honouring the life force within you. It is about saying yes to yourself again and again, from a place of love. This is self-love in action. This is daily empowerment. This is the heart of what it means to be *nourished*.

Reflection Exercise: Heart Focused Nutrition Challenge

I invite you to choose **two** of the following to commit to this week:

1. *Add one additional serving of vegetables or fruit each day.*

2. *Cook one homemade meal using only whole ingredients.*

3. *Drink at least 8 glasses of water per day.*

4. *Pause before each meal to take 3 breaths and express gratitude.*

5. *Reduce sugar or processed food intake for three consecutive days.*

I encourage you to commit to a daily reflection on how these changes affect your physical energy and emotional clarity.

Case Study Discussion – Mia's Journey

Mia was a single mother with two young children who was struggling to keep up with the demands of her life. She was constantly tired, irritable, and had low energy levels. Her children were also struggling with health issues, which made her worry even more. Mia knew that she needed to make a change in her life if she wanted to be able to provide for her family and give them a better life. I spoke with Mia about her self–talk, sleep, hydration, and her diet. We spent a little bit of time discussing the importance of nutrition and she decided to take a look at her diet and see if she could make some changes to improve her health. She started by cutting out processed foods and fast food and began cooking healthy meals at home with fresh ingredients. She also started drinking more water and making sure she was getting enough sleep each night. Within a few weeks, Mia began to notice a significant difference in how she felt. She had more energy throughout the day, and her mood had improved as well. She was more patient with her children and found herself enjoying time with them more than ever before. Another secondary benefit was that her children's health also improved, and they were no longer getting sick as often. As Mia continued to focus on her nutrition, she also found that she was becoming more connected with her heart. She started to listen to her body and pay attention to what it needed. She began practicing meditation and yoga, which helped her feel centred and at peace. Through her journey, Mia discovered that nutrition was a powerful tool for not only improving her physical health but also her emotional health and wellbeing. Mia's story is a reminder of the importance of taking care of yourself, listening to your body, and connecting with your heart. By making small changes in your nutrition and lifestyle, you can improve your physical and emotional health and live a happier, more fulfilling life.

Reflective Exercise – Mia's Journey

Here are four profound and reflective questions inspired by Mia's story to help you engage with your own nutrition journey:

1. What is your body trying to tell you right now, and have you been listening? *Mia's turning point came when she started paying attention to her body's messages. You, too, have an inner wisdom that speaks through fatigue, cravings, tension, or restlessness. When you listen with compassion, you begin to nourish not just your body, but your heart.*

2. In what ways has your current relationship with food supported or limited your energy and emotional wellbeing? *Like Mia, you may find that food habits formed out of stress or convenience do not always serve your deeper needs. You have the power to choose foods that support clarity, presence, and vitality. Small shifts can create ripples of healing.*

3. What simple daily rituals could you create to feed yourself with more love and intention? *Mia's healing began with fresh ingredients and hydration, but also with presence. What might change in your life if preparing and eating food became an act of care, rather than just another task? What would self-love look like on your plate?*

---

4. How could your personal healing ripple out and benefit those you care for most? *Mia's transformation did not just change her, it changed her children. When you nourish yourself, your capacity to show up with patience, presence, and love grows. Your healing becomes a gift that extends far beyond you.*

Affirmations For Integration (Heart Whispers)

Affirmations have the power to quiet the noise of doubt, open the doorway to self-trust, and draw you back into the wisdom of your heart. When practised daily, they nurture an inner dialogue based in love and truth, helping you live each day more aligned with who you truly are. I invite you to repeat silently or write:

- I honour my body by giving it the nourishment it deserves.

- I enjoy healthy foods that energise and sustain me.

- I treat my body with love through the choices I make.

- I am grateful for the food that supports my well-being.

- I create balance by eating in a way that feels good for me.

- I fuel my body with nutritious food.

- I choose foods that nourish my heart.

- I listen to my body's hunger cues.

- I drink plenty of water every day.

- I make mindful eating choices.

Nutrition Exercise – Eating with Heart Awareness

1. **Choose One Meal or Snack Today:** Select something nourishing, fruit, vegetables, whole grains, or a wholesome snack you enjoy.

2. **Pause Before Eating:** Take three slow breaths. Notice the colours, textures, and aromas of your food.

3. **Express Gratitude:** Silently thank everyone and everything that helped bring this food to your table, farmers, growers, the earth, sun, and rain.

4. **Eat Slowly and Mindfully:** Take small bites. Chew fully. Notice the flavours and how your body responds.

5. **Check In:** Halfway through, pause. Notice how you feel, satisfied, still hungry, or full.

6. **Close with Appreciation:** When finished, place your hand over your heart and say: *"I nourish my body with love, and my body loves me back."*

Closing Reflection

You have now been reminded that food is far more than fuel. It is story, connection, compassion, and care. Every meal you prepare, every sip of water you take, and every conscious choice you make in honour of your wellbeing is not simply an action, it is a declaration of self-respect. When you eat with awareness, you are not just filling your stomach, you are nourishing the clarity of your mind, calming your emotions, and restoring your spirit to wholeness. You are reminding yourself that nourishment is not just about survival, it is about living fully, deeply, and in alignment with your heart. Let this part of your journey be a turning point. Not a striving for perfection, but an invitation into presence. Let food become the sacred rhythm that anchors your day, a ritual of love that whispers, *"I deserve to feel well. I deserve to thrive."* Just as Mia discovered, healing is never found in grand leaps, it begins in the smallest of steps: in one fresh ingredient chosen with care, in one glass of water offered to a thirsty body, in one still and quiet moment where you pause long enough to listen to what your body truly asks of you. Carry this wisdom forward: that nourishment is not only what you eat, but also how you breathe, how you move, how you rest, and how you treat yourself with tenderness. To nourish is to honour your life as sacred, to respect the miracle that is your body, and to live each day as though your health and heart truly matter. You are worthy of feeling well. You are worthy of love, of rest, of joy, and of care, and every conscious meal you share with yourself or with others can become a quiet, powerful homecoming, a return to your heart, where healing, presence, and self-compassion live.

The Work Begins Where the Chapter Ends

Transformation is built one practice, one insight, one brave pause at a time. If this module stirred something in you, follow it. The rest of the Unbound Series, and the online programs, are designed to walk beside you as you continue the work – www.timetotransform.world

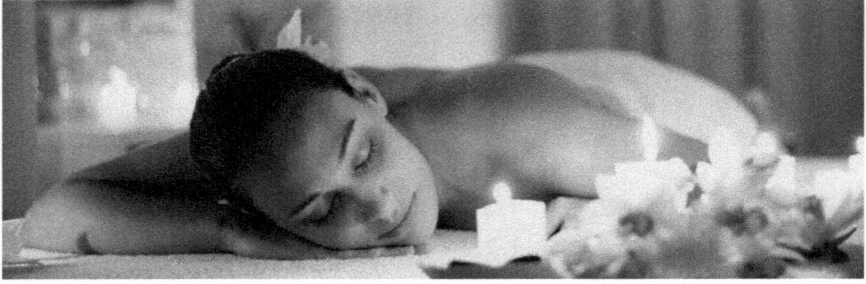

MODULE 3 – RELAXATION

Your Opening Reflection

Before you begin this module, give yourself permission to slow down. Take a gentle pause, soften your gaze or close your eyes, and let your attention rest on your breath. As you settle into this moment, allow yourself to truly feel into the following questions, not just with your mind, but with your heart. I invite you to undertake a short journaling session followed by optional pair-sharing or quiet reflection, and I encourage you to reflect on what prevents you from truly slowing down.

- "What is your current relationship with rest and stillness?"

- "When was the last time you felt deeply relaxed?"

- "When you slow down, what emotions or thoughts arise within you, comfort, unease, or something in between?"

- "How do you usually respond when your body asks for rest, do you honour it or push it aside?"

- "What beliefs do you hold about stillness, do you see it as valuable, or as wasted time?"

- "If you gave yourself permission to pause fully, what would that look and feel like for you?"

- "What simple practice could you invite into your daily life to create more space for rest?"

Let these questions open the doorway into presence. Every answer you give, whether in words, sensations, or silence, is a bridge between where you are and where you are going.

Learning Objectives

The learning objectives are included here to give you a clear focus for this module, ensuring that each practice you explore moves you closer to mastering the skills, insights, and heart-led awareness that will enrich your life well beyond the program. By the end of this module, you will:

- Recognise relaxation as an essential component of emotional well-being and resilience

- Understand the physiological and emotional benefits of restorative practices

- Identify personal signs of stress and burnout, and how to respond with compassion

- Develop a personalised relaxation routine aligned with inner balance and heart connection

Core Emotional Domains

The core emotional intelligence domains covered here are essential because they form the foundation for lasting heart connection, guiding you to deepen self-awareness, regulate emotions, build resilience, and strengthen the mind-body bond throughout your *Unbound* journey.

- **Self-Awareness:** You learn to recognise the subtle signs of stress and fatigue in your body, emotions, and thoughts, becoming more attuned to when you need rest and why it matters.

- **Self-Regulation:** You practise calming your nervous system through breath, stillness, and mindful relaxation, allowing you to respond to life with greater ease rather than react from overwhelm.

- **Emotional Resilience:** By prioritising rest and recovery, you build inner strength and the capacity to bounce back from emotional strain or life's demands with steadiness and clarity.

- **Empathy (Self and Others):** Relaxation opens space for compassionate listening, to your own needs and to the emotional states of those around you, deepening your relational presence.

- **Well-Being and Life Balance:** This part reminds you that rest is not a reward, but a vital rhythm of sustainable living, essential for clarity, creativity, and connection in your everyday life.

"Relaxation – The Art Of Letting Go"

Relaxation is more than just a mental break, it is a healing practice that brings you back into emotional, physical, and creative balance. In the busyness of your day-to-day life, it is easy to forget the power of simply pausing, but when you give yourself permission to slow down and soften, you begin to return to your natural state of calm presence. In this part of your *Unbound* journey, you are invited to explore what it means to truly rest, not just to disconnect, but to reconnect. Relaxation isn't about avoiding life, it is about creating space to feel, breathe, and restore. When you let go of tension, quiet the inner noise, and return to your breath, you allow your nervous system to reset. Your body heals. Your emotions settle. Your creativity reawakens.

You will draw from ancient practices and modern science to understand how rest activates your parasympathetic nervous system, your body's way of returning to safety and repair. Through stillness, you begin to hear the quieter parts of your heart. You reconnect with empathy, build emotional resilience, and honour your need for gentleness. Relaxation reminds you that you do not have to earn your rest. It is your birthright. When you prioritise stillness, you begin to find clarity, presence, and renewal. You become more balanced, not by doing more, but by choosing what truly matters. This is your invitation to pause, not as an escape, but as a sacred return. A return to your breath. A return to balance. A return to you.

Historical Roots: Egypt, Greece, India, China, How Cultures Viewed Rest As Sacred

Long before the modern world began glorifying busyness, many ancient cultures understood something profound, **rest was not laziness; it was sacred.** It was seen as essential to well-being, insight, healing, and spiritual connection. As you reconnect with your own need for rest, it is powerful to remember that you are returning to something deeply ancestral, something honoured and revered across time and cultures.

Ancient Egypt

In ancient Egypt, rest and sleep were seen not as passive states, but as sacred gateways into the divine. To the Egyptians, the hours of stillness were moments when the veil between the human and the spiritual thinned, allowing wisdom and healing to flow through dreams. Sleep was honoured as a bridge to the gods, a time when guidance, prophecy, and renewal could be received. Temples were constructed not only as places of worship, but also as sanctuaries for healing. Within their quiet chambers, priests and healers facilitated sacred sleep rituals known as **incubation**. These rituals invited individuals to enter a deeply restful state, lying down in a protected space, breathing slowly, and surrendering to the embrace of silence. In this state of openness, dreams were welcomed as divine messages, visions that could bring answers to life's struggles, insight into decisions, or even physical healing. To rest was not considered idleness. It was regarded as a **portal of wisdom**, a sacred act of aligning the body and soul with cosmic order. In surrendering to rest, the Egyptians believed you were surrendering to something higher, allowing your soul to speak in the language of dreams and symbols. Imagine yourself stepping into one of these ancient temples. The air is still and perfumed with incense. A quiet hush surrounds you as you recline on a simple bed of linen. Your breath deepens, your body softens, and slowly you drift into the realm of dream, trusting that in this space of rest, healing, and divine communication, you will receive exactly what your heart and soul need. Even today, you can carry this wisdom forward: rest is not wasted time, but a **sacred practice of restoration**. Each time you surrender to sleep or stillness with intention, you invite your inner world to reveal itself, and you open a doorway to insight, healing, and peace.

Ancient Greece

In ancient Greece, rest was not viewed as indulgence, but as medicine for both the body and the soul. Philosophers such as **Hippocrates**, often called the father of medicine, and later **Galen**, emphasised that true health could not exist without periods of balance, quiet, and renewal. They taught that exhaustion and overexertion disrupted the harmony of the four humours, blood, phlegm, yellow bile, and black bile, which were believed to govern physical and emotional wellbeing. To restore balance, the body required cycles of **rest, reflection, and stillness**. The practice of sacred rest was also central to the **temples of Asclepius**, the Greek god of healing. These sanctuaries, known as **Asclepieia**, were places where seekers came not only for physical cures but for spiritual renewal. Upon arrival, pilgrims would often bathe, fast, or engage in rituals to purify the body and mind. Then, they were invited to lie down in a sacred chamber and surrender to silence, stillness, and sleep. This ritual, called **incubation**, was believed to open the way for divine dreams, visions in which Asclepius himself or his healing spirits offered guidance, remedies, or reassurance. For the Greeks, healing was never separate from rest. **There was no healing without rest. There**

was no clarity without stillness. To pause was not weakness, but wisdom, an act of alignment with the natural rhythms of life and the divine order of the cosmos. Imagine walking into one of these sanctuaries, the air thick with the scent of herbs and oils, the sound of water echoing from a nearby fountain. You are guided to a quiet space where you lie down, close your eyes, and surrender to stillness. In that silence, the body begins to soften, the mind begins to slow, and the spirit opens to receive. Healing begins not through striving, but through the **art of resting deeply**. Even today, this wisdom calls to us. To slow down. To surrender. To remember that clarity does not come from doing more, but from allowing ourselves to pause long enough to hear what our body and soul have been trying to say all along.

India

In India, rest was not seen as absence of activity, but as a profound practice of presence. The ancient tradition of **Yoga Nidra**, often called the *yogic sleep*, guided practitioners into a state of deep conscious rest that lay between wakefulness and sleep. In this liminal space, the body could release tension, the mind could soften its constant activity, and the spirit could return to its natural state of wholeness. Unlike ordinary sleep, Yoga Nidra was a **spiritual discipline**, a practice of awareness. Practitioners were invited to lie down, close their eyes, and follow the rhythm of their breath inward. Step by step, the teacher would guide awareness through the body, gently relaxing each part, until the entire being entered into stillness. In this sacred state, the body rested deeply, yet consciousness remained awake and open, a unique meeting of **rest, renewal, and insight**. Here, healing was not forced but allowed to unfold naturally. Old wounds could surface gently, emotions could be released, and clarity could emerge from within. In Yoga Nidra, rest became more than recovery; it became a **pathway to transformation**. Rest in this tradition was a **sacred return to the self.** The breath was a bridge to inner calm. The body, once tense and striving, became an ally in letting go. Awareness itself became medicine, illuminating the layers of distraction and revealing the quiet light of the soul beneath. Imagine yourself lying on a mat in a quiet temple space, the air warm and still. A voice guides you to notice your breath, then your hands, your feet, your chest, your face. One by one, the parts of you soften and release. Your body sinks into rest, yet a part of you remains awake, luminous, and free. This is the gift of Yoga Nidra: the **union of stillness and awareness**, where renewal and insight flow without effort. Even today, this practice teaches us that rest is not laziness, but a

discipline of the heart. It is a conscious choice to surrender striving, to listen deeply, and to trust that in stillness, life itself restores you.

<u>Ancient China</u>

In ancient China, the wisdom of **Daoism** invited people to live in harmony with the natural rhythms of life. To the Daoists, existence itself was a dance between movement and stillness, light and dark, effort and rest, all flowing together in balance, like the yin and yang. To resist or force life's currents was to create struggle; to rest and flow with them was to return to alignment with the Dao, the great way of nature.Rest, in this tradition, was not seen as weakness or idleness. It was understood as a **vital rhythm within the cycle of life**. Just as the earth needs seasons of stillness for renewal, so too do human beings. Silence and stillness were cultivated as sources of clarity, wisdom, and transformation. A quiet mind was like a still pond, reflecting truth with precision and depth. Even warriors and scholars were taught the principle of **wu wei**, the art of effortless action. Wu wei was not inaction, but the state of acting in perfect harmony with the flow of life, without strain or resistance. From this place, rest and action became partners, not opposites. Rest prepared you for movement; movement returned you to rest. Both were essential for balance and vitality. Imagine yourself in a Daoist garden, where water flows gently over stones and bamboo bends with the breeze. You sit quietly, breathing with the earth, noticing how every leaf, every ripple, every birdcall arises and passes effortlessly.

In this stillness, you realise: you, too, are part of this natural rhythm. You do not need to force. You do not need to grasp. When you rest, you align with the great flow, and from this alignment, clarity, strength, and transformation naturally emerge. The wisdom of Daoism reminds us that stillness is not the absence of life, but the essence of life itself. To rest is to return to harmony with the Dao, to discover that the universe is already carrying you, if only you soften enough to let it. These ancient roots remind you that **rest is not something to fit in after you have done enough. It is foundational.** Sacred. Alive with possibility. In stillness, you reconnect with your wholeness. In relaxation, you meet yourself again, unmasked, unhurried, and whole. As you lie down or pause in silence today, know that you are part of a long, beautiful lineage that understood something our modern world is just beginning to remember: *Rest is a spiritual act. Rest is a return to the heart. Rest is a remembering of who you truly are.*

The Nervous System Explained: Parasympathetic Activation And Why it Matters

Your body is a masterpiece of wisdom, designed not only to keep you alive but to help you heal, grow, and return to balance. At the centre of this design is your **nervous system**, the intricate network of signals that governs how you respond to the world around you. One of its greatest gifts is the ability to shift between states, from activation to calm, from survival to safety, from reactivity to presence. Learning how to recognise and guide these shifts is key to emotional healing, resilience, and reconnecting with your heart. Your nervous system has **two main branches**:

The Sympathetic Nervous System (Fight-or-Flight)

This is your body's accelerator. When you face a challenge, danger, or even the stress of a crowded inbox, your sympathetic system switches on. Your breath becomes shallow, your heart races, your muscles tense. Your body is preparing you to fight, flee, or push through. This response is essential in true emergencies, but modern life keeps many of us in this state far too often, running on adrenaline, exhausted, and disconnected from peace.

The Parasympathetic Nervous System (Rest-and-Restore)

This is your body's natural brake and healer. When activated, your breath slows, your heart rate steadies, your digestion improves, and your whole system signals: *"You are safe now."* In this state, your body repairs itself, your mind clears, and your heart opens. It is here that healing, integration, and renewal happen. The vagus nerve, sometimes called the body's *"calm highway,"* plays a central role in activating the parasympathetic system. When stimulated through slow breathing, mindful movement, singing, humming, or even gentle touch, it helps you shift out of stress and into grounded calm. Why does this matter? Because when your nervous system feels safe, your **heart can speak**. Calm is not weakness, it is wisdom. Stillness is not idleness, it is the soil where clarity, compassion, and resilience grow. Think of it this way: when you are in survival mode, your world shrinks. You react. You grasp. You fight or flee, but when you activate your parasympathetic nervous system, your world expands again. You see more clearly. You feel more deeply. You respond rather than react. You become more present, more compassionate, more in tune with yourself and others. Simple practices can awaken this state within minutes:

- Slow, rhythmic breathing (especially longer exhales).

- Resting with your hand on your heart.

- Gentle yoga, tai chi, or mindful walking.

- Pausing in stillness with the intention to soften.

Each time you do this, you are reminding your body: *"You are safe. You are home."* In this part of your *Unbound* journey, you are not fighting your nervous system; you are partnering with it. You are reclaiming calm as your birthright. You are discovering that resilience is not about pushing harder, but about returning more gently, again and again, to safety and presence. When your body rests in calm, your heart's whispers become audible. When your nervous system softens, healing unfolds naturally, and in this sacred space, where breath slows, muscles release, and the heart opens, transformation begins.

The Myth Of "Busy" And The Cost Of Burnout

You have likely been told, perhaps since childhood, that being busy is a virtue. That a full calendar, a packed to-do list, and a life of constant motion are proof that you are valuable, productive, successful, and even lovable. Somewhere along the way, you may have learned to equate your worth with how much you do, how quickly you respond, how much you achieve, or how well you keep up, but this belief is not truth, it is a myth. *"Busy"* is not always purposeful. More often, it becomes a mask, hiding your exhaustion, your fear of stillness, or your disconnection from what really matters. You can be busy and empty. Busy and lonely. Busy and quietly breaking inside. You may be praised for how much you achieve, yet your soul knows the cost, and the cost is high. When you live in a constant state of *"on,"* your nervous system never has the chance to rest. Your breath becomes shallow, your mind scatters, and your emotions feel harder to manage. Your body begins to whisper: headaches, fatigue, irritability, anxiety. If you ignore the whispers, they grow louder, burnout, illness, disconnection, even collapse. Busyness without balance does not lead to joy, it leads to depletion. It erodes creativity, compassion, presence, and meaning. You stop hearing your own needs. You forget what it feels like to breathe deeply, to feel your heart, to live from the inside out, but it does not have to stay this way. You can choose to rewrite the story. To remember that rest is not laziness, it is medicine. That slowing down is not giving up, it is coming home to what matters. That your value is not measured by how much you do, but by how deeply you live.

In this part of *The Unbound Organisation*, you are invited to gently step away from the myth of *"busy"* and into a new rhythm. One that honours your energy, protects your peace, and gives your nervous system the exhale it has been waiting for. You are not a machine. You are a living, breathing, feeling, tender-hearted human being. You are allowed to pause. You are allowed to rest, and in fact, your healing, your joy, and your wholeness depend on it. You have also likely been conditioned to believe that insight comes from effort, thinking harder, working longer, pushing through, but what if the clarity you seek is not found in doing more... but in doing less? Stillness is not the absence of action. It is the presence of awareness. In stillness, your mind softens and your inner landscape becomes more visible. Like a muddy river settling after the storm, clarity does not come from stirring the water, it comes from letting it rest. When you pause long enough to truly *be*, the noise of the world fades, and the whispers of your heart can finally be heard. It is often in the quietest moments, a deep breath, a walk in nature, a few minutes with your eyes closed, that breakthrough insights rise. Not because you forced them, but because you created space for them to emerge. Stillness gives you perspective. It lets you step back from the overwhelm and see your life with fresh eyes. It invites intuitive knowing to surface, truths that cannot be accessed through logic alone. When you slow down, your nervous system rebalances, your body releases tension, and your inner wisdom is no longer drowned out by urgency. Paradoxically, when you do less, you *receive* more, more clarity, more creativity, more alignment. You begin to operate from depth, not just momentum. You become more intentional, more present, more grounded. In *The Unbound Organisation*, stillness is not a retreat from life, it is a return to it. It is where your next steps become clear, not because you rush toward them, but because you listen deeply for them. *So allow yourself to pause. To breathe. To trust the quiet* because sometimes, the greatest insights come not when you strive, but when you simply allow.

Creativity, Resilience, And Relationships: What Happens When We Recharge

When you allow yourself to rest, deeply, intentionally, without guilt, you do more than just recover from exhaustion. You begin to renew your most vital capacities: your creativity, your emotional resilience, and your ability to show up in your relationships with presence and care. **Creativity** does not thrive in burnout. It withers in stress. When you are constantly rushing, your mind becomes cluttered with noise and urgency, leaving little space for wonder, vision, or possibility, but when you slow down, breathe, and let your nervous system soften, something remarkable happens, your imagination reawakens. Ideas flow more freely. Solutions become clearer. The colours return to your inner world. Creativity is born not from pressure, but from spaciousness. **Resilience**, too, is restored in rest. Life is full of challenge, but when you are rested, you have the inner stability to face what comes. You bounce back more easily. You think more clearly. You feel more emotionally steady. The strength you need is not forged by pushing harder, it is nurtured by knowing when to pause, replenish, and begin again from a place of alignment, and then, there are your **relationships**.

The people you care about most benefit deeply when you are well-rested and present. When you are not surviving on empty, you listen better, love more patiently, and communicate more authentically. You are able to offer your full self, not a rushed, distracted version of you, but the real you. The you with space in your heart. When you recharge, you do not just feel better, you live better. You create more, connect deeper, and navigate life with more grace. So let rest be part of your rhythm. Let it be non-negotiable, because every time you choose to restore yourself, you are also choosing to renew your heart, your voice, and your relationships, and that is a gift to everyone, including you.

Body, Breath, and Balance – Expanded Practice

This practice is about creating harmony within yourself by reconnecting with your breath, your body, and the quiet presence of your heart. It is not about fixing or changing anything, it is about noticing, softening, and allowing yourself to rest in awareness.

Step 1: Balanced Heart Breathing (3 minutes)

Begin by returning to the foundation from Day 1. Place a hand on your heart and gently slow your breath. Inhale through your nose for a count of 4, and exhale softly through your mouth for a count of 6. With each breath, imagine you are nourishing your body with calm, safety, and presence. Feel your heart steady as your nervous system begins to relax.

Step 2: Gentle Body Scan Meditation (5 minutes)

Close your eyes and bring your attention slowly through the different parts of your body. Start at the top of your head and move downward, forehead, jaw, shoulders, arms, chest, belly, hips, legs, and feet. Notice any sensations, warmth, tightness, tingling, or stillness. You are not trying to

---

change them; you are simply becoming aware. This is an act of kindness toward yourself, letting your body be just as it is.

Step 3: Simply Be (Presence Without Judgment)

Now, allow yourself to rest in this awareness. Notice how your body feels when you release the need to do or perform. Can you welcome each sensation with curiosity instead of judgment? This gentle acceptance is balance: letting the body, mind, and heart come into alignment through awareness.

Optional Enhancement

If you wish, create an atmosphere of peace around you. Soft instrumental music, nature sounds, or even silence can become the backdrop for your practice. Allow these sounds to hold you, reminding you that you are safe, supported, and exactly where you need to be.

Reflection Prompt: After this practice, take a few moments to write in your journal:

- *What did I notice in my body that surprised me?*

- *How did my breath shift my sense of balance or presence?*

- *Where in my body did I feel most at ease?*

Case Study Discussion: Glen's Journey

To say that Glen was a hard worker was an understatement. He worked six days a week in his own business, and he never seemed to stop. Long days and sleepless nights had taken their toll on his physical and mental well–being, leaving him exhausted and disconnected from his true self. He was past burnout when we started journeying together and it took a long time to get him to a place that he could even realise he needed to slow down. Over several months we started introducing very simple routines into his daily life, such as balanced heart breathing and taking peaceful leisurely walks outside at a park near his work. As he gradually embraced these practices, Glen noticed a remarkable shift within himself. The relentless grip of stress began to loosen, replaced by a sense of calm and tranquility. Glen discovered the joy of being present in the moment, experiencing life's simple pleasures, and nurturing his relationships with his wife and children. He approached challenges with a clearer mind and a renewed sense of purpose. His productivity soared, and he achieved a greater work–life balance. The ripple effects of his relaxation practices positively influenced those around him, inspiring friends, and colleagues to prioritise their self–care and well–being. Through relaxation, Glen unearthed a deeper understanding of himself and his place in the world. He learned to listen to his body's needs and honour his own boundaries.   Glen's journey is a salutary reminder of the transformative power of relaxation and that by learning to relax, you can rediscover your true self, cultivate and nurture your own well–being, and live a more fulfilled and balanced life.

Reflective Exercise: Glen's Journey

Here are four profound and reflective questions inspired by Glen's story to help you engage with your own relaxation journey:

1. **What beliefs have you inherited about rest and productivity, and how might those beliefs be keeping you disconnected from your well-being?** Take a moment to reflect on whether you have attached your worth to being constantly busy. What would it mean for you to redefine success through presence, balance, and ease?

2. **When was the last time you truly listened to your body without rushing past its signals?** Your body holds quiet wisdom. Are there places within you asking to slow down, breathe, or soften, and are you willing to honour those needs today?

3. **What simple, restorative practice could you begin right now to help you return to yourself each day?** Think small: a walk, a breath, a pause. What could become your new ritual of calm, a sacred space in your routine that belongs just to you?

4. **How would your relationships shift if you began showing up more rested, present, and emotionally available?** Imagine how your energy, attention, and love might feel different when you are no longer running on empty. What becomes possible when you give from overflow rather than depletion?

Affirmations For You – (Heart Whispers)

Affirmations have the power to quiet the noise of doubt, open the doorway to self-trust, and draw you back into the wisdom of your heart. When practised daily, they nurture an inner dialogue based in love and truth, helping you live each day more aligned with who you truly are. I invite you to repeat silently or write:

- In relaxation, I find peace and refuge from life's demands.

- I embrace the calm of relaxation, letting go of tension.

- In stillness, I discover the profound beauty of relaxation.

- I prioritise self-care and carve out time for relaxation.

- Through relaxation, I recharge my spirit and rejuvenate my soul.

- I am at peace when I surrender to the gentle embrace of relaxation.

Create Your *"Relaxation Ritual Blueprint"*

Rest is not a luxury, it is a necessity for your mind, body, and heart. When you consciously create space for relaxation, you give yourself permission to replenish energy, restore balance, and return to life with more clarity and compassion. This blueprint is your personal guide to designing sustainable rituals of rest that align with your unique rhythm and lifestyle.

Step 1: Daily Micro-Moments of Rest

Relaxation does not have to wait for a weekend or a holiday. Small pauses throughout your day can make a profound difference. Try:

- Closing your eyes for one minute of deep breathing between tasks.

- Stepping outside to feel the sun, wind, or air on your skin.

- Stretching slowly while bringing awareness to your breath.

- Sipping a cup of tea or water with full presence, as if it were a sacred act.

These micro-moments reset your nervous system and remind you that rest can be woven into ordinary moments.

Step 2: Weekly Unplug Hours or "Sabbath" Practices

Choose a block of time each week where you step away from screens, work obligations, and busyness. This could be an afternoon in nature, a technology-free evening, or a few sacred hours dedicated to family, creativity, or stillness. By creating these boundaries, you gift yourself time for deeper restoration and reconnection.

Step 3: Restorative Tools

Gather tools that support you in relaxing deeply and intentionally. Your toolkit might include:

- Gentle music, sound baths, or nature soundscapes.

- A warm bath with calming scents like lavender or chamomile.

- Meditation or guided relaxation practices.

- Time in nature, walking, sitting by water, or simply lying on the grass.

- Creative outlets such as journaling, painting, or mindful cooking.

Notice which tools genuinely nourish you, and keep them close at hand.

Step 4: Boundaries with Technology and Overcommitment

Much of your fatigue comes not from doing too little, but from doing too much, or doing too much *for others* at the expense of yourself. Reflect on:

- When and how you use your phone or screens.

- Whether you need to say *"no"* more often to protect your energy.

- What commitments can be simplified, delegated, or released.

Setting boundaries is not selfish, it is essential for protecting your wellbeing and sustaining your capacity to give from a place of fullness.

Step 5: Your Ritual Declaration

Now, shape these elements into a personal blueprint that feels realistic and supportive for you. Write your responses to the following:

- *"My non-negotiable for relaxation is…"*

- *"When I honour rest, I feel…"*

Let this be your reminder that rest is not optional, it is your foundation. Every time you honour rest, you strengthen your ability to show up for life with presence, resilience, and joy.

Closing Reflection

As you arrive at the close of this part of your journey, pause and give yourself the gift of a deep, nourishing breath. Feel the stillness that lives beneath the surface of your busyness, the quiet sanctuary within you that is always available, waiting patiently for your return. Relaxation is not a reward for having done enough. It is your right, your rhythm, your refuge. In letting go of the myth of *"busy,"* you have opened space for something deeper: insight, healing, and presence. You have remembered that doing less does not mean being less, it often means becoming more. More attuned. More rested. More whole. As Glen's story reminds you, when you learn to slow down, you do not fall behind, you catch up with your heart. So keep choosing rest not just as a break from life, but as a way back to it. Let your breath be your anchor. Let stillness become your strength, and know this: *Every time you honour your need to pause, you honour your sacred aliveness. You are worthy of rest. You are worthy of peace. You are worthy of coming home to yourself.*

Your Story Is Unfolding

The chapter ends, but your story is still moving. If you want a deeper map, broader tools, and a community walking the same path, the next Unbound book or program will meet you there. Your story is calling. Answer it – www.timetotransform.world

MODULE 4 - GROUNDING

Your Opening Reflection

Invitation to Grounding - As you step into this module, I invite you to let the earth beneath you hold your weight, steady and sure. Imagine roots extending from your body into the ground, reminding you that you are supported, anchored, and safe. This is your moment to return to yourself, to release the rush, to soften the tension, and to remember that you are never separate from the strength and stability of the earth. Breathe deeply, feel your presence, and allow yourself to come home to your grounding.

- "When was the last time you felt fully anchored, steady, and safe in yourself?"

- "What practices, people, or places help you return to a sense of grounded calm when life feels overwhelming?"

- "In what areas of your life do you feel scattered or unsteady, and what might help you ground more deeply there?"

- "How does your body tell you when you are grounded, what sensations, rhythms, or signals arise?"

- "What does it mean to you to stand firmly in your truth, no matter what storms arise around you?"

Let these questions open the doorway into presence. Every answer you give, whether in words, sensations, or silence, is a bridge between where you are and where you are going.

Learning Objectives

The learning objectives are included here to give you a clear focus for this module, ensuring that each practice you explore moves you closer to mastering the skills, insights, and heart-led awareness that will enrich your life well beyond the program. By the end of this module, you will:

- Understand the emotional and physiological benefits of grounding.

- Learn and experience grounding techniques to reduce anxiety and stress.

- Deepen self-awareness by reconnecting with the physical body and present moment.

- Recognise grounding as a tool for emotional regulation and decision-making.

- Integrate grounding practices into daily life for ongoing balance and heart connection.

Core Emotional Domains

The core emotional intelligence domains covered here are essential because they form the foundation for lasting heart connection, guiding you to deepen self-awareness, regulate emotions, build resilience, and strengthen the mind-body bond throughout your *Unbound* journey.

- **Self-Awareness:** Grounding anchors you in the present moment, helping you notice your thoughts, sensations, and emotions as they arise.

- **Self-Regulation:** By connecting with your body and breath, you calm your nervous system and create space to respond rather than react.

- **Emotional Resilience:** Grounding builds inner stability, allowing you to navigate stress and uncertainty with greater clarity and strength.

- **Empathy:** When you are grounded, you are more attuned to others, your presence becomes deeper, and compassion flows with ease and authenticity *"Forgiveness - Releasing The Past"*

"Grounding – Finding Safety in the Present"

Grounding: Coming Home to the Body, the Moment, and Yourself

Grounding is both a **physical** and **emotional** process, a returning to what is real, stable, and present. In a world that often pulls you into the past with regret or into the future with anxiety, grounding gently invites you back into the *now*. It reminds you that safety, clarity, and calm are found not in racing thoughts, but in the stillness beneath them. When you ground yourself, you **anchor into your body**, your breath, your senses. You notice the earth beneath your feet, the rise and fall of your chest, the sounds and textures around you. This simple act of presence creates an immediate shift: your mind begins to settle, your nervous system calms, and the storm of emotion begins to soften. Emotionally, grounding is a tool for **self-regulation**. It helps you find your centre when you feel overwhelmed, disconnected, or scattered. It allows you to respond with intention rather than react from fear or fatigue. In this grounded state, you are more resilient, more clear, and more compassionate, with yourself and with others. Grounding is not about escaping your experience, it is about **embodying it fully**, without judgment. It teaches you that peace is not the absence of challenge, but the presence of groundedness. In grounding, you come back to yourself.

- To breath.

- To presence.

- To the steady truth that **this moment is enough,** and so are you.

What Is Grounding?

Across time and tradition, grounding has been more than a calming technique, it has been a sacred relationship between your human spirit and the living Earth. Long before science named the nervous system or psychology defined trauma, cultures around the world understood that healing begins by returning to the ground beneath you.

Indigenous Traditions: Grounding as Relationship and Reverence

In many Indigenous cultures, grounding is a deeply spiritual act, one of **connection, reciprocity, and respect** for the Earth as a living, breathing being. The land is not a resource to be used, but a relative to be honoured. Through practices such as walking barefoot, smudging, drumming, or placing hands on trees, grounding becomes a way of **coming back to wholeness,** not just as individuals, but as part of a greater web of life. The Earth is seen as a **source of wisdom and nourishment**, holding memory, energy, and guidance. When you feel overwhelmed, lost, or fragmented, you are often invited to "*go back to the land*", to sit in silence, feel the soil, listen to the wind, or immerse yourself in ceremony. These are not passive acts of escape, but intentional pathways to **embodied remembrance**. Grounding in this context is about restoring **right relationship,** with the self, with community, and with the more-than-human world. It is about listening with your feet, breathing with the trees, and remembering that **you belong.**

Ayurveda and Traditional Chinese Medicine: Grounding as Energetic Balance

In **Ayurveda**, grounding is associated with the **root chakra** (*Muladhara*), the energetic centre located at the base of your spine, which governs your sense of safety, stability, and survival. When this chakra is balanced, you feel **secure, present, and anchored**. When imbalanced, you may feel anxious, scattered, or disconnected. Practices like **prāṇāyāma** (breath control), restorative yoga, warm foods, daily rituals, and time in nature are used to stabilise and nourish your root chakra, reconnecting you with your body and the rhythms of the Earth. In **Traditional Chinese Medicine**, grounding is tied to the **Earth element**, which governs digestion, nourishment, and emotional equilibrium. When the Earth element is strong, it offers inner centredness and clarity. Grounding practices in this tradition often include **qigong**, **earthing exercises**, **tai chi**, and mindful eating, methods that restore **harmony between body, emotion, and environment**.

Monastic and Contemplative Traditions: Grounding as Inner Stillness

In Christian, Buddhist, and other monastic traditions, grounding was cultivated through **structured ritual and silent practice**. Walking meditations in cloisters, the rhythm of chanting, breath-focused prayers like the *Jesus Prayer*, and time in nature were all ways of **stilling the mind and rooting the soul**. These practices were not escapes from the world, but portals into the **inner sanctuary of presence**. Grounding in this context became a **spiritual discipline,** a path to humility, surrender, and alignment with the divine.

A Shared Wisdom

Across all these traditions, grounding was never just a practice. It was a **return,** to the Earth, to the self, to the sacred. It reminds you that healing is not about striving upward, but about **deepening downward**.

- That clarity is not always in thinking more, but in **feeling more**.

- That strength is found not in resistance, but in **groundedness**.

Grounding invites you to come back to what has always held you: *The Earth. Your breath. The moment. Your body. Your truth.*

Modern Psychological and Somatic Approaches to Grounding

Healing the Mind by Reconnecting to the Body

In modern psychology, particularly in trauma-informed, somatic, and mindfulness-based practices, **grounding is now understood as a vital and evidence-based strategy** for emotional regulation, safety, and mental clarity. It has become a cornerstone of therapeutic interventions for anxiety, trauma, dissociation, and chronic stress, not just as a coping mechanism, but as a pathway to long-term healing.

What Is Grounding in Psychological Terms?

Grounding refers to any technique that brings your awareness back into the *present moment* by reconnecting you with your body, breath, senses, and surroundings. When a person is emotionally overwhelmed, by stress, anxiety, trauma triggers, or intrusive thoughts, the brain can easily slip into **fight, flight, freeze, or fawn** responses. Grounding interrupts this physiological cascade by helping you regulate your nervous system and re-engage with safety. Common techniques include:

- **Breathwork** (e.g., extended exhale, box breathing)

- **Sensory orientation** (e.g., the 5-4-3-2-1 method)

- **Movement** (e.g., walking, stretching, shaking out tension)

- **Touch-based techniques** (e.g., holding a warm mug, pressing your feet into the floor)

- **Visualisation** (e.g., imagining roots growing from your feet into the earth)

These practices help shift attention **from spiraling thoughts into embodied awareness**, creating an internal pause, just long enough to access clarity, resilience, and self-agency.

The Neuroscience Behind Grounding

From a neurological perspective, grounding activates your **parasympathetic nervous system**, also known as the *"rest-and-digest"* system. This calms the stress response (regulated by your sympathetic nervous system), lowering cortisol and adrenaline levels, slowing the heart rate, and stabilising blood pressure. By drawing awareness back to the present moment, grounding can interrupt your neural pathways associated with trauma flashbacks or rumination. It also engages your **prefrontal cortex**, your brain's centre for reasoning, planning, and self-regulation, restoring executive function after emotional flooding. In short, grounding supports **neuroplasticity,** your brain's ability to rewire and recover from dysregulation, by building new, safer associations with embodiment and presence.

The Somatic Approach: Reclaiming the Wisdom of the Body

Somatic therapists recognise that trauma is not only a psychological wound, it is stored in your **nervous system and the body**. Grounding becomes a way for you to **return safely to your body**, especially if you have dissociated from it due to past pain or overwhelm. Rather than analysing thoughts or reliving traumatic memories, somatic grounding gently guides you to feel your feet on the floor, your breath in your chest, or your spine rising with strength. These micro-moments of safety begin to re-establish trust in your body's ability to hold experience without collapsing under it. This work is especially powerful in helping you move from **numbness to aliveness**, from **hyperarousal to regulation**, and from **survival to embodiment**.

From Coping Skill to Healing Practice

While grounding is often introduced as a short-term coping technique, its **long-term practice opens a doorway to deeper healing**. As you develop a daily grounding rhythm, whether through meditation, nature walks, sensory awareness, or movement, you begin to feel more grounded, more spacious, and more connected. This shift allows emotional experiences to **flow rather than flood**, making space for self-compassion, insight, and transformation. In a world that can often feel chaotic, fast-paced, and overstimulating, grounding becomes more than a practice, it becomes a way of being. *A quiet return to presence. A place of inner safety. A daily commitment to coming home to yourself.*

Benefits of Grounding: Physical Health, and Emotional Clarity

Grounding is more than a calming technique, it is a **holistic practice** that supports your wellbeing on multiple levels. When you ground yourself, you return to your natural state of presence: a place where your body feels safe, your emotions are balanced, and your spirit is attuned to its deeper wisdom. Let us explore how grounding nurtures **your whole self**:

Physical Health: Regulating the Nervous System and Energising the Body

At its core, grounding supports **physiological equilibrium,** helping your body return to a natural state of balance after the wear and tear of chronic stress, overstimulation, or emotional overload. In today's fast-paced world, many people live in a prolonged state of **sympathetic nervous system dominance**, also known as the **fight, flight, or freeze** response. This can lead to fatigue, insomnia, digestive issues, inflammation, and suppressed immune function. Grounding counteracts this by **activating the parasympathetic nervous system,** your body's built-in *rest, digest, and restore* mode. This shift results in a cascade of positive physiological effects:

1. **Lowered Heart Rate and Blood Pressure**: As your body begins to feel safe and supported, your cardiovascular system relaxes. Grounding helps reduce the physical markers of stress, allowing your heart to beat more steadily and efficiently.

2. **Improved Sleep and Circadian Rhythm**: Grounding practices, especially those performed in nature or with intentional breath, help regulate melatonin production and rebalance disrupted sleep cycles. When you are grounded, your body re-attunes to its natural rhythms, making rest deeper and more restorative.

3. **Reduced Cortisol Levels**: Chronic stress elevates cortisol, which over time can contribute to weight gain, mood swings, inflammation, and immune suppression. Grounding has been shown to reduce cortisol production, allowing the body to repair and regenerate more effectively.

4. **Enhanced Energy and Vitality**: When your nervous system is calm and balanced, more energy is available for life. Grounding clears internal tension, improves oxygenation, and restores clarity, leading to increased stamina and a greater sense of aliveness throughout the day.

Earthing: Grounding with the Earth Itself

In recent years, scientific studies on *"earthing",* the direct physical connection with the Earth's surface, have brought new insight into ancient practices. Research indicates that **barefoot contact with soil, sand, grass, or natural stone** allows the body to absorb negatively charged electrons from the Earth, which may help:

- Reduce systemic **inflammation**

- Improve **immune function**

- Normalise **blood viscosity**

- Support **electromagnetic balance** in the body

While more research is emerging, many report subjective benefits such as quicker recovery from fatigue, improved mood, and reduced physical pain after regular time spent connecting physically with the Earth. Even a few minutes a day, **feet in the grass, hands on a tree, or sitting quietly outdoors,** can have cumulative and profound health effects.

Grounding And Emotional Intelligence: Enhancing Presence And Choice

When you ground yourself, you give your emotional intelligence the space it needs to grow. Grounding is not just about calming down, it is about **coming back to yourself** so you can respond to life with clarity rather than react from stress or fear. In moments of overwhelm, your nervous system can hijack your thoughts and actions. You might feel scattered, reactive, or disconnected, but when you pause, take a breath, feel your feet on the floor, and **anchor into your body**, you interrupt that automatic pattern. You return to the present moment, and with that presence comes **the power to choose** how you show up. Grounding deepens your **self-awareness** by helping you notice what you are actually feeling, not just what you are thinking. It supports **self-regulation**, allowing you to move from reaction to reflection. When you are grounded, you are more likely to pause before speaking, to listen deeply, and to respond with compassion, toward yourself and others. This grounded awareness enhances **empathy**, **resilience**, and **relational intelligence**. You are no longer swept away by the noise around you; you stand in the calm centre of your own truth. From that place, you can lead, connect, and live with integrity and emotional clarity. Every time you ground yourself, you reclaim choice, and with choice comes freedom, power, and presence.

The Neuroscience Of Stress And How Grounding Activates The Parasympathetic Nervous System

When you are under stress, whether from a deadline, an emotional trigger, a conflict, or even an old memory, your body responds instantly. Without you needing to think about it, your brain signals your nervous system to protect you. You may feel your heart race, your breath quicken, your muscles tighten, or your thoughts spiral. This is your **sympathetic nervous system** kicking in: the part of your body designed to keep you alive through the **fight, flight, or freeze response**. This response is meant for short bursts of danger, but in your modern world, threats are not always physical. They are emotional, relational, digital, or imagined, and they can last all day. If you do not reset, your nervous system can stay stuck in overdrive. This is when you feel burned out, anxious, overwhelmed, disconnected, or numb. Here is the good news:

your body also has a built-in healing mechanism, your **parasympathetic nervous system**. This is your **rest, digest, and restore** mode. It slows your heart rate, deepens your breath, supports digestion, improves immune function, and calms your brain. When you ground yourself, you send a new signal to your brain: *"It is okay. I am safe now."* You do this by bringing your awareness back into your body:

- You feel your feet on the floor.

- You take a slow, intentional breath.

- You notice the sensation of your hand on your chest or belly.

- You orient your senses. What can you see, hear, feel?

These small acts may seem simple, but they **rewire your brain**. They activate your **prefrontal cortex,** the part of your mind responsible for awareness, compassion, decision-making, and self-regulation. When you ground yourself, you do not bypass stress, you **transform your relationship to it**. You become the calm in the storm. You reconnect with your body as a safe place, not just a container for tension, and from that calm space, you can think more clearly, feel more honestly, and choose how to move forward, on your terms. So the next time life feels too much, pause:

1. Ground yourself.

2. Feel your breath.

3. Feel the Earth beneath you.

Remember, you are not stuck in stress. You have the power to return to safety, clarity, and strength. This is the neuroscience of self-empowerment. This is the wisdom of grounding in action.

Integrating Grounding Into High-Performance Environments And Daily Rituals

Grounding is not just something you turn to in a crisis, it is a practice you can weave into the rhythm of your day, especially in **high-performance environments** where focus, clarity, and emotional balance are essential. Whether you are leading a team, presenting to stakeholders, managing clients, or studying under pressure, you are constantly being asked to perform, decide, and respond, and while your mind may be sharp, your **nervous system needs stability** to sustain excellence without burnout. That is where grounding becomes your secret edge. When you integrate grounding into your daily rituals, you begin to **regulate your energy, sharpen your attention, and increase your emotional intelligence,** even in demanding situations.

<u>Start with Small Anchors Throughout the Day</u>

You do not need hours of meditation or a quiet retreat to ground yourself. You can build **micro-moments of reconnection** into your day:

- **Before a meeting** – Take 3 slow breaths. Feel your feet on the floor. Say quietly, *"I am present."*

- **When giving feedback** – Place one hand over your chest or stomach. Speak from grounded clarity, not reactivity.

- **After back-to-back calls or emails** – Stand, stretch, and breathe. Let the tension leave your shoulders and jaw.

- **At the start of your day** – Write a short intention like: *"I choose calm under pressure."*

These rituals do not interrupt performance, they **sustain it**. When you are grounded, you do not rush decisions. You do not get easily hijacked by stress. You speak with authority **without losing empathy**.

<u>Why It Works in High-Performance Settings</u>

Grounding activates your **prefrontal cortex,** allowing you to make smarter, more emotionally balanced decisions under pressure. It also quiets the noise of fear, perfectionism, and urgency, so you can lead, communicate, and execute with clarity. The more you practice, the more you train your nervous system to come back to balance quickly. Over time, you become the kind of person who can stay **calm in the storm,** adapt with grace, and lead others by your presence, not just your position.

<u>Grounding as a Leadership and Lifestyle Practice</u>

When you integrate grounding into your lifestyle, it is no longer just a tool, it becomes a way of being. You begin to show up **more present in your relationships, more attentive with your teams,** and **more connected to your own needs.** Grounding becomes the space between stimulus and response. It becomes your reset button, your pause, your return, and in high-performance environments, that makes all the difference. So whether you are navigating deadlines, studying under pressure, leading meetings, or managing emotional complexity, come back to your breath. Come back to your body.

Come back to the ground beneath you.

Sensory Awareness Walk (Outdoor or Simulated)

I invite you to:

1. Walk slowly, paying close attention to the sensations in your feet, the pressure, texture, and rhythm of each step.

2. Tune into the sounds, smells, and textures around you, allowing each sense to awaken fully.

3. At intervals, pause, close your eyes if comfortable, and take three deep grounding breaths, feeling your body anchored in the present moment.

Debrief: After your walk, take a few minutes to reflect: *What emotions or insights emerged during your walk? How did your body feel? What changed in your mind or heart?*

Case Study Discussion: Lucas's Journey

After a lifetime of working long hours as a long–haul truck driver, and always being on the go, Lucas found himself in a state of constant stress and anxiety. He had tried everything from medication to therapy, but nothing seemed to work. One day, Lucas contacted me and after 3–4 weeks I chatted with him about trying grounding. I asked Lucas to connect with the earth's natural energy by walking barefoot or lying on the ground. At first, Lucas was highly skeptical, but he decided to give it a try. Lucas took off his shoes and walked on the grass in his backyard, feeling the cool blades between his toes. As he walked, he focused on his breath and let his mind clear. He felt a sense of calm and peace within him that he had not experienced in years. From that day forward, Lucas made grounding a daily practice. He spent time in nature, whether it was walking barefoot on the beach or lying in a park. Lucas found that his stress and anxiety levels decreased significantly, and he felt more balanced and centred in his life. He also discovered that grounding had other benefits. He felt more connected to the world around him and more in tune with his own emotions (this was massive for Lucas). Lucas began to appreciate the small moments of beauty and joy that he had previously overlooked. He felt more present in the moment and was able to connect with others on a deeper level. He also found that he had more energy and focus for the things that truly mattered to him. Lucas realised that grounding was not a cure–all, but it was an important tool in his toolbox for managing stress and anxiety. It was something that he could always turn to when he needed to find balance in his life.

Reflective Exercise: Lucas's Journey

Here are four profound and reflective questions inspired by Lucas's story to help you engage with your own grounding journey:

1. When was the last time you allowed the earth to hold you, without rushing, fixing, or thinking?

Reflection: Like Lucas, you may have spent much of your life in motion, driven by responsibility, pressure, or habit, but grounding reminds you that rest is not weakness; it is wisdom. When you let yourself slow down, even for a few moments, you invite in calm, clarity, and healing that your body has longed for.

2. What would it feel like to reconnect with the ground beneath your feet, not just physically, but emotionally?

Reflection: Your body knows how to return home to presence. Each breath, each barefoot step, each moment of stillness is a pathway back to your centre. When you take time to ground, you give your nervous system the safety it needs to regulate, and your heart the space it needs to soften.

3. Where in your day do you most need a pause, a moment to breathe, feel, and return to yourself?

Reflection: Lucas found that a few minutes barefoot in the grass changed everything. You do not need perfect conditions, just a willingness to pause. These micro-moments of grounding can become sacred rituals that restore your energy, reduce anxiety, and remind you that you are not just surviving, you are allowed to feel alive.

4. What might open up for you if you truly believed that you are supported, by the ground, by the moment, by life itself?

Reflection: Grounding is not just a technique, it is a shift in trust. It is the quiet knowing that you do not have to carry everything alone. Just like Lucas, you can find stability not by gripping harder, but by surrendering to what's already holding you. The ground is always there. So is your breath. So are you.

Affirmations For Integration: (Heart Whispers)

Affirmations have the power to quiet the noise of doubt, open the doorway to self-trust, and draw you back into the wisdom of your heart. When practised daily, they nurture an inner dialogue based in love and truth, helping you live each day more aligned with who you truly are. I invite you to repeat silently or write:

- *I feel more centred and calmer after grounding exercises.*
- *I notice a decrease in anxiety when I practice grounding.*
- *I am more in tune with my body when I ground myself.*
- *I find it easier to focus on the present moment with grounding.*
- *I feel more connected to the earth when I practice grounding.*
- *I release tension more easily when I practice grounding.*
- *Grounding helps me respond to challenges with greater clarity and patience.*
- *My thoughts feel more organised and steady after grounding.*
- *Grounding reconnects me to my inner strength and stability.*

Optional Extension Activity

Here are **3 original grounding exercises**. Each exercise includes **three parts,** a physical action, a mindful practice, and a heart-centred integration:

Exercise 1: Tree Lean + Grounding Intention + Heart Touch

1. Tree Lean: Stand or sit with your back gently resting against a tree or solid wall. Feel the support behind you and allow your body to relax into it. Let the earth carry your weight.

2. Grounding Intention: Silently repeat an intention such as: *"I am safe. I am supported. I am here."* Let this intention settle into your body like roots beneath the surface.

3. Heart Touch: Place one hand on your heart and the other on your belly. Breathe slowly. With each breath, invite yourself to feel grounded, present, and connected to the now.

Exercise 2: Stone Hold + Stillness Scan + Anchoring Phrase

1. Stone Hold: Find a small stone or natural object. Hold it in your palm

---

and observe its weight, texture, and temperature. Let it represent steadiness in your life.

2. Stillness Scan: Close your eyes and scan your body slowly from head to toe. Notice where tension lives and where ease flows. Stay curious, not critical.

3. Anchoring Phrase: Repeat quietly: *"In this moment, I return to myself."* Feel the energy of the stone and your breath grounding you into your inner calm.

Exercise 3: Spiral Walk + Sensory Awareness + Grounded Statement

1. Spiral Walk: Mark a small spiral pattern in the sand, grass, or with objects. Slowly walk the spiral path inward. With each step, let go of distraction or stress.

2. Sensory Awareness: Pause in the centre. Tune into 3 things you can feel, 3 sounds you can hear, and 3 natural elements around you. Let your senses awaken presence.

3. Grounded Statement: Say softly to yourself: *"I am grounded. I belong to this earth. I am at peace."* Then walk the spiral path back out with renewed focus.

Closing Reflection

As you come to the end of this part of your journey, remember: grounding is not something outside of you, it is within you, always. When life feels too fast, too loud, or too much, you can pause. You can feel your breath. You can feel the ground beneath your feet. You are **not** lost. You are not disconnected. You are simply being called back to the place you never truly left, **your body, your breath, your being**. Grounding is a quiet act of power. It brings you back into the present, where peace begins, where clarity returns, where your heart can speak again. No matter what is happening around you, you now have a way to return home to yourself. So take this with you:

- **You are safe to pause.**

- **You are safe to feel.**

- **You are safe to come back to now.**

Let every step forward be grounded in presence. Let every breath remind you, you are here, and that is enough.

The Journey Doesn't Stop Here

This moment is a threshold. Every Unbound book is another doorway into clarity, courage, connection, and purpose. If you feel the pull, step further in – www.timetotransform.world

Finding Purpose and Identity

Part 2

PART 2 – FINDING PURPOSE AND IDENTITY

Cultivating Connection, Belonging & Compassion in a Divided World

(Time to Transform: Living Unbound - Chapters 5 Mirror • 7 Self-Love • 12 Kindness • 15 Compassion)

A Moment of Awareness

Somewhere in the rhythm of your daily interactions, between the polite greetings, the virtual meetings, and the unspoken expectations, you start to sense something deeper, a quiet divide that cannot be fixed by policies or training alone. You notice the subtle ways people hold back, the pauses before they speak, the glances that carry hesitation, the ideas that never make it to the table. You recognise it not because you have read about it, but because you've felt it too, that moment of being unseen, unheard, or misunderstood. This is where real inclusion begins: not in strategy, but in awareness. It starts when you look honestly in the mirror and acknowledge your own filters, stories, and biases. When you choose to see not just the differences in others, but the humanity that connects you. Welcome to the heart of inclusion. This part of your journey is not about compliance, it is about connection. It invites you to see leadership not as holding power, but as holding space. Space for authenticity, for difference, for belonging.

Why Inclusion Matters

Inclusion is not about who you invite to the table, it is about how you make them feel when they get there. It is not a box to tick; it is a culture to live. When people feel safe to be themselves, creativity rises. When they feel seen and valued, collaboration deepens, and when they feel trusted, performance flourishes, but when fear or judgment linger in the background, people shrink to fit rather than expand to contribute. Diversity brings the potential.

Inclusion unlocks it, and compassion, the ability to feel with, not just for, others, sustains it. You cannot build belonging from the outside in; it must begin within you. The courage to face your own biases, to forgive your own blind spots, and to extend that same understanding outward, that is where transformation starts. Inclusion, at its deepest level, is not a project. It is a practice. A daily act of empathy. A moment-to-moment choice to lead with heart.

When you open your heart to difference, you do not lose your identity, you expand it.

The Four Pillars of Inclusion

1. Mirror – The Practice of Self-Awareness

The mirror never lies. It reflects what is there, both your light and your shadow. To look into it honestly takes courage. When you pause to see yourself clearly, you begin to recognise the unconscious habits and patterns that shape how you see others. Awareness does not bring shame; it brings freedom. You cannot transform what you cannot see. This is where inclusive leadership begins, with humility, reflection, and the willingness to keep learning. The mirror invites you to replace defensiveness with curiosity, judgment with understanding.

The mirror does not ask you to be perfect. It asks you to be present.

2. Self-Love – The Foundation of Empathy

You cannot offer acceptance if you do not extend it to yourself. Self-love is not arrogance; it is acknowledgement. It says, *"I am enough as I am, and so are you."* When you meet yourself with kindness, you dismantle the inner critic that projects judgment outward. You begin to understand that confidence and compassion are not opposites, they are allies. Inclusive cultures are born from individuals who know how to hold space for their own imperfections. When you treat yourself with gentleness, you create a ripple of permission that allows others to be real too.

The way you speak to yourself teaches others how to speak to you, and how to speak to each other.

3. Kindness – The Language of Respect

Kindness is not weakness. It is strength expressed with grace. It is how you communicate respect without needing to agree on everything. In a diverse workplace, differences will always exist. Kindness bridges them. It softens hard edges, diffuses tension, and opens conversations that might otherwise close too soon. True kindness is active, it listens, it notices, it responds. It is holding the door for another voice, asking the question that helps someone feel seen, offering feedback that heals rather than harms.

Kindness is inclusion in action, small gestures with extraordinary impact.

4. Compassion – The Bridge to Belonging

Compassion is empathy in motion. It's what happens when understanding meets courage. It does not just feel for someone; it stands with them. When you lead with compassion, you cultivate psychological safety, the invisible thread that allows people to speak truth without fear. Teams that feel safe are more innovative, more loyal, and more human. Compassion transforms inclusion from a value to a lived experience. It says, *"I see you, I care, and I am willing to understand."*

Belonging is not built by similarity, it is sustained by compassion.

The Synergy of the Four Pillars

Self-awareness, self-love, kindness, and compassion are not just emotional virtues; they are organisational catalysts. Together, they create a workplace where difference becomes a source of strength, not division. When you look inward **(Mirror)**, you cultivate awareness. When you accept yourself **(Self-Love)**, you develop authenticity. When you extend warmth **(Kindness)**, you create connection, and when you act with empathy **(Compassion)**, you create belonging. This is the heart of inclusive leadership, a coherence between who you are and how you lead. It is how trust is built, innovation thrives, and teams move beyond tolerance into genuine unity.

Diversity may open the door, but inclusion invites people to stay.

A Closing Reflection

Take a moment and imagine a workplace where everyone feels safe to be themselves. Where voices are heard without interruption. Where difference is not feared but welcomed as fuel for growth. Now imagine that begins with you. With the way you listen, the way you respond, and the way you choose to see others. Inclusion is not a policy you apply, it is a presence you bring. Every time you pause before reacting, every time you choose understanding over judgment, every time you speak from empathy instead of ego, you strengthen the invisible culture of belonging.

You cannot create belonging for others until you belong fully to yourself.

A Heart Invitation

As you step into this second part of *The Unbound Organisation*, may you lead with openness. When the world feels divided, be the one who connects. When conversations get uncomfortable, stay curious. When you feel unseen, remember that seeing others begins with seeing yourself. Let the mirror guide you, let love ground you, let kindness move through you, and let compassion unite you. This is how organisations heal. This is how cultures transform. This is how inclusion moves from policy to pulse.

You are not here to manage diversity; you are here to embody unity, through the heart.

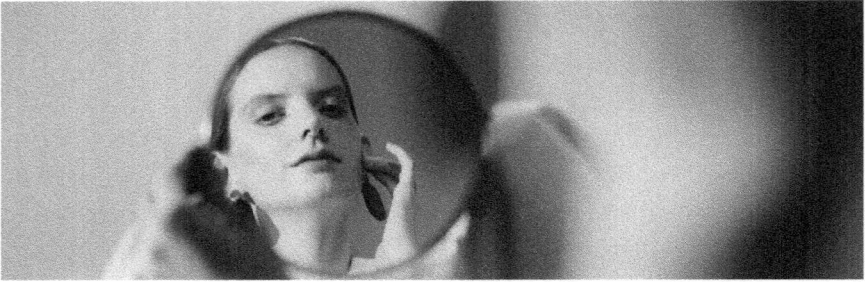

MODULE 5 - MIRROR

Your Opening Reflection

An Invitation to See Yourself with Gentle Eyes - As you step into this module, I invite you to pause and soften. Take a breath, and allow yourself to meet the mirror not as an enemy, but as a friend. The reflection before you is not asking for perfection, only honesty, tenderness, and presence. Let this moment be an opening, a chance to see yourself not through judgment, but through love.

- "Are you willing to see the parts of yourself you usually hide?"

- "What truths about yourself are you ready to accept today?"

- "When you meet your own gaze, do you recognise your inherent worth?"

- "When you look in the mirror, what do you really see?"

- "Do you offer yourself love and kindness... or judgment?"

Let these questions open the doorway into presence. Every answer you give, whether in words, sensations, or silence, is a bridge between where you are and where you are going.

Learning Objectives

The learning objectives are included here to give you a clear focus for this module, ensuring that each practice you explore moves you closer to mastering the skills, insights, and heart-led awareness that will enrich your life well beyond the program. By the end of this module, you will:

- Understand the emotional impact and science behind mirror work.

- Apply mirror work techniques to build yourself-worth, self-love, and emotional resilience.

- Identify internal resistance to self-acceptance and begin the process of transformation.

- Practice heart-connected affirmation and forgiveness through eye-gazing and mirror-based self-dialogue.

- Recognise how mirror work supports long-term emotional intelligence development and heart connection.

Core Emotional Domains

The core emotional intelligence domains covered here are essential because they form the foundation for lasting heart connection, guiding you to deepen self-awareness, regulate emotions, build resilience, and strengthen the mind-body bond throughout your *Unbound* journey.

- **Self-Awareness:** Helps you honestly see and acknowledge your emotions and inner dialogue as you face yourself.

- **Self-Regulation:** Enables you to stay grounded and calm when uncomfortable feelings surface during mirror work.

- **Motivation:** Fuels your commitment to personal growth and keeps you returning to the practice with intention.

- **Self-Compassion:** Encourages a kind, gentle response to your reflection, replacing criticism with understanding.

- **Emotional Resilience:** Strengthens your ability to move through vulnerability and transform emotional pain into healing.

"Mirror - Facing Yourself With Love"

The Psychological, Emotional, and Spiritual Value of Mirror Work

Mirror work is a courageous act of self-witnessing. It invites you to stand before your own reflection and meet the person who looks back, not with judgment, but with awareness, honesty, and compassion. This seemingly simple practice holds profound **psychological**, **emotional**, and **spiritual** value, especially when integrated into a heart-led path of healing and self-affirmation.

Psychological Value

From a psychological standpoint, mirror work is a powerful tool for increasing **self-awareness**. When you consciously look into your own eyes and speak to yourself with intention, you confront the often unconscious inner dialogue that runs beneath your surface thoughts. Over time, you begin to notice the beliefs you have inherited, the wounds you have carried, and the stories you have internalised about your worth. By practicing positive affirmations like *"I am enough"* or *"I am worthy of love,"* you start to **reprogram negative self-beliefs** and create new neural pathways through the science of **neuroplasticity**. This consistent, mindful reinforcement can shift your self-perception and support long-term cognitive and emotional growth.

Emotional Value

Emotionally, mirror work helps you build **emotional resilience**. It allows you to feel what you have suppressed, grief, shame, anger, joy, and to welcome those feelings without turning away. When you stand in front of the mirror and acknowledge your emotional truth, you begin to **regulate your emotional responses** with more clarity and compassion. This act of presence with your own emotional experience cultivates **self-acceptance** and nurtures a profound connection between your inner world and outer expression. Over time, this emotional honesty strengthens your capacity to hold space for others as well, enhancing empathy and relational depth.

Spiritual Value

Spiritually, mirror work becomes a sacred space, a daily ritual where you meet your soul. As you look into your own eyes, you begin to see not just your physical self, but the deeper essence that lives beneath your skin. This connection awakens your **inner wisdom**, your **divine light**, and the quiet voice of your heart. You begin to **recognise yourself as whole and loved**, regardless of past mistakes or external validation. In this space, the mirror becomes a metaphor for truth, reflecting not just who you are, but who you are becoming. It is a practice of **remembrance**, returning you to the truth that you are enough, just as you are. **In essence**, mirror work integrates psychological insight, emotional healing, and spiritual connection into a daily act of self-honouring. It helps you rewrite your internal narrative, build compassion from the inside out, and live with greater authenticity, presence, and love. When you dare to face yourself, gently, bravely, and consistently, you begin to unbind your heart and unlock the sacred power that lives within you.

The Origin Of Mirror Work: Louise Hay's Legacy

Mirror work, as a transformative healing practice, finds its modern roots in the pioneering work of **Louise Hay,** an internationally renowned author, speaker, and the founder of Hay House Publishing. Often called the "*Queen of Affirmations*," Hay revolutionised the self-help landscape by introducing a profoundly simple yet emotionally powerful method: **mirror work,** the practice of looking into your own eyes in a mirror while speaking affirming, loving, and healing words to yourself. At the heart of Hay's philosophy was the belief that **self-love is the key to healing**. In her seminal book, *You Can Heal Your Life* (1984), she taught that most suffering, whether emotional, physical, or spiritual, stems from **negative self-beliefs, self-criticism, and unhealed emotional wounds**, often based in childhood. Mirror work, she believed, was a way to gently bring those wounds to the surface and meet them with compassion rather than judgment. The mirror became, in Hay's hands, a **sacred tool for self-confrontation and self-connection**. It bypassed the intellect and tapped directly into the heart. When you stand before a mirror and say, *"I love you,"* or *"I am willing to change,"* you are not just speaking words, you are rewiring beliefs, rewriting narratives, and restoring trust in yourself. Hay often said, *"The mirror reflects back to us the feelings we have about ourselves,"* and that reflection, when met with courage and consistency, becomes a gateway to healing.

The emotional impact of mirror work can be immediate and intense. Many people experience tears, resistance, even anger, as long-buried shame, fear, or grief rises to the surface. Yet with continued practice, mirror work becomes a daily ritual of **self-reclamation,** a way to rebuild inner safety, validate your worth, and awaken to your true nature. From a **psychological perspective**, mirror work helps interrupt cycles of negative self-talk, strengthens self-compassion, and promotes emotional regulation. From a **spiritual perspective**, it aligns you with the divine within, reminding you that you are inherently worthy, lovable, and whole. Hay's legacy lives on not just in her writings but in the countless lives transformed through her teachings. Her work paved the way for a generation of coaches, therapists, and spiritual leaders who continue to use mirror work as a foundation for emotional intelligence, trauma recovery, and self-love. To engage in mirror work is to return home to yourself. It is a commitment to **see, hear, and honour the person looking back at you,** not as broken, but as beautifully becoming. Through this practice, you are invited to dissolve the layers of fear, shame, and self-doubt and remember this fundamental truth: **your heart is the most powerful healer you have.**

The Science Behind Mirror Work: Neuroplasticity, NLP, And

Emotional Reprogramming

<u>1. Neuroplasticity - Rewiring the Brain Through Repetition and Intention</u>

At the core of mirror work lies the principle of **neuroplasticity,** your brain's innate ability to change and reorganise its neural pathways in response to thoughts, experiences, and behaviors. When you stand in front of a mirror and repeat empowering affirmations like *"I am enough"* or *"I am worthy of love,"* you are not just speaking words, you are sending new signals through your brain's emotional and cognitive circuits.

Repeated mirror affirmations:

- Activate regions such as the **ventromedial prefrontal cortex** (associated with self-referential thinking and emotional regulation).

- Begin to **overwrite old narratives** stored in your subconscious, often tied to shame, rejection, or inadequacy.

- **Strengthen neural connections** that align with self-worth, compassion, and inner peace.

This consistent rewiring process gradually **shifts your inner default** from self-criticism to self-acceptance. It creates a new emotional baseline where confidence and calm become more natural responses.

<u>2. NLP - Anchoring and Reframing Limiting Beliefs</u>

Neuro-Linguistic Programming (NLP) is a psychological approach that studies how language and behavior influence your brain. Mirror work draws from two powerful NLP techniques:

- **Anchoring**: By placing your hand over your heart, making eye contact with your reflection, and pairing these gestures with positive affirmations, you create an anchor, a physiological and emotional cue that triggers feelings of safety, warmth, and empowerment. Over time, just returning to the mirror with this gesture can evoke those same emotional states.

- **Reframing**: Many people carry internal scripts like *"I am not good enough,"* *"I do not matter,"* or *"I always fail."* NLP teaches that by consciously **replacing these limiting beliefs** with affirmations such as *"I am growing,"* *"I am loved,"* or *"I am resilient,"* you shift your perception of self and reality. Mirror work makes this reframe **visceral and immediate**, amplifying its effectiveness through direct self-confrontation.

3. Emotional Reprogramming - Healing Through Presence and Self-Compassion

Mirror work also accesses your **limbic system**, your brain's emotional centre. When you speak to yourself with sincerity, while making gentle eye contact, your nervous system receives the message that **you are safe, seen, and accepted**. This is emotionally powerful, especially for those who never received that validation from others. Emotional reprogramming through mirror work:

- Creates **new emotional memory patterns** that create trust and compassion.

- Reduces cortisol and supports parasympathetic nervous system activation, bringing **calm and regulation**.

- Encourages the release of **suppressed emotions** in a safe and self-directed environment.

Over time, the act of meeting yourself in the mirror with love helps you **dismantle shame**, **release stored trauma**, and **cultivate deep emotional resilience**.

Final Insight: A Whole-Person Transformation

When combined, neuroplasticity, NLP, and emotional reprogramming make mirror work a truly integrative healing modality. This is not about vanity, it is about **visibility**: truly seeing yourself, acknowledging your worth, and creating a new, embodied relationship with who you are. By returning to the mirror day after day, you are not only reprogramming your thoughts, you are **reclaiming your voice**, **rewriting your story**, and **rebuilding your identity** from the inside out.

Mirror Work As A Daily Emotional Intelligence Ritual

Mirror work is more than just a moment in front of your reflection, it is a sacred ritual that invites you to reconnect with your inner self. When you look into your own eyes and speak words of affirmation or truth, you are choosing to see yourself with clarity, compassion, and courage. You give yourself permission to be fully seen, not just by the world, but by you. As a daily emotional intelligence ritual, mirror work helps you build **self-awareness**. You begin to notice how you feel as you speak to yourself, how your body responds, and what thoughts arise. This awareness becomes a powerful guide, helping you better understand the emotional patterns that shape your life. You also develop **self-regulation**. As difficult emotions surface, like shame, fear, or self-doubt, you learn to sit with them, breathe through them, and respond with love instead of judgment. This daily practice teaches you how to pause, reflect, and choose kindness, even in moments of inner conflict. Your **motivation** is reignited. By affirming who you are and who you are becoming, you strengthen your commitment to live with purpose and integrity. You begin to show up for yourself in ways you once reserved only for others.

Self-compassion deepens. Through consistent mirror work, you begin to soften toward yourself. You realise that the love, encouragement, and forgiveness you have offered others is something you deeply deserve too. You learn to be your own ally, and over time, your **emotional resilience** grows. You face yourself daily, with all your wounds and wisdom, and instead of turning away, you lean in. You find strength in your softness and courage in your honesty. When you practice mirror work regularly, you create space for healing, integration, and growth. You start each day by declaring: *I see you. I hear you. I am here for you,* and in doing so, you transform the mirror from a place of judgment into a sacred space of self-connection and heart-led transformation.

The Three Phases Of Mirror Work

Awareness • Courage • Embodiment

1. Awareness - Meeting Yourself with Presence

You begin by simply showing up. Standing in front of the mirror, you allow yourself to be seen, not just physically, but emotionally and energetically. You become aware of the stories you have been telling yourself, the critical thoughts that arise, the resistance in your body, and the way you have been avoiding your own gaze. This phase is about *honest observation*. You do not need to change anything, just notice. You are learning to witness yourself with curiosity rather than judgment.

2. Courage - Leaning into Discomfort with Love

It takes real bravery to stay. As you continue mirror work, emotions may surface, grief, anger, shame, or sadness. In this phase, you are called to *remain present* despite discomfort. You begin to say words that feel foreign, like "*I am enough*" or "*I am lovable,*" even if a part of you does not yet believe them. This is the work of the heart, stepping beyond old patterns and daring to believe in your own worth. Courage means trusting that you are safe to feel and safe to heal.

3. Embodiment - Living the Truth of Who You Are

Over time, what once felt difficult becomes natural. You begin to *live* your affirmations. You do not just say *"I am worthy"*, you move through the world with that truth in your body. This is embodiment: when love, self-trust, and confidence move from thoughts into action. You find yourself making aligned choices, setting healthy boundaries, expressing your truth, and embracing your life with compassion and presence. You become a living mirror of the love you have discovered within.

Why Facing Yourself Can Be So Confronting, And Liberating

Facing yourself can feel like stepping into uncharted territory, because when you slow down and truly see yourself, without judgment or distraction, you come face-to-face with everything you have tried to suppress, avoid, or ignore. It can be deeply confronting because it invites you to witness not only your strengths and successes, but also your wounds, insecurities, regrets, and unmet needs. You might feel exposed, vulnerable, or even overwhelmed, because mirror work asks you to meet your inner world with honesty and compassion. You may hear the old narratives you have carried for years: *"I am not enough," "I am unlovable," "I failed."* These stories can be hard to confront, but when you do, you begin to reclaim your power. You learn that your worth is not defined by the past, by perfection, or by other people's opinions. You realise that your heart has always held the wisdom and strength to heal, and this is where the liberation begins. By facing yourself with presence and kindness, you open the door to deep emotional freedom. You stop running from who you are and start embracing every part of your being. In that reflection, you start to see not just flaws or pain, but your resilience, your capacity for love, and your divine potential. You give yourself permission to be human, to grow, to feel, to transform. This brave act of self-meeting does not just change how you see yourself. It changes how you live. It grounds you in authenticity, empowers your choices, and strengthens your relationships with others. The very mirror that once felt intimidating becomes a sacred space, a space where you come home to yourself, again and again.

Mirror Exercise

Purpose: To cultivate self-acceptance, dissolve limiting self-beliefs, and reconnect with your heart through the healing power of eye contact and affirmations.

Step-by-Step Guide:

1. **Find Your Mirror Space:** Choose a quiet, private space where you can stand or sit comfortably in front of a mirror. Make sure you will not be disturbed. Gently dim the lights if you wish to create a softer, heart-held atmosphere.

2. **Place Your Hand on Your Heart:** Take three slow, deep breaths. As you inhale, feel your chest rise. As you exhale, feel your body soften. Bring your awareness to your heart and place your hand over it.

3. **Look Into Your Eyes:** Gaze into your own eyes, not with judgment or critique, but with curiosity and tenderness. Allow yourself to simply *see* the person in the mirror.

4. **Speak the Following Affirmations Aloud (or Create Your Own):**

    1. *"I see you."*

    2. *"You are worthy of love."*

    3. *"I forgive you."*

    4. *"I am here for you."* **Repeat each one slowly. Pause between statements to breathe and feel.**

5. **Notice the Resistance or Emotion**

    Do not rush past discomfort. If tears come, let them flow. If resistance arises, acknowledge it gently: *"I see you, too."* You are meeting parts of yourself that have long been waiting to be held.

6. **Close with This Statement:**

    "Every time I return to the mirror, I return to myself."

7. **Journal Reflection (Optional):**

    Write about what you noticed, felt, resisted, or accepted during the practice.

This is not about perfection, it is about presence. Do this daily for one week and watch how your relationship with yourself transforms.

Case Study Discussion: Michael's Journey

Michael was a larger-than-life character with an infectious personality. Michael was a self–made man in his mid-40s and anybody looking at Michael and his life would have been left with the impression that he was someone who was in a good place. However, this was not the case. Michael liked helping others, but his self–talk was brutal, and he did not love himself at all. I journeyed with Michael for quite a few months, and we did some deep healing. One of the things I requested of Michael was to feel into his heart and make a list of all the things he truly loved about himself. Over time this list grew, and I asked Michael to read his list out loud to himself in front of a mirror. I still recall the conversation I had with Michael after I asked him to read his list to himself in front of the mirror. His response, *'there is no f...n way I am reading anything out to myself in front of the mirror.'* The mere thought of this terrified him. Michael had conditioned himself over decades to believe that he was wholly unworthy, an imposter. I then asked Michael to read his list to me over our Zoom call and he did. I then asked him to just stand in front of his mirror for 60 seconds every day for a week and say nothing. Michael agreed, and over the next 6 months Michael found the courage to take small steps, to heal, learn and grow. He got to a point where he could face himself in the mirror, speak out loud and truly believe the words he was saying.

(Authors note: Please note that every person is different, and every person has different hurts, pains, woundings and traumas. The point I would like you take from Michael's story is to never give up on yourself. You are a precious gift, and your life is to be lived and not merely survived. Living an authentic life off integrity is more than just existing!)

Reflective Exercise: Michael's Journey

Here are four profound and reflective questions to help you deeply engage with Michael's story and the power of mirror work:

1. **When you look into the mirror, what is the first thought or feeling that arises, and is it truly yours, or a reflection of someone else's voice from your past?** *This question invites you to notice old programming and become aware of whose expectations or judgments you have internalised.*

2. **What part of yourself have you struggled to face, and what might happen if you chose to meet that part with compassion instead**

> **of criticism?** *This encourages emotional courage and opens the door to deep self-acceptance and healing.*
>
> 3. **How has avoiding your own gaze affected your relationship with yourself and others?** *This helps you explore the link between self-awareness and how authentically you connect with the world around you.*
>
> 4. **If you could speak one truth into the mirror that your younger self longed to hear, what would it be, and how would it change the way you live today?** *This helps you engage in self-reparenting and step into a more empowered, heart-led identity.*

Affirmations For Integration (Heart Whispers)

Affirmations have the power to quiet the noise of doubt, open the doorway to self-trust, and draw you back into the wisdom of your heart. When practised daily, they nurture an inner dialogue based in love and truth, helping you live each day more aligned with who you truly are. I invite you to repeat silently or write:

- I use the mirror to practice positive self–talk.
- I avoid judging myself when I look in the mirror.
- I find peace when I meditate in front of a mirror.
- I see my progress in my reflection during workouts.
- I remind myself of my worthiness when looking in the mirror.
- I show myself love and kindness in front of the mirror.
- I honour the person I see in the mirror as a work in progress and a work of art.
- I embrace my reflection as a true expression of my authentic self.
- I look into the mirror and recognise the strength within me.
- I celebrate the unique beauty that is mine alone.
- I use my reflection as a reminder of how far I have come.

> ## Mirror Exercise – Meeting Yourself with Love
>
> 1. **Find Your Mirror:** Stand or sit comfortably in front of a mirror. Look directly into your own eyes.

2. **Breathe and Soften:** Take three slow, deep breaths. With each exhale, release any tension in your shoulders, jaw, or chest.

3. **Speak Your Name:** Gently say your name out loud, as if greeting a dear friend.

4. **Affirm Your Worth:** Choose one phrase to repeat slowly three times, such as:

   - *I see you, and you are enough.*

   - *I love and accept you, exactly as you are.*

   - *You are worthy of kindness and joy.*

5. **Close with Gratitude:** Place your hand over your heart, smile softly, and thank yourself for showing up in this moment.

Closing Reflection

The mirror is not merely glass, it is a sacred space where your deepest truths await. Each time you meet your own eyes, you are offered an invitation: to see beyond the surface and witness the essence of who you truly are. In this reflection, you face not only your image but the stories, wounds, and beliefs you have carried, some yours, some not. It takes courage to look and even more to stay, but as you soften your gaze and open your heart, what once felt confronting becomes liberating. You begin to see not what is wrong with you, but what has always been right, your resilience, your beauty, your worth. Through mirror work, you reclaim the power to rewrite your inner narrative. You unlearn shame. You meet your pain with tenderness. You awaken self-compassion, and gradually, you return home to yourself. May your mirror become a place of presence, healing, and truth, and may you always remember: the reflection you see is not just who you are, it is who you are becoming.

Keep Walking the Unbound Way

You are not meant to do this work alone. There are more practices, more chapters, more companions, and more guidance waiting across the Unbound Series and its programs. When you are ready, take the next stride – www.timetotransform.world

MODULE 6 – SELF LOVE

Your Opening Reflection

An Invitation to Honour Yourself - As you step into this module, let it be a gentle reminder that you are worthy of your own tenderness. Self-love is not selfish, it is the soil from which your strength, compassion, and joy grow. Allow yourself to be embraced by your own kindness, to listen softly to your needs, and to remember that you are already enough, just as you are.

- "In what ways have you honoured yourself this week?"

- "How do you speak to yourself when no one else is listening?"

- "What boundaries do you set to protect your well-being?"

- "When you think of your best qualities, how do they make you feel?"

- "What does self-love mean to you today?"

Let these questions open the doorway into presence. Every answer you give, whether in words, sensations, or silence, is a bridge between where you are and where you are going.

Learning Objectives

The learning objectives are included here to give you a clear focus for this module, ensuring that each practice you explore moves you closer to mastering the skills, insights, and heart-led awareness that will enrich your life well beyond the program. By the end of this module, you will:

- Understand the role of self-love in emotional well-being and authentic living.

- Distinguish self-love from narcissism and selfishness.

- Identify barriers to self-love and cultivate compassionate self-awareness.

- Practice heart-centred exercises to deepen self-worth and emotional resilience.

- Integrate daily rituals that nourish and protect emotional and spiritual wellbeing.

Core Emotional Domains

The core emotional intelligence domains covered here are essential because they form the foundation for lasting heart connection, guiding you to deepen self-awareness, regulate emotions, build resilience, and strengthen the mind-body bond throughout your *Unbound* journey.

- **Self-Awareness**: You recognise your thoughts, feelings, and needs without judgment.

- **Self-Regulation**: You respond to emotions with care, not reactivity.

- **Empathy (towards self)**: You treat yourself with kindness, especially in pain or failure.

- **Social Skills**: You honour your worth by setting and respecting healthy boundaries.

- **Motivation**: You act from a place of inner truth, guided by your heart and values.

"Self Love – Returning To Your Worth"

Self-love is the foundation of your emotional intelligence and heart connection. The inner ground from which your authenticity, resilience, and ability to truly connect with others can grow. Self-love is not about vanity, self-indulgence, or trying to be better than anyone else. It is the quiet, steady commitment to honouring your own humanity. It means recognising your worth, even when you feel like you have fallen short. It means tending to your own needs without guilt and offering yourself grace in moments of struggle. When you practice self-love, you begin to deepen your self-awareness. You start to notice the patterns in your thoughts, the emotions that rise within you, and the needs hiding beneath your reactions. You stop hiding from yourself and instead meet yourself with honesty and curiosity. That awareness becomes the foundation for self-regulation, it helps you respond to life's challenges with more presence, calm, and compassion, rather than reactivity or harsh self-judgment. Through self-love, you begin to build empathy toward yourself. You learn to forgive your past, to soften your inner dialogue, and to acknowledge your pain without becoming consumed by it. You become both the witness to your wounds and the source of your healing. From this place of grounded self-love, you gain the strength to set and honour healthy boundaries. You no longer feel the need to shrink, please, or overextend yourself. Instead, you speak your truth with clarity, and you hold space for relationships that reflect mutual respect and emotional honesty. This deepens your social intelligence, because you are connecting from a place of wholeness, not lack. Perhaps most powerfully, self-love awakens your intrinsic motivation. You begin to take action not from fear or pressure, but from alignment with your values, your heart, and your inner sense of purpose. You feel moved to grow, not to prove yourself, but to honour the unique potential that lives inside you. In the end, self-love is a return to your truth. It anchors your emotions, softens your inner critic, and empowers you to live from the inside out. You no longer have to be perfect, you just have to be present, and from that presence, your transformation begins.

The Historical Basis Of Self-Love: From Ancient Greece's *Philautia* To Modern Self-Compassion Research

The concept of self-love is far from a modern invention. Its roots stretch deep into human history, appearing across philosophy, spirituality, and psychology as a vital part of living a meaningful and balanced life. Understanding where self-love began, and how it has evolved, helps you appreciate its deeper purpose: not as self-indulgence, but as a foundation for wisdom, connection, and inner peace.

Ancient Greece: *Philautia* as Noble Self-Regard

In the wisdom traditions of Ancient Greece, love was understood as a multifaceted force, expressed in different ways depending on its object and purpose. Among the various forms of love identified by Greek philosophers, such as *agape* (universal love), *eros* (romantic love), and *philia* (deep friendship), there was *philautia*: love of the self. Aristotle and other classical thinkers considered *philautia* essential to a well-lived life, but they were careful to distinguish between two distinct types. The **first**, virtuous *philautia*, was based on self-respect, self-knowledge, and moral character. This kind of self-love was considered **noble and necessary**, a balanced and rational regard for one's own worth that served as the **foundation for all other forms of love**. In essence, if you could not love or care for yourself wisely, you would struggle to love others well. The **second** type of *philautia* was self-centred and excessive, a form of egoism or narcissism that was destructive to both the individual and the community. This distorted self-love was seen as corrosive, a kind of hubris that disconnected a person from truth, humility, and relational harmony. Greek philosophers such as Socrates and Plato also emphasised the importance of **knowing oneself** (*gnōthi seauton*) as the gateway to ethical action and inner harmony. Self-love, when grounded in self-awareness and virtue, was not seen as indulgent or vain, it was considered the root of all personal integrity, emotional balance, and wise decision-making. For the Greeks, to live ethically and contribute meaningfully to society, you had to cultivate *philautia* in its truest sense: not as a pursuit of personal gain or admiration, but as a **disciplined love for your own soul**, your potential, and your responsibility to others. In this way, Ancient Greek philosophy teaches you that genuine self-love is not about superiority or separation, it is about cultivating the inner conditions that allow you to show up in the world with wisdom, compassion, and strength.

Modern Self-Compassion Research

While ancient philosophies like *philautia* laid the groundwork for understanding self-love as noble self-regard, modern psychology has brought this concept into clearer focus through decades of rigorous research, especially in the field of self-compassion. Spearheaded by Dr. Kristin Neff, self-compassion research has redefined how you can relate to your inner world, particularly during moments of failure, shame, or struggle. It has helped reveal that true self-love is not about perfection, ego, or inflated self-esteem, it is about how kindly and honestly you meet yourself when life gets hard. Self-compassion involves three powerful and interconnected elements:

1. **Self-Kindness:** Instead of berating yourself when you make a mistake, self-kindness invites you to soften, to speak to yourself as you would to a dear friend. This includes recognising your efforts, forgiving your shortcomings, and honouring your pain without judgment. It is about treating yourself with care and respect, even when you feel like you have fallen short.

2. **Mindfulness:** At the heart of self-compassion is presence. Mindfulness teaches you to acknowledge what you are feeling, whether it is sadness,

anger, fear, or disappointment, without exaggerating it or pushing it away. It gives you space to observe rather than react, to witness your experience with clarity and tenderness.

3. **Common Humanity:** Self-compassion reminds you that you are not alone. Your struggles, imperfections, and doubts are not signs of personal failure, they are part of what it means to be human. Recognising this shared vulnerability helps dissolve isolation and opens the door to connection and empathy.

What makes self-compassion so powerful in the modern era is its grounding in scientific evidence. Research shows that individuals who practice self-compassion are more emotionally resilient, less prone to anxiety and depression, and better equipped to cope with adversity. It strengthens your emotional regulation, lowers stress hormones, improves motivation, and promotes healthier relationships. Unlike self-esteem, which often depends on performance, comparison, or external validation, self-compassion is unconditional. It does not require you to be flawless. Instead, it meets you exactly where you are and offers the radical permission to be human. Modern therapeutic practices, including mindfulness-based stress reduction (MBSR), compassion-focused therapy, and acceptance and commitment therapy (ACT), now integrate self-compassion as a core component. These approaches teach you how to pause, breathe, and meet your suffering not with fear, but with presence and love. In a world that often pressures you to do more, be more, and achieve endlessly, self-compassion becomes a quiet, powerful act of rebellion. It is a way of reclaiming your worth, not because of what you produce, but because of who you are. By embracing self-compassion, you are continuing a long lineage of heart wisdom, from ancient teachings to modern neuroscience. You are giving yourself what you have always deserved: grace, kindness, and the freedom to be whole, just as you are.

Differentiating Self-Love from Selfishness Or Narcissism

It is easy to feel conflicted about self-love, especially if you have been taught to associate it with selfishness or arrogance. Maybe you were conditioned to always put others first, to dismiss your own needs, or to believe that taking care of yourself meant you were being self-absorbed, but here is the truth: real self-love is not about elevating yourself above others, it is about coming home to yourself with honesty, compassion, and responsibility. When you love yourself, you are not saying, *"I am better than everyone else."* You are saying, *"I am worthy, just as I am."* You learn to honour your feelings without suppressing them, to rest when you are tired without guilt, and to speak your truth with clarity and respect. This is not self-indulgence, it is emotional maturity. It is recognising that your well-being matters, not so you can isolate or dominate, but so you can contribute, relate, and live from a place of wholeness.

Selfishness, in contrast, often disregards the impact of your actions on others. It comes from scarcity, the belief that if you do not take care of your own needs at any cost, no one will, but when you embody self-love, you begin to trust that there is enough. Enough time, enough worth, enough space for both your needs and the needs of others. You no longer act from desperation or defensiveness. You begin to respond to the world with presence and grace.

Narcissism masks deep insecurity. It demands constant admiration and external validation, often at the expense of real connection. The narcissistic self says, *"I must be the best. I must always win. I must not be vulnerable."* But your self-loving self says, *"I am enough, even when I fall short. I am whole, even when I feel broken. I am worthy, even when I am growing."*

Self-love gives you the **courage to be honest with yourself**, to take responsibility for your emotions and actions, and to forgive yourself when you make mistakes. It is not about being perfect, it is about being *present*. With yourself. With others. With life. From a grounded place of love, you can create boundaries without guilt. You can say no without fear. You can show up in relationships with less need for approval and more space for authenticity. You stop trying to earn love by performing or pleasing, and you start offering love freely, because your cup is no longer empty.

When you love yourself, **you become more generous**, not less. More empathetic. More compassionate. You no longer love others in ways that drain or diminish you, you love in ways that uplift and empower both of you. So do not confuse self-love with selfishness or narcissism. They are not the same. One is based in fear and separation; the other is grounded in truth and connection. When you choose to love yourself, you are choosing to live in integrity, with your values, your needs, and your heart, and from that place, you give the world something far more powerful than perfection, you give it your real, open, and beautifully human self.

The Neuroscience Of Self-Affirmation And The Benefits Of Positive

Self-Regard

When you speak kindly to yourself, affirm your values, or remind yourself of your inner strength, you are doing more than just *"thinking positively."* You are reshaping the very structure of your brain. The science of self-affirmation shows that how you relate to yourself, especially in moments of stress, challenge, or self-doubt, can significantly influence your emotional health, cognitive performance, and even physical well-being.

How Self-Affirmation Works in the Brain

Self-affirmation practices, such as repeating *"I am"* statements, reflecting on core values, or journaling about what matters most to you, activate regions of the brain associated with **self-processing, emotional regulation, and reward**. In particular, the **ventromedial prefrontal cortex (vmPFC)** plays a central role. This part of your brain integrates information about your identity and values and helps modulate your response to stress and threat. When you affirm something meaningful about yourself, such as *"I am resilient," "I am a caring person," or "I choose to live with integrity"*, you reinforce the neural circuits that support **confidence, security, and value-based decision-making**. fMRI studies have shown that people who engage in regular self-affirmation practices show **increased activity in the vmPFC**, along with **reduced activation in the threat centres of the brain**, like the amygdala.

Physiological Benefits of Self-Affirmation

Self-affirmation does not just affect your brain, it influences your body, too. Research has demonstrated that positive self-regard through affirmation can:

- **Lower cortisol levels**, reducing the impact of chronic stress on the body.

- **Improve heart rate variability (HRV)**, a key marker of emotional resilience.

- **Enhance immune function**, particularly during high-pressure situations.

By soothing your physiological stress response, self-affirmation helps you stay calm, focused, and grounded, especially when you are facing criticism, uncertainty, or internal doubt.

Cognitive and Emotional Benefits

Affirming your values and self-worth has a measurable impact on your ability to think clearly and regulate emotions. People who regularly engage in self-affirmation:

- **Perform better under pressure**, particularly on complex or evaluative tasks.

- **Experience less defensiveness**, allowing them to receive feedback with greater openness.

- **Recover more quickly from failure**, as they see mistakes as part of the growth process rather than as evidence of inadequacy.

- **Cultivate intrinsic motivation**, aligning their actions with personal meaning rather than external pressure.

Positive self-regard, grounded in affirmation, also builds **emotional agility,** the ability to stay curious, open, and non-reactive to difficult emotions. You become more skilled at acknowledging discomfort without being consumed by it.

Why Self-Affirmation Is not Just Fluff

Contrary to popular myths, self-affirmation is not about denial or blind positivity. It is not pretending everything is fine when it is not, nor is it about ignoring real challenges or difficult emotions. Instead, it is about anchoring yourself in what is true, enduring, and life-giving within you, even in the midst of hardship. Self-affirmation is a conscious practice of inner alignment, a way of reminding yourself of your worth, your values, and your capacity to navigate life with integrity. When you say, *"This is who I am, even now,"* you reaffirm your identity beyond circumstances. This steadying act helps you face reality with courage, rather than avoidance, because you are grounded in your own truth. Over time, this practice reshapes the way you speak to yourself and the lens through which you view your life. It strengthens resilience, builds self-trust, and keeps you connected to your heart, ensuring that even when the world around you feels uncertain, you have an unshakable place within to return to.

Common Self-Love Blockers

Despite your deep longing for self-love, certain inner barriers can quietly and persistently block your ability to truly embrace yourself. These self-love blockers are often based in past experiences, inherited beliefs, and cultural messages that have shaped how you see yourself, and they can keep you stuck in cycles of self-judgment, guilt, or emotional numbness. Understanding these blockers with compassion is the first step to releasing them.

1. Internalised Shame

Shame is the deep belief that you are unworthy, not because of what you have done, but because of who you are. It often begins in childhood, when love or acceptance felt conditional. Over time, you may have internalised the message that being *"you"* was not enough. Shame says, *"There's something wrong with me,"* and that belief can quietly sabotage your self-worth. Until shame is gently met with compassion, it will keep you from receiving your own love.

Healing Path: *Practice radical self-acceptance. Speak to your shame with understanding, not judgment. Affirm your worthiness even in imperfection.*

2. Unprocessed Trauma

When you have experienced emotional, physical, or psychological trauma, your nervous system learns to protect you, sometimes by disconnecting from your own feelings or body. This can make self-love feel unsafe, unfamiliar, or even impossible. You may struggle with trust, vulnerability, or believing that you deserve gentleness.

Healing Path: *Ground in safety first. Use somatic practices, therapy, or trauma-informed mindfulness to reconnect with your body and restore inner safety. Self-love grows in secure ground.*

3. Perfectionism

Perfectionism tells you that you must earn love by being flawless. It sets impossible standards, then criticises you when you fall short. It creates fear of failure and fuels constant self-pressure. Perfectionism says, *"You are only worthy when you succeed,"* robbing you of the chance to love yourself as you are, especially when you need it most.

Healing Path: *Learn to celebrate effort over outcome. Practice self-compassion when things go wrong. Replace "I am not enough" with "I am learning, and that is enough."*

4. Societal Conditioning

You have been taught, sometimes subtly, sometimes loudly, what beauty, success, worthiness, and value *"should"* look like. These external standards often drown out your inner truth. Messages about productivity, appearance, gender roles, or comparison can disconnect you from your authentic self and develop self-rejection.

Healing Path: Begin to question the stories you have inherited. Whose voice is shaping your self-worth? Choose to redefine your value on your own terms. Self-love starts by coming home to your own truth.

Final Thought

Each of these blockers, shame, trauma, perfectionism, and conditioning, is not a flaw in you. They are wounds that can be healed, voices that can be softened, and beliefs that can be rewritten. With presence, compassion, and courage, you can unlearn what no longer serves you and remember the love that has always been your birthright. **Self-love is not something you earn. It is something you return to.**

Reflective Exercise: Six self-love rituals

I invite you to select two of the following to commit to for the week:

1. Spend time in nature.

2. Listen and respond to your body's needs.

3. Engage in a creative outlet.

4. Set a boundary and honour it.

5. Celebrate a recent achievement.

6. Reflect in stillness on a feeling you have been avoiding.

"Which of these acts of self-love do you resist the most, and why?"

Case Study Discussion – Roger's Journey

Roger's self-talk began to shift in small, almost imperceptible ways at first. He caught himself in moments of harsh inner criticism and chose instead to speak words of kindness, the kind he would offer to a dear friend. Each time he extended compassion to himself, he felt a little lighter, a little less burdened by the weight of old wounds. Through this process, he discovered a deep and nourishing sense of self-love, one he had never known before. For the first time in his life, Roger began to believe he was truly worthy of love and belonging, even without a traditional family of his own. As the days unfolded, the ripple effect of his practice became clear. He noticed that he was attracting more positive people and uplifting experiences into his world. He found himself surrounded by conversations that inspired him, by relationships that respected and valued him. Confidence grew quietly but steadily within him, and with it came the courage to pursue long-held dreams.

He began to create, to explore, to step into opportunities with a newfound sense of purpose and passion. Over time, Roger learned to trust himself deeply. No longer did he chase approval or validation from others, instead, he tuned in to the steady, guiding voice within. He started making decisions not out of fear, but from a place of alignment with his own truth. He came to see that his worth was not something to be earned; it had been his birthright all along. Day after day, week after week, Roger committed to his self-love practices. They became as natural as breathing, small, intentional acts that reminded him of who he was, and in doing so, he discovered a part of himself that shone with love, light, and unwavering self-acceptance. This part of him was no longer fragile or hidden; it was the foundation upon which he would build the rest of his life, and he knew, with absolute certainty, that he would never let it go again.

Reflective Exercise: Roger's Journey

Here are four profound and reflective questions inspired by Roger's story to help you engage with your own self-love journey:

1. **When did you first learn to measure your worth by achievement, and how has that shaped your inner dialogue?** *Roger's story may mirror your own if you have tied your value to success. This question invites you to explore where that belief began, and whether it is still serving the person you are today.*

2. **How do you respond to yourself when you feel vulnerable, unproductive, or imperfect?** *Self-love is often most needed when you feel least worthy of it. Reflecting on how you treat yourself in difficult moments can reveal whether your love is conditional or growing toward compassion.*

3. **What part of you is still waiting to be accepted, just as it is?** *Like Roger, you may carry pieces of yourself that feel unworthy of love. This question invites you to turn toward those parts, not to fix them, but to embrace them with understanding.*

4. **What would it feel like to speak to yourself with the same kindness you offer to others?** *Roger's transformation began when he softened his inner voice. Reflect on how your life might change if you gave yourself the same empathy, patience, and grace you freely give to those you love.*

Affirmations For Integration (Heart Whispers)

Affirmations have the power to quiet the noise of doubt, open the doorway to self-trust, and draw you back into the wisdom of your heart. When practised daily, they nurture an inner dialogue based in love and truth, helping you live each day more aligned with who you truly are. I invite you to repeat silently or write:

- I feel alive when I dance to my favourite song.

- I am free when I let my body move to the rhythm.

- I find joy in the expression of movement through dance.

- I feel connected to my body and emotions when I dance.

- I am confident in myself when I dance with passion.

Self-Love Exercise – Speaking to Yourself with Kindness

1. **Find a Quiet Space:** Sit comfortably and take three slow, deep breaths. Place your hand gently over your heart.

2. **Acknowledge Yourself:** Close your eyes and think of one thing you appreciate about who you are, not what you have done, but who you are at your core.

3. **Speak Your Love Whisper to yourself:** *"I see you. I value you. I love you."* Repeat it slowly three times, letting the words sink in.

4. **Anchor the Feeling:** Smile softly and imagine a warm light filling your chest, expanding with each breath, wrapping you in compassion.

5. **Carry It Forward:** Before you finish, promise yourself one small act of kindness you will give to yourself today.

Closing Reflection

As you gently close this module on self-love, take a deep breath and honour just how far you have already come. Choosing to explore self-love is not a sign of weakness or self-obsession, it is a bold and healing act of self-remembering. In a world that often teaches you to seek your worth outside of yourself, self-love is how you return home. It is not about ego, vanity, or pretending to have it all together. True self-love is quiet. Grounded. Compassionate. It is the moment you stop measuring your worth by what you achieve, how you appear, or who approves of you. It is the moment you choose to listen inward, soften your self-talk, and extend grace to the parts of you that are still growing. Self-love is how you begin to break the cycle of self-rejection. It is how you build trust with yourself, by showing up, again and again, even when it is hard. It is how you stop abandoning your own needs, your own voice, your own heart, and as you deepen in this practice, you start to see the ripple effects. You stop settling for relationships, environments, or beliefs that diminish you. You begin to protect your peace, honour your boundaries, and move through life with more confidence and clarity. You lead from wholeness rather than from wounds. Loving yourself does not mean you will never feel doubt or pain again. It means you will walk through those moments with greater strength and compassion. You will know how to pause, breathe, and return to the truth: *you are not broken, you are becoming.* So let self-love be the anchor you return to, the voice that steadies you, and the light that guides you through uncertainty. You are worthy of joy, rest, respect, and tenderness, and most importantly - **You are worthy of your own love. Always.**

Let the Next Chapter Find You

Sometimes the story that changes us isn't the one we planned to read.One of the other Unbound books, or one of the online journeys, may be the next voice your heart is waiting for. Stay open. The next chapter is already reaching toward you – www.timetotransform.world

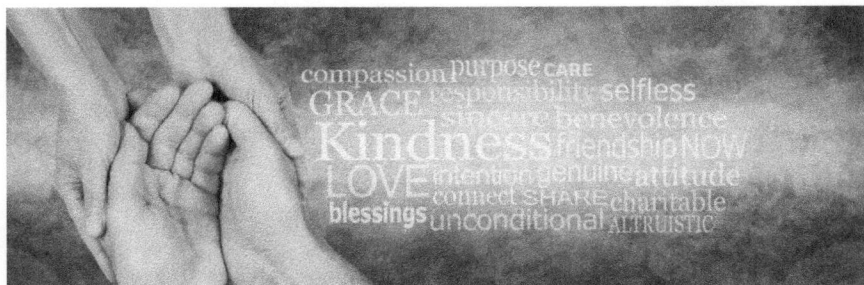

MODULE 7 - KINDNESS

Your Opening Reflection

Invitation to Kindness - As you enter this module, I invite you to soften your heart toward yourself. Let go of the urge to strive or judge, and instead welcome the gentleness that kindness offers. Imagine speaking to yourself the way you would to someone you deeply love, with tenderness, patience, and compassion. This is your chance to practice kindness not as a fleeting act, but as a way of being, beginning with how you meet yourself in this very moment.

- "When was the last time you were truly kind to yourself?"

- "What does kindness toward yourself look and feel like in your daily life?"

- "When you think of being kind to others, do you extend the same grace to yourself?"

- "What beliefs or habits sometimes stop you from treating yourself with kindness?"

- "How does your body respond when you speak to yourself with compassion instead of criticism?"

- "If a loved one were in your shoes today, how would you show them kindness, and can you offer that to yourself?"

Let these questions open the doorway into presence. Every answer you give, whether in words, sensations, or silence, is a bridge between where you are and where you are going.

Learning Objectives

The learning objectives are included here to give you a clear focus for this module, ensuring that each practice you explore moves you closer to mastering the skills, insights, and heart-led awareness that will enrich your life well beyond the program. By the end of this module, you will:

- Understand the emotional and relational impact of kindness on yourself and others.

- Explore the role of kindness in building emotional resilience and connection.

- Practice self-kindness as a foundation for empathy and compassion.

- Identify opportunities to integrate kindness into your everyday choices.

- Recognise kindness as a transformative force for living a heart-led life.

Core Emotional Domains

The core emotional intelligence domains covered here are essential because they form the foundation for lasting heart connection, guiding you to deepen self-awareness, regulate emotions, build resilience, and strengthen the mind-body bond throughout your *Unbound* journey.

- **Self-Awareness:** Kindness invites you to pause and notice your internal state, your emotions, assumptions, and judgments, so you can choose to respond with intention and care.

- **Empathy:** By practicing kindness, you attune more deeply to the emotions and needs of others, strengthening your ability to connect, listen, and relate with compassion.

- **Self-Regulation:** In moments of tension, kindness helps you shift from reactivity to presence. It softens harsh responses and creates space for grace under pressure.

- **Social Skills:** Kindness enhances your ability to build trust, nurture meaningful relationships, and create emotionally safe environments where others feel seen and valued.

- **Motivation (Intrinsic Growth through Compassion):** When guided by kindness, your growth becomes heart-led. You are motivated not by external rewards, but by the joy of contributing, uplifting, and embodying your values.

"Kindness – Gentle Strength In Action"

Kindness is more than a moral virtue, it is a transformative emotional intelligence practice that awakens connection, inner strength, and authentic leadership. In today's fast-paced, outcome-driven world, kindness is often misunderstood as soft or passive, but in truth, kindness is courageous. It takes strength to slow down, to listen, and to respond with compassion when reacting with criticism would be easier. It requires emotional maturity to stay grounded in empathy, even when you are under pressure or facing misunderstanding. Kindness begins within. It starts with your willingness to speak gently to yourself, to forgive your own missteps, and to create space for growth without harshness. This inner kindness builds a **healthy, grounded sense of self-worth,** not based on how much you achieve, but on how deeply you honour your own humanity. From that space, kindness naturally extends outward. It becomes the bridge between you and others, enhancing your ability to understand their needs, emotions, and perspectives.

You become more attuned in conversation, more responsive in conflict, and more intentional in your presence. This nurtures trust, strengthens relationships, and develops emotional safety, core foundations of **social intelligence**. In leadership, whether you lead a team, a classroom, a family, or your own life, kindness becomes a guiding force. It does not dilute effectiveness; it amplifies it. When you lead with kindness, people feel seen, respected, and inspired. Your influence grows not through control, but through care. Ultimately, kindness is not something you perform. It is something you embody. It shapes how you live, relate, and serve. It invites you to return to the heart again and again, to respond to life not from fear or ego, but from empathy, integrity, and compassion. *Kindness is a practice. Kindness is power. Kindness is the courage to lead, live, and love with humanity.*

Kindness As An Emotional Regulation Tool

Kindness is not just an outward gesture, it is a powerful internal mechanism for emotional regulation. When you choose to respond with kindness, especially in emotionally charged situations, you activate parts of your brain associated with empathy, connection, and calm. This helps to quiet the amygdala, your brain's threat detector, and reduces the fight, flight, or freeze response that often fuels reactivity, defensiveness, or aggression. When you are overwhelmed or frustrated, pausing to practice kindness, toward yourself or others, creates a physiological and psychological shift. It lowers your cortisol (the stress hormone), slows your heart rate, and brings your nervous system back into balance. This allows you to move from reaction to reflection, from anger to curiosity, from fear to care. Importantly, kindness does not mean ignoring boundaries or denying difficult feelings. Instead, it invites you to meet those emotions with gentleness, compassion, and self-awareness. Whether you are speaking kindly to yourself during moments of shame or extending grace to someone who has hurt you, kindness becomes a choice to stay regulated and present. Over time, using kindness as a regulation tool strengthens your resilience. It builds your inner muscle to stay grounded under pressure, to repair relationships with humility, and to speak truth without harm. It becomes a steady anchor that helps you navigate life with clarity, connection, and emotional maturity. In this way, kindness is not just a reaction, it is a conscious practice of returning to your centre, softening your edges, and choosing the heart over the impulse.

The Neuroscience Of Kindness: Oxytocin, Serotonin, And Social Bonding

Kindness does not just feel good, it is wired into your brain and body as a deeply healing and connecting experience. When you offer or receive a kind gesture, a cascade of neurochemical activity is activated that supports emotional wellbeing, resilience, and human connection.

Oxytocin - The *"Connection Hormone"*

Oxytocin is often called the *love* or *bonding hormone*. Acts of kindness, like a warm smile, a thoughtful message, or a compassionate touch, stimulate the release of oxytocin. This hormone promotes trust, emotional openness, and social bonding. It reduces stress, lowers blood pressure, and creates a sense of safety. In both giver and receiver, oxytocin enhances feelings of closeness and belonging, reinforcing positive social behaviours. When you consciously engage in acts of kindness, you are not only nurturing someone else's wellbeing, you are also nourishing your own body and mind at a biological level. Oxytocin does not just make you feel connected, it strengthens your ability to empathise, to listen deeply, and to respond with compassion, even in moments of tension. Over time, these small but powerful hormonal boosts create a feedback loop: the more kindness you give and receive, the more naturally your heart opens, and the more your relationships flourish with trust, warmth, and authenticity.

Serotonin - The Mood Stabiliser

Serotonin plays a key role in regulating your mood, satisfaction, and emotional stability. When you engage in kind, generous behaviour, serotonin levels rise, creating a sense of calm, optimism, and inner balance. Serotonin also contributes to resilience, helping you handle challenges with greater equanimity. Kindness becomes a self-reinforcing practice, boosting your mood while improving your perception of social interactions. As serotonin levels increase, your brain naturally begins to associate kindness with safety and wellbeing, making it more likely that you will repeat those behaviours. Over time, this creates an upward spiral, small acts of kindness not only brighten the moment but also strengthen your long-term emotional stability. By actively cultivating kindness, you are building a mental and emotional foundation that supports patience, perspective, and a steady inner peace, even when external circumstances are uncertain or stressful.

The Kindness Feedback Loop

Neuroscientists have identified a positive feedback loop: when you perform an act of kindness, you feel good, which makes you more likely to be kind again. This cycle builds emotional intelligence, strengthens neural pathways for empathy, and develops long-term wellbeing. Repeated kindness reinforces patterns in the brain that promote connection, trust, and cooperative behaviour. Over time, this feedback loop becomes self-sustaining. The more kindness you practice, the more your brain associates generosity with personal reward and emotional fulfilment. Even small acts, holding a door open, offering a genuine compliment, or listening without judgment, can trigger this cycle. With consistent repetition, your capacity for empathy and compassion deepens, creating a ripple effect that not only enhances your own mental health but also contributes to a more caring and cooperative environment around you.

Kindness and Social Bonding

Humans are social beings, and kindness acts as a bridge between nervous systems. Brain imaging studies show that giving and receiving kindness activates reward centres in the brain, particularly the **ventromedial prefrontal cortex,** an area associated with value-based decisions and social connection. This neurological activity reinforces shared humanity, building stronger personal and community relationships. **In essence**, kindness is not only an emotional or moral virtue, it is a biological imperative. It is a neurochemical strategy for your wellbeing, resilience, and belonging. When you practice kindness regularly, you are not only helping others, you are reshaping your brain, regulating your emotions, and becoming more deeply connected to yourself and the world around you. When you engage in acts of kindness, whether through a simple smile, a listening ear, or a generous act, you are essentially participating in a shared biological dance. Your brain and body synchronise with others in a subtle but profound way, creating a sense of safety and mutual trust. Over time, this builds a reservoir of goodwill that strengthens not only your personal connections but also the collective wellbeing of the groups you belong to. This shared kindness becomes contagious, inspiring others to act with compassion, thus creating a ripple effect that extends far beyond the initial moment of generosity.

Historical And Spiritual Foundations Of Kindness Across Traditions

Kindness is not a modern invention, it is a timeless principle based deeply in the wisdom traditions, philosophies, and spiritual teachings of cultures across the world. From ancient scriptures to oral traditions, acts of compassion and benevolence have long been recognised as both sacred duty and powerful pathways to personal and collective transformation.

Christianity

In the Christian tradition, kindness is a core fruit of the Spirit (Galatians 5:22–23) and a central commandment. Jesus' teachings consistently emphasise mercy, love for one's neighbour, and forgiveness. The parable of the Good Samaritan embodies kindness beyond boundaries of race or religion, showing that true compassion is unconditional. Christians are taught that to be kind is to reflect the nature of God: *"Be kind and compassionate to one another, forgiving each other, just as in Christ God forgave you"* (Ephesians 4:32).

Hinduism

In Hindu philosophy, kindness is expressed through the principle of **ahimsa**, or non-violence. Based in the Vedas and embraced by sages like Mahatma Gandhi, ahimsa extends beyond refraining from harm to actively choosing compassion in thoughts, words, and deeds. Acts of kindness are seen as expressions of **dharma,** right action, and contribute to the spiritual growth of both giver and receiver.

Buddhism

Buddhist teachings place **metta**, or loving-kindness, at the heart of spiritual practice. Metta meditation involves sending intentions of goodwill to oneself and all beings, even those who are difficult to love. The Buddha taught that cultivating loving-kindness dissolves anger, softens the heart, and leads to liberation from suffering. Kindness is not seen as passive, it is courageous, conscious, and transformative.

Judaism

In Judaism, kindness is a form of **chesed,** a covenantal love and steadfast kindness that mirrors God's relationship with humanity. The Torah is filled with injunctions to care for the widow, the orphan, and the stranger, making kindness a divine command and a social responsibility. The Talmud teaches: *"The world is built on kindness"* (Psalm 89:2), affirming its role in sustaining communities and spiritual life.

Islam

In Islam, kindness is both a spiritual virtue and a daily obligation. The Prophet Muhammad (peace be upon him) said, "*Kindness is a mark of faith, and whoever is not kind has no faith.*" The Qur'an urges believers to respond to evil with good, and to treat others with mercy, even when they differ. Allah is described as **Ar-Rahman, Ar-Rahim,** the Most Compassionate, the Most Merciful, encouraging Muslims to embody divine compassion in all interactions.

Indigenous and Earth-Based Traditions

Across Indigenous cultures, kindness is intimately woven into the fabric of life. It is expressed through **reciprocity,** giving back to the Earth, to the ancestors, and to one's community with humility and gratitude. In many traditions, elders teach that kindness is not optional but essential for harmony and survival. It is a sacred duty to walk gently, speak with care, and uphold the dignity of all beings.

A Shared Moral Thread

Though cultures and languages differ, the essence of kindness remains remarkably universal. Whether called **karuna**, **chesed**, **metta**, or **compassion**, it reflects the deep human understanding that love, empathy, and care are essential for both spiritual growth and societal wellbeing. To live kindly is to participate in the ancient rhythm of humanity, one that honours dignity, connection, and the sacredness of life. When you choose kindness, you are not just following a personal value, you are stepping into a global, intergenerational legacy of healing, hope, and heart.

Kindness To Others *And* Self As A Path To Wholeness

Kindness is often celebrated as a virtue we extend outward, but its true power lies in its ability to transform us from within. When you choose kindness, not only toward others but also toward yourself, you are actively participating in your own healing and integration. Kindness becomes a bridge, from fragmentation to wholeness, from harshness to harmony.

To Others: Building Bridges of Belonging

When you act kindly toward others, you affirm their worth and humanity. Simple acts, listening deeply, offering help, speaking gently, send the message: *You matter. You are seen.* In a world that often feels disconnected or competitive, kindness restores trust. It creates spaces of psychological safety, encourages cooperation, and strengthens bonds of empathy and belonging. You begin to realise that your kindness is not a gift from a place of superiority, it is a mutual recognition of shared vulnerability, and in that mutual recognition, something powerful happens: you see yourself in the other. Compassion is no longer abstract. It becomes the language of your heart.

To Yourself: Returning to Inner Safety

True wholeness cannot be achieved if you only extend kindness outward while withholding it from yourself. Many of us are our own harshest critics. We replay mistakes, dwell in guilt, or measure ourselves against impossible standards, but when you learn to speak to yourself with gentleness, to say *"It is okay,"* *"I am doing my best,"* or *"I deserve rest"*, you shift the entire tone of your inner world. Kindness to self softens inner rigidity. It welcomes your imperfections and reminds you that healing is not linear. It creates space for rest, recovery, and renewal. It is not indulgent, it is intelligent, because when you are kind to yourself, you are more resilient, more present, and more capable of showing up fully for others.

The Healing Synergy

Kindness creates a feedback loop between your self and others. When you offer compassion outward, you are more likely to internalise it. When you nurture yourself, you are more grounded and generous in how you relate to the world. This synergy creates emotional intelligence, relational depth, and a grounded sense of purpose. Wholeness is not about perfection. It is about integration, bringing all parts of yourself, including your wounds, into the light of compassion. Kindness is the light. It does not fix everything instantly, but it melts what is frozen, mends what is torn, and reconnects what has been lost.

Kindness In High-Performance, High-Pressure Environments

Kindness Builds Stronger Teams

In high-pressure environments, the temptation to isolate, micromanage, or push harder can backfire. Kindness enables psychological safety, an environment where people feel comfortable expressing concerns, making mistakes, and being human. This is the foundation of high-functioning teams. When kindness is practiced through active listening, genuine recognition, or supportive feedback, teams become more cohesive, adaptive, and innovative. Kindness also develops mutual trust, which strengthens collaboration and reduces conflict. When you lead with empathy and offer encouragement instead of criticism, you invite others to bring their best ideas forward without fear of judgment. This not only boosts morale but also inspires creativity and problem-solving. In moments of stress or uncertainty, your kindness becomes a stabilising force, reminding your team that they are valued as people, not just as performers. Over time, this builds a resilient, connected culture where everyone feels invested in shared success.

Kindness to Self: Preventing Burnout

High achievers often extend compassion to others but struggle to show it to themselves. Overwork becomes a badge of honour, and self-kindness is mistaken for weakness. Yet, research consistently shows that self-compassion enhances motivation, perseverance, and wellbeing. In high-stakes roles, self-kindness is not a luxury, it is a lifeline. When you treat yourself with understanding rather than criticism during times of failure or fatigue, you recover faster and return stronger. By practicing kindness toward yourself, you build an inner foundation that can weather pressure without collapsing. You give yourself permission to rest, recharge, and reflect without guilt, allowing your mind and body to heal. This compassionate self-awareness helps you sustain your passion, sharpen your focus, and approach challenges with clarity instead of depletion. When you honour your own needs, you are not only preserving your energy, you are also modelling to others that resilience is built through care, not constant strain.

Kindness as a Leadership Imperative

Great leaders do not just demand results, they create conditions where people thrive. Kindness in leadership is not about being permissive or avoiding hard conversations. It is about delivering truth with humanity, making decisions with integrity, and recognising the inherent dignity in every team member. In the long run, kindness sustains performance by fuelling loyalty, engagement, and purpose. In high-performance environments, kindness is not an afterthought or a sign of weakness. It is a conscious choice that strengthens culture, enhances outcomes, and builds resilient, emotionally intelligent people. ***When pressure rises, let kindness lead. It is both your edge and your anchor.***

When you embody kindness as a leader, you set a tone that ripples through the entire organisation. Your example invites openness, develops mutual respect, and encourages others to step into their best selves. You create a climate where people feel valued for more than just their output, and as a result, they give more of themselves, not out of fear or obligation, but out of genuine commitment. This type of leadership does not just achieve short-term goals; it nurtures long-term growth, trust, and loyalty that endure far beyond any single project or performance review.

Forgiveness Exercise: *"The Mirror of Gentle Words"*

Purpose: To cultivate self-kindness and rewire the internal dialogue through embodied practice, this gentle exercise helps you see yourself with compassion and speak to yourself as a trusted friend would.

Step 1: *Speak 3 Kind Truths Aloud (2 minutes)*

Say three heartfelt affirmations to yourself, slowly and aloud. Choose from these or create your own:

- *"I am learning to love myself."*

- *"I am doing the best I can, and that is enough."*

- *"I deserve kindness, especially from myself."*

Let your words settle into your heart. If emotions rise, allow them to move through you gently.

Step 2: *Write a Letter to Yourself (5 minutes)*

Using a journal, write a short note to yourself as if you were writing to someone you deeply care about. Start with:

"Dear [Your Name], I want you to know..."

Let kindness guide your pen. No need to fix or change anything, just witness yourself with love.

Integration Reflection

Kindness to yourself is not indulgence, it is nourishment. This practice grounds you in compassion and begins to replace old inner criticism with acceptance and truth. Repeat this ritual as needed, especially on days when your heart feels tender or unseen.

Case Study Discussion: Isabella's Journey

Isabella was always there for others. She was the first to offer help and the last to leave when someone needed her. She was kind, compassionate and caring, but she had a hard time showing that same kindness to herself. Isabella self–talk was brutal, constantly telling herself that she was not good enough, smart enough or pretty enough. Isabella felt that she was not worthy and did not deserve kindness or love from herself or anyone. Over time in our sessions, Isabella realised that she could not keep giving to others if she did not give to herself. She started by practicing self–compassion and self–care. She began to treat herself with the same kindness and respect she showed to others. It was not easy for her at first, but with practice, she started to change the way she talked to herself and the way she treated herself._ As Isabella's heart opened up to kindness, she began to see and feel into herself differently. She started to believe that she was lovable, just as she was. Isabella discovered that showing herself kindness allowed her to be more patient, understanding, and accepting of others. Her relationships with her family and friends deepened, and she felt more connected to the people around her. Isabella learned that kindness started with herself. She had to be kind to herself before she could be truly kind to others. She realised that she had to fill her own cup before she could pour into others. By gifting kindness to herself, Isabella was able to live a more heart–led life, where love and compassion flowed freely. Today, Isabella continues to practice self–kindness and uses her experience to help others who may be struggling with the same issues she once faced. She knows that living a heart–led life means being kind to yourself and others, and that kindness is the key to unlocking a life full of love and joy.

Reflective Exercise: Isabella's Journey

Here are four profound and reflective questions inspired by Isabella's story to help you engage with your own kindness journey:

1. **What would change if you spoke to yourself with the same compassion you offer others?** *Reflection:* You often give others grace,

---

comfort, and encouragement, but what if you gave that same gift to yourself? Your inner voice shapes your emotional landscape. When you soften it with kindness, you create space for healing, growth, and joy. You become your own ally, not your harshest critic.

2. **When was the last time you truly acknowledged your own worth?** *Reflection:* Worthiness is not something you earn, it is something you already possess. Like Isabella, you may have learned to be kind to others while overlooking yourself, but you deserve love, rest, and recognition. Your value is not conditional. Begin by honouring yourself, gently and consistently.

3. **In what ways has withholding kindness from yourself affected your ability to give it freely to others?** *Reflection:* You cannot pour from an empty cup. If your self-kindness is lacking, giving to others may start to feel exhausting or transactional, but when you fill your heart with compassion for yourself, you do not run dry you overflow. True kindness is sustainable when it starts within.

4. **What daily ritual could help you nurture self-kindness as a way of life?** *Reflection:* Self-kindness does not require grand gestures, it lives in your small, intentional choices: how you speak to yourself in the mirror, how you rest, how you forgive your mistakes.

Start simple. Let kindness become a habit, a rhythm, a sacred return to your heart each day.

These questions and reflections are designed to gently guide you inward, to recognise that kindness is not only what you give, but also what you allow yourself to receive. Like Isabella, you too can open your heart to yourself and live more freely, more fully, and more compassionately.

Affirmations For Integration: (Heart Whispers)

Affirmations have the power to quiet the noise of doubt, open the doorway to self-trust, and draw you back into the wisdom of your heart. When practised daily, they nurture an inner dialogue based in love and truth, helping you live each day more aligned with who you truly are. I invite you to repeat silently or write:

• I show kindness to everyone I meet.

- I believe in the power of kindness.

- I feel happy when I show kindness to others.

- I practice self–kindness every day.

- I believe that kindness can change the world.

- I feel grateful for acts of kindness shown to me.

- I choose kindness even in challenging situations.

- I create a ripple of kindness wherever I go.

The Kindness Ripple Exercise:

I invite you to commit to one small act of kindness for yourself and one for someone else over the next 24 hours. Write it down, reflect on intention, and share with a partner if comfortable. Example acts:

- Writing a forgiveness letter to yourself

- Paying for someone's coffee

- Setting a firm but loving boundary

- Saying something kind to yourself in the mirror

When you consciously choose and act on kindness, you plant a seed that can grow far beyond the moment. The person you help may go on to help someone else, and the kindness you show yourself may inspire deeper self-respect and healthier boundaries in the days ahead. In this way, even the smallest gesture can ripple through lives, touching people you may never meet and creating waves of compassion that extend far beyond your immediate circle.

Closing Reflection

In a world that often glorifies speed, achievement, and self-interest, your choice to slow down and lead with compassion is not just countercultural, it is a profound act of strength. It is the decision to be a source of light in a landscape that can sometimes feel cold and unyielding. Today, as you have reflected on kindness, toward others and, perhaps most importantly, toward yourself, remember this: the gentleness you offer yourself becomes fertile soil. From that soil, your empathy blossoms, your patience deepens, and your courage takes root. This is where true resilience grows, not in the relentless pushing, but in the tender tending of your own heart. When you choose to soften instead of harde. When you speak to yourself with care instead of criticis. When you see others not as threats, but as fellow humans doing their best. You create ripples of healing, connection, and peace, not just for others, but for yourself. Kindness is not a task to check off; it is a way of moving through the world. Carry it forward as a steady rhythm in your words, in your actions, in your pauses, and in your presence. Let kindness shape your relationships, your work, and the way you see the world. Let kindness be your anchor in storms and your light in darkness. Let it be the language your heart speaks, in quiet moments, in challenging moments, in every moment, to every soul you meet, including your own, and as you live this way, you may discover something extraordinary: kindness not only changes the lives it touches, it transforms the one who gives it most of all.

Strength Meets You in Stages

Each chapter builds capacity; each book builds a life. If this work is awakening something in you, follow that thread. The wider Unbound library and programs will meet you at the next level of your growth — www.timetotransform.world

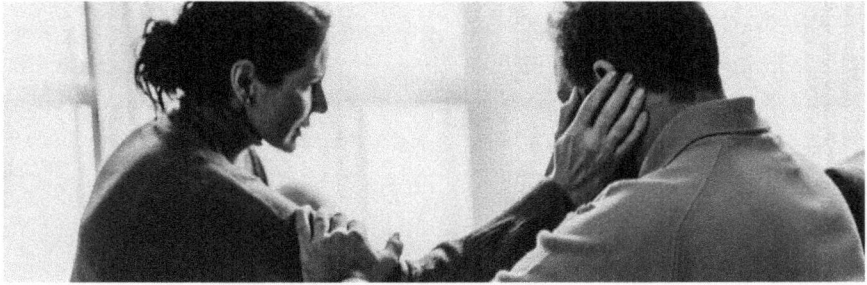

MODULE 8 - COMPASSION

Your Opening Reflection

Invitation to Compassion - As you open this module, I invite you to place your hand over your heart and breathe gently into the space beneath your palm. Imagine compassion as a warm light, flowing first toward yourself, then radiating outward to others. This is your reminder that compassion is not weakness but strength, the courage to meet pain with tenderness, to hold yourself and others with kindness, and to soften instead of harden. Let this moment be your entry point into a deeper practice of living with an open heart..

- "Think of a time when you struggled. How would it have felt if someone had offered you kindness instead of judgment?"

- "What does compassion look like in action for you, toward yourself, toward others, or toward the world

- "When you witness suffering, big or small, what is your first instinct? To turn away, to fix it, or to connect with it?"

- "If compassion were a language, what words or gestures would you use to speak it more fluently in your everyday life?"

- "When was the last time someone showed you compassion? How did it make you feel?"

- "What would change in your life if you showed yourself the same compassion you offer others?"

Let these questions open the doorway into presence. Every answer you give, whether in words, sensations, or silence, is a bridge between where you are and where you are going.

Learning Objectives

The learning objectives are included here to give you a clear focus for this module, ensuring that each practice you explore moves you closer to mastering the skills, insights, and heart-led awareness that will enrich your life well beyond the program. By the end of this module, you will:

- Understand the emotional and neurological benefits of practicing compassion.

- Develop skills in self-compassion, empathy, and compassionate communication.

- Explore the relationship between compassion and healing, connection, and leadership.

- Apply compassion in both personal and professional contexts to create positive change.

Core Emotional Domains

The core emotional intelligence domains covered here are essential because they form the foundation for lasting heart connection, guiding you to deepen self-awareness, regulate emotions, build resilience, and strengthen the mind-body bond throughout your *Unbound* journey.

- **Self-Awareness:** invites you to recognise your own pain and humanity as the starting point for compassion.

- **Self-Regulation:** helps you respond rather than react, creating space to hold others' emotions without being overwhelmed.

- **Empathy:** deepens as you see beyond the surface and honour the shared experiences that unite us all.

- **Social Skills:** are enriched as compassion develops genuine connection, healing conflict, and strengthening trust.

- **Motivation:** becomes heart-aligned as your drive to act is fuelled by kindness, service, and the desire to uplift others.

"Compassion – The Heart Of Connection"

Compassion is more than a kind gesture, it is a transformative force of emotional intelligence that elevates both personal well-being and collective humanity. At its core, compassion is the deep awareness of suffering, your own and others', combined with the heartfelt desire to relieve it. When turned inward, compassion becomes a powerful tool for healing. It helps you soften the inner critic, dissolve shame, and acknowledge your struggles without judgment. Instead of pushing yourself to 'get over it,' you learn to sit gently with your pain, to listen with tenderness, and to honour your human experience. This self-compassion builds true emotional resilience. It develops confidence not through perfection, but through kindness. When expressed outwardly, compassion becomes the bridge between people. It breaks down barriers of fear, anger, and misunderstanding. Compassionate communication allows for deeper listening, clearer understanding, and stronger, more authentic relationships. In high-performance environments like corporate settings, universities, or government departments, compassion enables more inclusive decision-making, reduces conflict, and fuels purpose-driven collaboration. Leaders who lead with compassion are not weak, they are strong enough to care. They are emotionally attuned to the needs of others, can hold space during conflict, and inspire trust and loyalty. Compassion transforms performance cultures into human-centred ones, where people are seen, heard, and valued. Compassion is not passive. It is active. It is not just a feeling, it is a conscious choice to be present, kind, and responsive, even when it is hard. It is the fuel for courageous conversations, the anchor during times of uncertainty, and the heartbeat of every act of service. In a world that is too often fractured by comparison, competition, and fear, compassion reminds you that you are not alone, and neither is anyone else. It invites you to be the one who listens deeper, who softens the edge, and who dares to care. This is how healing happens. This is how heart-led transformation begins.

The History And Universality Of Compassion Across Cultures And Spiritual Traditions

Compassion is one of humanity's oldest and most revered virtues, an emotional and spiritual force that transcends time, geography, and belief systems. Across ancient civilisations and sacred traditions, compassion has been upheld as a path to both personal transformation and collective peace.

In **Buddhism**, compassion (karuṇā) is one of the Four Immeasurables, essential for liberation from suffering. It calls for active empathy and loving-kindness toward all beings. In **Christianity**, Jesus taught, *"Love your neighbour as yourself,"* embedding compassion at the heart of faith through parables, forgiveness, and service to the poor and vulnerable. **Islam** begins nearly every chapter of the Qur'an with *"In the name of God, the Most Compassionate, the Most Merciful,"* affirming rahmah (mercy) as a divine attribute to be lived by the faithful. **Hinduism** emphasises ahimsa, non-violence and compassion toward all living beings, as a foundational principle of spiritual life. **Judaism** teaches tikkun olam, or *"repairing the world,"* often through acts of compassion and justice. **Sikhism** speaks of daya, or compassionate sensitivity, as a vital expression of devotion to God and service to humanity.

In **Indigenous traditions** around the world, compassion is expressed through a deep kinship with all life, people, animals, the Earth, and ancestors. The sacred principle of reciprocity reminds us that care must flow in all directions for harmony to exist. Even in secular philosophy, from Confucian ethics to Stoic thought, compassion is seen as a key to ethical living and wise leadership. Modern psychology now echoes what ancient wisdom has always known: compassion is essential for mental health, community, and resilience. Despite differences in language, rituals, or belief, compassion remains a universal bridge, uniting hearts across continents, inviting people to rise above fear, and reminding you of your shared humanity. It is not bound to any one religion or culture. It is a sacred thread woven through them all, whispering the same truth: that to live fully is to love deeply, and to be truly human is to care.

Compassion vs. Empathy: Understanding The Distinction And Synergy

Empathy and compassion are often used interchangeably, but they are distinct emotional capacities, each powerful on its own, and transformative when combined. **Empathy** is the ability to feel or understand what another person is experiencing. It comes in two primary forms:

- **Emotional empathy**: where you actually *feel* another's emotions, as if they were your own.

- **Cognitive empathy**: where you intellectually *understand* what someone is feeling, even if you do not feel it yourself.

Empathy allows you to tune in, to walk in another's shoes, and to resonate with their internal world, but without boundaries or action, empathy alone can lead to **empathic distress,** an emotional overload that can result in burnout, especially in caring professions or high-stress environments. **Compassion**, on the other hand, takes empathy a step further. It adds two crucial ingredients: **a desire to alleviate suffering** and **a conscious choice**

to act with care. Compassion is empathy in motion. It includes warmth, perspective, and intentional response. Where empathy feels *with*, compassion feels *for*, and *moves toward*.

The **synergy** between them is profound. Empathy creates the connection. Compassion channels it into wise, heartful action. In emotionally intelligent relationships, workplaces, and leadership, this blend creates not only mutual understanding but also resilience, inclusion, and trust. In short:

- **Empathy says**: *"I feel what you are feeling."*

- **Compassion says**: *"I see your pain, and I want to help ease it."*

When you learn to navigate both, empathising without being overwhelmed, and responding with compassionate intention, you open the door to deeper connection, sustainable caregiving, and a more heart-led way of being.

The Science Of Compassion: Effects On The Brain, Body, And Emotional Wellbeing

Compassion is not only a spiritual virtue or moral ideal, it is a **biological capacity** wired into your human system. Thanks to advances in neuroscience, Compassion is not only a spiritual virtue or moral ideal, it is a **biological capacity** wired into your human system. Thanks to advances in neuroscience, psychology, and mind-body medicine, we now know that compassion has **measurable, transformative effects** on your brain, body, and emotional health.

Compassion and the Brain: Rewiring for Connection

Compassion activates specific regions of your brain associated with empathy, reward, and emotional regulation:

- Your **anterior cingulate cortex** and **insula** light up during compassionate responses, facilitating emotional awareness and motivation to help.

- The **ventral striatum,** a key part of your brain's reward system, is activated when you act with compassion, reinforcing pro-social behavior with a sense of pleasure or satisfaction.

- The **prefrontal cortex**, responsible for your executive function and impulse control, is strengthened by compassion meditation, enhancing emotional regulation and mindful decision-making.

Repeated acts of compassion, even imagined or intentional ones, **retrain**

neural pathways toward care, presence, and connection. Through a process called **neuroplasticity**, your brain literally reshapes itself to become more compassionate over time.

Compassion and the Body: Healing Through Heartfulness

Biologically, compassion enables a shift from stress to safety. When you act compassionately, whether toward yourself or others, your body enters a state of calm and repair:

- **Oxytocin**, known as the *"bonding hormone,"* is released, increasing trust and lowering blood pressure.

- **Heart rate variability (HRV)** improves, a sign of emotional resilience and nervous system balance.

- **Cortisol**, the body's stress hormone, decreases significantly during compassionate states.

- The **immune system** strengthens, as chronic inflammation, the root of many illnesses, is reduced.

- Compassion literally **heals your body**, reinforcing the link between emotional connection and physical vitality.

- Participants in **Compassion Cultivation Training (CCT)** reported greater empathy, reduced emotional reactivity, and enhanced wellbeing in as little as 8 weeks.

These findings offer hope: no matter your starting point, **you can become more compassionate**, toward yourself and others.

The Takeaway

Compassion is not weakness; it is your greatest neurobiological strength. When you allow yourself to meet your pain or another's suffering with kindness, you activate powerful systems in your brain and nervous system that restore balance, safety, and healing. Compassion is not indulgence; it is a force that reconditions your mind and soothes your heart. It is not optional; it is essential, for your health, your heart, and your humanity. Each time you choose compassion, you are teaching your body to soften stress, your mind to let go of fear, and your soul to remember what matters most. In a world that often demands performance, perfection, and pressure, compassion becomes your quiet revolution. It rewires your nervous system, strengthens your resilience, and awakens your courage. It shows you that love is not only an emotion but also the most intelligent response you can make. When you embody compassion, you step into alignment with the truth of your heart. You liberate yourself from judgment and create space for connection, healing, and peace, within yourself and in the world around you.

Compassion As A Leadership Quality And Driver Of Emotional Maturity

In the evolving landscape of leadership, compassion is no longer viewed as a soft or optional trait, it is a core competency for effective, emotionally intelligent leaders and a catalyst for meaningful human connection, organisational wellbeing, and sustained performance.

Compassionate Leadership: Leading with Heart and Strength

True leadership is not just about authority or vision, it is about presence, relational intelligence, and trust. Compassionate leaders:

- **See the person, not just the role.** You recognise the humanity behind the job title, and respond with empathy when others are struggling.

- **Listen deeply** and respond with care, not to fix, but to understand and empower.

- **Model psychological safety**, allowing others to be vulnerable, take creative risks, and speak their truth without fear of judgement.

- **Balance accountability with empathy**, knowing that high performance grows best in a culture of respect and care.

Far from making leaders appear weak, compassion earns respect, builds loyalty, and creates environments where people want to give their best.

Compassion as a Sign of Emotional Maturity

Compassion is emotional intelligence in action. It draws on and strengthens key EI domains:

- **Self-awareness**: Compassion requires you to notice your internal reactions, judgement, impatience, or defensiveness, and pause before responding.

- **Self-regulation**: Rather than reacting harshly, you choose a response that supports growth, for yourself and others.

- **Empathy**: You actively imagine what it feels like to be in someone else's shoes, without needing to agree or fix.

- **Motivation**: Compassionate leaders are motivated by a desire to serve a purpose greater than themselves.

- **Social skills**: Compassion deepens your ability to manage relationships, navigate conflict, and inspire teams.

Choosing compassion, especially in difficult moments, is a sign of **emotional strength**, not softness. It reflects maturity, humility, and wisdom. Compassion is not only a spiritual virtue or moral ideal, it is a **biological capacity** wired into your human system. Thanks to advances in neuroscience, Compassion is not only a spiritual virtue or moral ideal, it is a **biological capacity** wired into your human system. Thanks to advances in neuroscience, psychology, and mind-body medicine, we now know that compassion has **measurable, transformative effects** on your brain, body, and emotional health.

Compassion And The Brain: Rewiring For Connection

Compassion activates specific regions of your brain associated with empathy, reward, and emotional regulation:

- Your **anterior cingulate cortex** and **insula** light up during compassionate responses, facilitating emotional awareness and motivation to help.

- The **ventral striatum,** a key part of your brain's reward system, is activated when you act with compassion, reinforcing pro-social behavior with a sense of pleasure or satisfaction.

- The **prefrontal cortex**, responsible for your executive function and impulse control, is strengthened by compassion meditation, enhancing emotional regulation and mindful decision-making.

Repeated acts of compassion, even imagined or intentional ones, **retrain neural pathways** toward care, presence, and connection. Through a process called **neuroplasticity**, your brain literally reshapes itself to become more compassionate over time.

Why Self-Compassion Is The Foundation Of True Compassion For Others

You cannot pour from an empty cup, and in the realm of emotional intelligence, this truth becomes even more profound. Self-compassion is not self-indulgence or weakness. It is the very foundation upon which authentic compassion for others is built.

You Cannot Give What You Do Not Have

When you are harsh with yourself, judging, criticising, or berating your mistakes, it becomes harder to offer genuine understanding to others. Why? Because unacknowledged inner pain often leads to projection, burnout, or emotional distance. Self-compassion softens your inner world. It teaches you to:

- Embrace imperfection as part of being human.

- Respond to your struggles with kindness, not condemnation.

- Honour your needs and emotional landscape without guilt.

In doing so, you create space, emotional spaciousness, to meet others with the same grace.

Compassion Begins in the Mirror

People often assume compassion is outward-focused, but it starts within. When you treat yourself with warmth, patience, and understanding, you rewire your nervous system for safety and trust. You stop seeing others through a lens of comparison, competition, or judgement, and instead view them through a shared humanity. Self-compassion allows you to say:

- *"Just like me, they make mistakes."*

- *"Just like me, they are trying."*

- *"Just like me, they long to be seen and loved."*

This recognition dismantles barriers. It dissolves *"otherness."* It makes empathy more than a thought, it makes it embodied.

The Science of Self-Compassion

Research by Dr. Kristin Neff and others has shown that self-compassion:

- Activates the parasympathetic nervous system (calm, grounded state).

- Lowers cortisol and reduces chronic stress.

- Builds resilience and emotional regulation.

- Enhances motivation, not through fear, but through inner support.

People who practice self-compassion are more likely to:

- Offer help to others without resentment or martyrdom.

- Apologise and repair relationships.

- Maintain healthy boundaries.

- Act with courage, even after failure.

<u>Self-Compassion Cultivates Emotional Generosity</u>

When you are kind to yourself, your compassion becomes more spacious. You are less likely to take things personally, react from pain, or withdraw when others struggle. Instead, you offer presence. Understanding. A heart that says, "*I have been there too. I see you.*" In this way, self-compassion does not limit your compassion, it **amplifies** it.

Compassion-in-Action Toolkit

This week, I invite you to choose *at least two* of the following acts of compassion. Each small action you take has the power to ripple outward, nurturing your own heart while touching the lives of others.

1. **Self-compassion ritual** – Write a compassionate affirmation just for you and place it near your mirror. Each morning when you see it, pause, breathe, and let those words settle into your heart.

2. **Active listening moment** – In your next conversation, give the gift of your full presence. Put away distractions, soften your attention, and truly listen, not just to the words spoken, but to the feelings behind them.

3. **Forgiveness practice** – Reflect on one burden you have been carrying, a hurt, a resentment, a grudge. Write a letter of forgiveness, not to condone or excuse, but to release your own heart from its weight. You do not need to send it; the act of writing is enough.

4. **Service contribution** – Offer one hour of your time this week to help someone without expectation. It could be assisting a colleague, supporting a friend, or volunteering in your community. Let your service be an expression of love without condition.

5. **Kindness ripple** – Choose a simple, anonymous act of kindness. It could be leaving a kind note, paying for someone's coffee, or sending encouragement without signing your name. Trust that your gesture, though unseen, will brighten someone's day.

Case Study Discussion: Grace's Journey

Grace was a 42 year–old woman who had always lived a fairly self–centred and disconnected life. By her own admission she was consumed by her own desires and needs, rarely considering the feelings and struggles of others. During one of our sessions, she told me about a series of events that led her to question the way she had been living and about a chance encounter where she witnessed an act of kindness between strangers. It was only a small thing in the overall scheme of life, but she told me that she had seen a man offer his coat to a homeless woman on a cold winter night. The compassion displayed in that moment struck a chord deep within her heart. It was a wake-up call that made her realise the emptiness of her own existence. Grace was inspired by this encounter, and she embarked on a powerful journey of self–reflection and transformation. She started by practicing self–compassion, learning to be kind, and forgiving towards herself. As she extended this compassion to herself, she discovered a newfound sense of peace and acceptance. In time, Grace began to extend her compassion to others. It was difficult for her at the start, but she volunteered at a local charity store, offering her time and support to those in need. She spent time and listened to their stories, held their hands, and offered words of encouragement. In each act of compassion, she experienced a deep connection with others and a profound sense of purpose.

As Grace continued on her path of compassion, she encountered profound changes in her life. Relationships that were once strained (especially with her parents) started to heal as she approached them with understanding and empathy. She also became a trusted confidante and a source of comfort for her friends and family. In her professional life, Grace's newfound compassion transformed the dynamics of her team. She became a source of inspiration, encouraging her workmates to work together and support one another. Outside of her immediate circle, Grace found herself drawn to causes that championed social justice and equality. In time she became an advocate for homeless teenagers in her area, using her voice to raise awareness and bring about change. Her acts of compassion extended beyond individuals, encompassing the broader community. Through her journey of embracing compassion, Grace experienced a profound shift in her life. The once self–centred woman that I had first encountered had evolved into a beautiful beacon of light and love. Her heart overflowed with kindness, and she radiated a warmth that touched the lives of those around her and she was a joy to be around. In the process of embracing compassion, Grace discovered the true essence of her being. She realised that life's true purpose was about connecting with others, offering support, and showing kindness. It was through compassion that she found fulfillment, joy, and a profound sense of belonging. Grace's story is a testament to the transformative power of compassion. It demonstrates that when you choose to open your heart to others and embrace empathy and kindness, you not only transform your own life but also create a ripple effect of positive change in those around you.

Reflective Exercise: Grace's Journey

Here are two profound and reflective questions inspired by Grace's story to help you engage with your own compassionate journey:

1. **When was the last time you offered yourself compassion instead of criticism?** *Supportive Reflection:* Just like Grace, your journey begins with how you treat yourself. Your inner voice matters. Are you offering yourself the same kindness and patience you give to others? When you make a mistake or feel overwhelmed, could you try saying to yourself, "I'm doing the best I can, and that's enough"?

2. **How might you see the humanity in others more clearly today, even those who challenge you?** *Supportive Reflection:* That simple moment Grace witnessed, a man offering his coat, reminds you that small acts of kindness can awaken deep truths. Every person you encounter is carrying invisible struggles. When you choose to meet them with curiosity and compassion, you open the door to deeper connection and healing.

Affirmations For Integration: (Heart Whispers)

Affirmations have the power to quiet the noise of doubt, open the doorway to self-trust, and draw you back into the wisdom of your heart. When practised daily, they nurture an inner dialogue based in love and truth, helping you live each day more aligned with who you truly are. I invite you to repeat silently or write:

- I choose to show compassion to people in my life.
- I am committed to doing acts of kindness for others.
- I open my heart to the pain and struggles of others.
- I embrace forgiveness to embrace compassion and healing.

- I strive to listen deeply and validate the experiences of others.

- I believe in the power of compassion to create positive change in the world.

Compassion Reflection Exercise

Take a 30-minute walk with the clear intention of awakening your heart to compassion. As you step outside, allow yourself to slow down and notice the people passing by, the rhythms of nature, the quiet details of your surroundings. With each step, ask yourself:

- *Where is compassion needed here?*

- *Where can I offer kindness, within me and around me?*

If you see someone rushing, instead of judging, breathe in patience. If you notice an elderly person or a child, silently bless them with safety and love. If you witness tension, offer an inward prayer for peace. If you pass by a tree, flower, or bird, acknowledge the gift of life it holds and the interconnectedness you share.

As you walk, extend compassion inward too. Notice if self-criticism or restlessness arises, and gently replace it with kindness toward yourself. Let your heart guide your gaze, your breath, and your thoughts. When you return, take a few moments to journal. Write down what you noticed, how the walk made you feel, and whether compassion shifted the way you saw the world. Ask yourself:

- *What action am I called to take now, from this heart-awakened place?*

This walk is not just an exercise, it is a living practice, training your mind and heart to choose compassion as your natural way of seeing.

Closing Reflection

Compassion is not something you simply give away, it is a force that reshapes you from within. Every time you choose compassion, whether toward yourself or others, you send ripples through your nervous system, calming fear and dissolving judgment. You rewire your brain for connection rather than separation, for healing rather than harm. Remember: compassion is not weakness, it is courage. It is not indulgence, it is intelligence. It is not optional, it is essential, for your heart, your health, and your humanity. As you walk this path, let compassion become both your anchor and your compass.

Notice how it changes your inner dialogue, softens your relationships, and expands your presence in the world. When pressure rises, return to compassion. When criticism echoes, return to compassion. When the world feels heavy, return to compassion. In doing so, you are not only offering love to others, you are offering love to yourself, and in that simple, profound choice, you awaken the quiet revolution of the heart.

The Invitation Continues

You have begun something meaningful. Every Unbound offering, book or program, is an invitation to go deeper. If something in you whispered "yes" while reading this chapter, honour it. Continue the journey — www.timetotransform.world

PART 3 – THE CORPORATE RESET

Creating Space, Stillness & Sustainable Momentum in a World of Motion

(Time to Transform: Living Unbound – Chapters 9 Nothingness • 23 Declutter • 11 Forgiveness • 28 Reflection)

A Moment of Recognition

You have probably felt it, that invisible heaviness that comes when everything in the organisation is "urgent." The days fill with meetings that leave no time to think, inboxes overflow with information but not insight, and success becomes measured by how busy everyone looks rather than how aligned they feel. It is a strange irony: the faster you move, the more you risk losing your way. The Corporate Reset begins with this simple truth, sometimes the most productive act is to pause. To stop long enough to see where your energy is leaking. To make space for the ideas, connections, and clarity that cannot emerge in chaos. You are not being asked to slow down progress, you are being invited to ensure it still has purpose. - *Momentum without meaning is motion without direction.*

Why Resetting Matters

In the relentless pursuit of growth, many organisations mistake noise for achievement, but just as a cluttered desk clouds the mind, a cluttered culture clouds vision. When every initiative is top priority, focus fractures. When forgiveness is absent, teams hold invisible tension that drains creativity. When reflection is skipped, learning disappears. Resetting is not weakness, it is wisdom. It is the practice of regularly clearing the mental, emotional, and operational clutter that builds up over time. Just as your body needs rest, your organisation needs rhythm, moments of stillness between the surges of action. When you give yourself and your team permission to pause, something remarkable happens: innovation breathes again, relationships repair, and people remember *why* they do what they do. - *The most effective organisations are not the ones that never stop; they are the ones that know when to stop, breathe, and begin again.*

The Four Pillars of the Corporate Reset

1. Nothingness – The Power of Stillness

Nothingness sounds empty, but it is not. It is space, the fertile silence where new ideas are born. In leadership, this looks like creating moments where you do nothing *on purpose*: a quiet minute before a meeting, a team check-in that begins with breath instead of agenda, a week where strategy takes precedence over speed. Stillness is where innovation takes root. It is the pause between notes that makes the music of an organisation audible again. - *When you embrace stillness, you invite clarity.*

2. Declutter – Clearing the Path for What Matters

Decluttering is not just about physical space, it is about mental, emotional, and organisational space. It is asking hard questions: Which processes genuinely serve purpose? Which meetings add meaning, and which repeat noise? Which expectations drain rather than drive? When you declutter, you reclaim energy. You model discernment, the ability to say no with grace so that what remains can flourish. - *What you release creates room for what truly matters.*

3. Forgiveness – Releasing the Weight of the Past

Every organisation carries unspoken history, projects that failed, relationships that strained, words that lingered. Without forgiveness, these memories calcify into resistance. Forgiveness does not mean forgetting; it means freeing. It allows teams to move forward unburdened, to trust again, and to create without fear of blame. For you as a leader, forgiveness might mean forgiving yourself, for the decision you made under pressure, the conversation you avoided, the pace you could not sustain. When you extend that same grace to others, you build a culture that learns rather than judges. - *Forgiveness is the quiet force that transforms accountability into growth.*

4. Reflection – Turning Activity into Insight

Reflection is the moment when doing turns into learning. It is how experience becomes wisdom and momentum becomes mastery. In a corporate context, reflection might take the form of post-project debriefs that focus not on fault but on discovery; leadership journaling that captures lessons in real time; or shared conversations that honour both success and struggle. Reflection gives you perspective, a chance to see the arc of your efforts, to celebrate progress, and to refine purpose. - *Without reflection, even the best strategies lose their meaning.*

The Synergy of the Four Pillars

Stillness, decluttering, forgiveness, and reflection form a natural sequence a rhythm of renewal. You pause (Nothingness), you clear (Declutter), you release (Forgiveness), and you learn (Reflection). Together, they create a culture that can breathe. This is how organisations evolve, not through endless acceleration, but through conscious renewal. A reset is not a retreat; it is how you prepare for the next level of growth with clarity, cohesion, and heart. - *When you make space, what truly matters rises naturally to the surface.*

A Closing Reflection

Close your eyes for a moment and imagine your organisation at its best calm, clear, creative. Notice the difference in tone, pace, and presence. That vision isn't a dream; it's a direction. It begins with you. Take a breath before you act. Delete one task that no longer aligns. Forgive one frustration you've been carrying. Reflect on one lesson worth keeping. Every small reset strengthens the whole. - *You do not need to start over. You just need to start clean.*

A Heart Invitation

As you move through *The Corporate Reset*, give yourself permission to lead differently. When the world demands urgency, offer steadiness. When confusion grows, create space. When exhaustion spreads, model forgiveness. When progress feels hollow, pause and ask why. This is how corporate cultures heal, not through new systems alone, but through new awareness. You are not leading machines; you are leading humans, and humans need space to breathe, reflect, and reconnect with purpose. - *Resetting is not stopping. It is remembering who you are and what truly matters.*

MODULE 9 - NOTHINGNESS

Your Opening Reflection

An Invitation to Breathe - Before you move forward, allow yourself this simple gift: pause, soften, and breathe. Your breath is not just air, it is life moving through you, a gentle reminder that you are here, alive, and connected. Let each inhale welcome you home to your heart, and let each exhale release what no longer serves you. With every breath, you are reminded that presence, peace, and renewal are always within reach.

- "How comfortable are you with simply being, without needing to achieve or produce?"

- "What fears or discomforts arise when you slow down completely?"

- "When was the last time you sat in silence and truly listened to your own breath?"

- "What would it feel like to release all expectations for a moment?"

- "How might doing nothing actually restore your energy and clarity?"

- "When was the last time you allowed yourself to do absolutely nothing, with no guilt?"

Let these questions open the doorway into presence. Every answer you give, whether in words, sensations, or silence, is a bridge between where you are and where you are going.

Learning Objectives

The learning objectives are included here to give you a clear focus for this module, ensuring that each practice you explore moves you closer to mastering the skills, insights, and heart-led awareness that will enrich your life well beyond the program. By the end of this module, you will:

- Understand the emotional and psychological benefits of embracing stillness and nothingness.

- Recognise how overstimulation and busyness interfere with your emotional clarity and self-awareness.

- Practice techniques to invite silence, spaciousness, and simplicity into your daily life.

- Develop inner awareness through intentional disengagement from constant doing.

- Cultivate greater presence, peace, and heart connection by creating space for nothingness.

Core Emotional Domains

The core emotional intelligence domains covered here are essential because they form the foundation for lasting heart connection, guiding you to deepen self-awareness, regulate emotions, build resilience, and strengthen the mind-body bond throughout your *Unbound* journey.

- **Self-Awareness:** You learn to observe your inner landscape in stillness, noticing thoughts, emotions, and sensations without needing to fix or judge them.

- **Self-Regulation:** By resting in quiet, you calm your nervous system, release reactivity, and create space for thoughtful, heart-aligned responses.

- **Mindful Presence:** In the spaciousness of nothingness, you practise simply being, fully present, unattached to outcomes, grounded in the now.

- **Motivation:** In the pause, clarity returns. You reconnect with what truly matters, realigning your energy with purpose rather than pressure.

"Nothingness – Embracing the Sacred Pause"

The Sacred Power of Nothingness

Modern life demands constant stimulation. You are bombarded by notifications, responsibilities, background noise, and the pressure to always be doing. In a world that rarely stops, stillness can feel uncomfortable, even foreign, but within that discomfort lies a profound invitation: to come home to yourself.

<u>Nothingness is not emptiness. It is spaciousness.</u>

It is the pause between the inhale and exhale, the moment before a thought forms, the sacred silence behind your heartbeat. When you allow yourself to rest in nothingness, you are not abandoning life, you are rediscovering it. In this space, your nervous system begins to settle:

1. Your mind becomes less chaotic.
2. Your heart becomes more audible.

From this quiet place, wisdom arises, not from effort, but from presence. You begin to hear the deeper questions:

- What truly matters to you?

- What can you release?

- What is asking to emerge?

<u>Embracing nothingness is a radical act of self-regulation and emotional intelligence.</u>

It is a conscious choice to step away from the relentless demands of doing and into the quiet sanctuary of being. In this space, you interrupt the cycle of reactivity that so often drives exhaustion, disconnection, and overwhelm. Nothingness becomes a healing pause, a moment where clarity can rise, where the edges of your mind soften, and where you stand in your own sovereignty, unshaken by the noise around you. Here, time is no longer measured by productivity, but by alignment with your soul's natural rhythm. You begin to notice the steady pulse of your own breath, the subtle language of your body, and the quiet wisdom of your heart. When you allow yourself to simply be, you uncover a profound truth: you are already enough, exactly as you are, and from this stillness, your most authentic actions emerge, not from urgency, but from peace. So the next time you feel yourself swept up in the current of constant doing, choose the sacred pause. Sit in the fullness of nothing, without guilt or resistance. Let yourself be held by the silence, for it is in this space that the heart remembers what the noise once made you forget, that your worth was never in what you produced, but in the truth of who you are.

The Science and Spirituality of Nothingness

Honouring the art of rest, presence, and spacious being. In a world driven by productivity, performance, and endless achievement, the idea of doing *nothing* often feels indulgent, even shameful, but both modern science and ancient spiritual wisdom reveal a beautiful truth: nothingness is not laziness, it is medicine.

Dolce far niente - "The sweetness of doing nothing"

From the Italian tradition comes *dolce far niente*, a phrase that celebrates the joy and soulfulness found in intentional rest. It is not laziness, nor is it avoidance, it is the conscious decision to step out of the current of busyness and into the quiet flow of the present moment. It might look like sipping tea in the afternoon sun without rushing to the next task, watching clouds drift across the sky, or sharing peaceful silence with a loved one. In these moments, nothing is being *"achieved"* in the traditional sense, yet everything essential is being nourished. *Dolce far niente* is a reminder that your worth has never been measured by your output. Your soul does not thrive on relentless pressure; it blossoms in presence, in being fully here, and in allowing life to unfold without force.

Niksen - The Dutch art of purposeless rest

In the Netherlands, this practice takes the form of *niksen*, the art of doing absolutely nothing, on purpose. It is a radical permission slip to put down your phone, step away from emails, silence the *"to-do"* list, and simply exist in the moment with no objective other than being. Science now affirms what tradition has long known: when you give your mind space to wander without direction, creativity sparks, stress dissolves, problem-solving skills sharpen, and your overall emotional well-being improves. *Niksen* invites your nervous system to recalibrate, allowing tension to melt away and making room for insight to arise naturally. This is the fertile ground where your subconscious processes life's events, where resilience takes hold, and where clarity emerges, not from doing more, but from allowing more stillness. In *niksen*, you learn that rest is not an interruption to your life's journey; it is an essential part of the path itself.

The Neuroscience of Nothingness

When you allow yourself to enter a state of restful awareness, whether through daydreaming, meditating, or simply sitting still, a remarkable thing happens in your brain. You activate what is known as the *default mode network*, a system linked to self-reflection, creativity, emotional processing, and meaning-making. Contrary to the myth that idleness is a waste of time, neuroscience shows that it is in these very states of non-doing that your brain quietly integrates your experiences, makes sense of them, and sparks deeper insight. In other words, when you step back from the noise, your mind begins to connect the dots that busyness keeps scattered.

In this intentional rest, your body also shifts into repair mode. Cortisol, your primary stress hormone, decreases, giving your system a much-needed break from chronic pressure. Your heart rate variability, a key marker of emotional resilience, begins to balance, and your parasympathetic nervous system, the *"rest and restore"* branch of your body's wiring, takes the lead, calming you from the inside out. By giving yourself permission to pause, you are not doing *"nothing"*, you are creating the optimal conditions for your mind to heal, your body to recover, and your spirit to reconnect with what truly matters.

The Spiritual Roots of Stillness

Across spiritual traditions around the world, from Buddhism and Taoism to Christian monasticism and Sufi mysticism, stillness is not seen as an absence, but as a profound presence. It is not emptiness, but fullness, the quiet space in which you can meet your truest self and listen to the wisdom that cannot be heard in the noise of everyday life.

Zen Buddhism

In Zen, the practice of silence and sitting meditation (*zazen*) is a direct path to awakening, a way of stripping away illusions and resting in the essence of reality. The focus is not on achieving a specific state, but on simply sitting with what is, allowing thoughts to rise and fall like waves without clinging to or rejecting them. This stillness is not passive; it is alive with awareness. Each breath is a doorway into the present moment, each heartbeat a reminder of life's impermanence and beauty. Through this sustained attention, Zen teaches that enlightenment is not somewhere else to be reached, but here, already present, revealed when the mind quiets enough to see it.

Christianity

In Christianity, contemplative prayer becomes a meeting place with the divine, where the heart communes with God beyond words, beyond asking, simply in the openness of being. This form of prayer invites you to rest in God's presence without agenda, to be still and know. Christian mystics such as St. Teresa of Ávila and Thomas Merton wrote of stillness as a sacred intimacy, where the soul is nourished not by doing, but by abiding. It is here that love deepens, faith matures, and grace flows freely. The stillness is an act of surrender, trusting that God's presence is enough.

Taoism

In Taoism, quiet observation of nature is a teacher, revealing the effortless flow of life and the harmony of all things. By watching the seasons shift, rivers carve valleys, and trees grow without striving, you begin to see the Tao, the Way, unfolding without force. Stillness in Taoism is not withdrawal from life, but attunement to its rhythms. When you slow down to truly witness the natural world, you begin to mirror its balance. You learn that life is not meant to be pushed into shape, but trusted to find its own. In this way, stillness is not escape but alignment.

Indigenous Traditions

In Indigenous traditions, time spent on the land is sacred, not for doing, but for listening, for receiving guidance from the earth, the ancestors, and the unseen. This listening is an active relationship with the world, one built on reciprocity, respect, and belonging. Stillness here is not solitary; it is communal. It connects you to the web of life and reminds you that you are part of something far greater. Sitting by a river, walking through the forest, or lying under the night sky becomes ceremony, restoring your place in the circle of life and deepening your responsibility to care for it.

Sufi Mysticism

In Sufi mysticism, stillness is a lover's embrace with the Divine Beloved, where the soul is dissolved into unity and love. The Sufi seeks not just to know about God, but to taste God directly, and stillness is the chalice from which that love is drunk. Poets like Rumi and Hafiz spoke of this union as a silence so full it overflows. In the quiet, the heart hears the music of the soul, and the self melts away into the greater Self. It is here that longing meets fulfilment, and the seeker becomes the sought.

Stillness is where the soul breathes. It is where the heart remembers what the mind forgets. It is the space where you come home to yourself, and, in that homecoming, to the sacred.

Why "Doing Nothing" Is A Radical And Emotionally Intelligent Act In A Hyperproductive World

In a culture that glorifies hustle, output, and achievement, choosing to pause, even briefly, is not just a break from the norm. It is a bold, countercultural act of emotional intelligence. You have likely been conditioned to equate your worth with your productivity. The more you do, the more valuable you feel. Rest becomes something to *"earn,"* and idleness is mistaken for laziness, but emotional intelligence asks something deeper:

- Can you be with yourself when there is nothing to achieve?
- Can you slow down enough to hear what your heart is really saying?

Doing nothing invites you into that space. It teaches you to tolerate stillness, to sit with discomfort, and to meet yourself without distractions. It interrupts the nervous system's overdrive and gently regulates your emotions, thoughts, and breath. It reconnects you with your intuitive self, the one that does not shout, but whispers. Emotionally intelligent people know that clarity does not come from constant motion. It emerges in stillness. Insight does not arise from rushing, it flows when you create space. Choosing to *"do nothing"* is how you begin to hear your inner world. It is where your values rise to the surface, where rest meets reflection, and where the next step can reveal itself, not through force, but through alignment. This act of non-doing is a declaration:

- I am enough, even in stillness.
- It is self-awareness in action.
- It is self-regulation without suppression.
- It is presence over performance.

In a world that rewards exhaustion, doing nothing becomes a form of resistance. In a world that forgets how to feel, doing nothing becomes a return to self, and in a world driven by noise, doing nothing is how you learn to listen again. So give yourself permission to pause, not as an escape, but as a homecoming.

Let your stillness be a statement.

Let it be a revolution grounded in grace.

Let it remind you that you are already whole.

The Difference Between Nothingness And Laziness

In a world that moves at lightning speed, where being "*busy*" is often mistaken for being valuable, slowing down can feel unnatural, even shameful. Yet there is a profound distinction between **nothingness** and **laziness,** a distinction that speaks to presence, intention, and emotional intelligence.

Laziness is avoidance.

It often stems from fear, apathy, or disconnection. When you are lazy, you may resist action not because your soul is asking for stillness, but because you are overwhelmed, unmotivated, or uncertain of your direction. Laziness numbs. It disconnects you from purpose, but nothingness is conscious. It is the intentional choice to pause. To step away from the noise of striving so you can come back into alignment with what truly matters. Nothingness is presence without performance. It is where your nervous system rests, your clarity returns, and your heart speaks. When you sit in stillness, not because you are avoiding life, but because you are making space for it, you are not being lazy. You are listening. You are allowing. You are trusting that your worth is not found in constant output, but in your ability to be with yourself. *Laziness dulls the senses. Nothingness sharpens awareness. Laziness drains your spirit. Nothingness nourishes it.* Choosing nothingness is an act of courage in a hyper productive world. It requires self-awareness to know when to stop, self-regulation to let go of urgency, and self-worth to know you are valuable, even in stillness. So the next time you pause, breathe, and simply *be*, remind yourself: This is not laziness. This is leadership from within. This is how you reset, realign, and return to the life you want to live, awake, aware, and grounded in what truly matters.

How Intentional Stillness Reduces Stress And Develops Resilience

In a world that rarely stops moving, **intentional stillness** is one of the most powerful tools you have to reduce stress and build lasting emotional resilience. It is more than just taking a break, it is a conscious return to the present moment, where healing begins, and clarity is restored. When you choose stillness, not as avoidance, but as *presence,* you send a powerful message to your nervous system: *"You are safe. You can slow down. You do not have to be on high alert."* This shift activates the **parasympathetic nervous system**, also known as the *"rest and restore"* state.

- Your heart rate softens.
- Your breath deepens.
- Cortisol levels begin to drop.
- Blood flow returns to the prefrontal cortex, the part of your brain responsible for insight, reasoning, and empathy.

In stillness, your body recalibrates. Your mind finds space, and your emotions begin to settle. This quiet space between thoughts and actions becomes your training ground for resilience, because when life gets chaotic or painful, it is not the absence of stress that defines your strength, it is your ability to **pause,**

breathe, and respond instead of react. Stillness gives you that ability. It helps you meet life with **inner steadiness**, even when the world around you feels uncertain. It allows you to hear your intuition, process your emotions, and reconnect with your values before making decisions. Over time, the practice of intentional stillness strengthens your emotional core. You become less shaken by pressure. More anchored in your truth. More able to navigate change, disappointment, or challenge with compassion and clarity. Resilience is not about pushing through at all costs. It is about knowing when to stop. When to breathe, and when to *be with yourself* in the quiet, so that you can return to the world not depleted, but renewed.

Nothingness As A Space For Creative Insight And Emotional Regulation

In a culture that often measures success by output and achievement, nothingness can feel useless, even threatening, but nothingness, true, intentional spaciousness, is not emptiness. It is potential. It is the fertile ground from which insight, healing, and transformation quietly emerge. When you allow yourself to pause, to be without performing, planning, or producing, you create a rare kind of space. A space where your nervous system can decompress, and your mind can finally breathe. This is not a void, it is a womb of possibility. From this sacred stillness, two powerful forces awaken - creative insight and emotional regulation.

Creative Insight

Creativity does not thrive in chaos. It thrives in space. Your most meaningful ideas often arise when you are not trying to find them, when you are walking without purpose, daydreaming by a window, or simply resting in the stillness of being. Neuroscience confirms this: when your brain enters its default mode network during restful states, it begins to form new connections, solve complex problems, and unlock subconscious wisdom. Stillness invites your imagination to speak. It creates the conditions where you can hear your soul's voice, free from noise, urgency, or comparison. It is in doing nothing that your next meaningful something often reveals itself.

Emotional Regulation

Nothingness also offers something gentler but just as powerful: emotional clarity. When you sit in stillness, your feelings have room to rise, not to overwhelm you, but to be acknowledged, felt, and gently processed. You create the space to observe your inner world with compassion rather than judgment. This is the heart of emotional regulation, not pushing emotions down, not being ruled by them, but allowing them to move through you. In stillness, you become a safe container for your experience. You learn to respond with presence, not reactivity. You soften your grip. You breathe deeper. You become more whole. In the stillness of nothingness, you are not wasting time. You are resetting your system. You are reclaiming your rhythm. You are allowing life to speak, not through noise, but through silence, and from that silence comes the truth, the vision, the insight, and the peace, that was waiting patiently for you to stop running, and simply be.

Nothingness - Reflection Exercise

The Five-Minute Nothingness Challenge:

I invite you to sit in silence for five full minutes.

- No music
- No phones
- No goals
- Just presence

I ask you to notice your breath, thoughts, sensations, without judgment or control. Now, write down how it felt:

- Restless?
- Peaceful?
- Difficult?
- Surprising?

Case Study - Ash's Journey

I remember when Ash, a very intelligent and spiritually aware young man, told me that doing nothing was easy and that he would do nothing for an hour. At the end of his first week of doing the 28–day challenge I spoke with Ash and asked him how he was going. Ash told me that he found it exceptionally difficult to sit and do nothing even for 2 minutes. He said that he, 'started getting agitated and nervous and felt like he needed to be '*doing something*'. Ash's experience is very common and even if you gifted yourself time and space and only spent 5 seconds doing nothing, really ask yourself why you cannot do it and write it down. Next time you gift yourself the opportunity to do nothing be courageous and claim the full 5 minutes, the journey to connect with your heart is worth the effort, and so are you. Every day make the choice to add on an extra minute and by the end of twenty–eight days you can gift yourself around 30 minutes of nothingness.

Reflective Exercise: Ash's Journey

Here are four profound and reflective questions inspired by Ash's story to help you engage with your own journey into nothingness:

1. When was the last time you allowed yourself to truly stop, not to escape, but to simply be? *Ash discovered that stillness was not about doing nothing, it was about meeting himself without distraction. When you give yourself space to pause, you meet parts of yourself that have been longing to be heard.*

2. What do you notice in the silence that you do not hear in the noise? *In the quiet moments, Ash began to hear truths he had been too busy to feel. Stillness reveals wisdom hidden beneath the surface of routine and noise. What is your silence trying to tell you?*

3. How do you usually respond to the feeling of emptiness? With resistance, or with curiosity? *Ash realised he had spent years filling every empty space with distraction, but when he leaned into the emptiness, it softened, and became a source of calm. Emptiness is not something to fear, it is something to explore.*

4. What might become possible in your life if you stopped needing to be productive all the time? *Ash found that his greatest insights came when he stopped pushing. When you release the pressure to perform, you create room for creativity, clarity, and peace. Sometimes the most powerful growth happens in the stillness between actions.*

Affirmations For Integration: (Heart Whispers)

Affirmations have the power to quiet the noise of doubt, open the doorway to self-trust, and draw you back into the wisdom of your heart. When practised daily, they nurture an inner dialogue based in love and truth, helping you live each day more aligned with who you truly are. I invite you to repeat silently or write:

- I find peace in the nothingness of a quiet mind.
- Nothingness allows me to let go of stress and anxiety.
- In nothingness, I discover the beauty of the present moment.
- Nothingness is where I find clarity and focus.

- In the void of nothingness, I find my true self.
- Nothingness helps me to release attachment to outcomes.
- I am grateful for the peace that nothingness brings to my life.

Optional Nothingness Extension Activity - The Nothingness Space Challenge

1. **Create Your "Nothingness Zone":** Choose a small, quiet spot in your home, a chair, a window seat, a cushion in the corner. Make sure it is free from screens, books, and other distractions.

2. **Prepare It with Intention:** Keep it simple and uncluttered. You may wish to add a single candle, a plant, or an object that brings you calm. This is a space for stillness, not stimulation.

3. **Commit to Daily Use:** Visit your nothingness zone each day, even if only for 3–5 minutes. Sit in stillness. Breathe slowly. Let thoughts pass without chasing them.

4. **Anchor to the Heart:** Place a hand over your heart. Feel its rhythm. Imagine this is the centre of your stillness, expanding gently with each breath.

Close with Gratitude: When you leave, silently thank yourself for showing up and honouring your inner space.

Closing Reflection

In a world that glorifies doing, you chose to simply be. By stepping into the sacred space of nothingness, you have taken a radical step, not away from life, but into its deepest current. This is not an escape; it is an arrival. You have let yourself pause, rest, and listen to the stillness beneath the noise. In this gentle act of surrender, you have remembered something both ancient and essential: you are not here to earn your worth. You already are enough. You do not need to prove yourself to life; you are already woven into its fabric. Nothingness is not empty. It is overflowing, with presence, with breath, with the quiet truths long buried beneath the clutter of busy days. It is here, in this stillness, that you regulate your nervous system, soften the grip of your mind, and allow your heart to breathe again. Here, you create the spaciousness for insights to rise unforced, for clarity to dawn without struggle, for wisdom to arrive in its own time. As you carry this part of your journey forward, may you continue to honour the pause, not as a luxury to be earned, but as a necessity for a life well-lived. Not as weakness, but as the courage to meet life on your own terms. Not as doing less, but as opening to receive more, because in the space of nothingness, you come home to everything that truly matters, and in that homecoming, you remember: the stillness was never separate from you. It was always here, waiting for you to return.

Your Future Self Is Waiting in the Next Book

You do not need to rush, but you also do not need to wait. The man or woman you are becoming is already alive in the pages ahead, and in the practices held across the Unbound programs. Step toward them – www.timetotransform.world

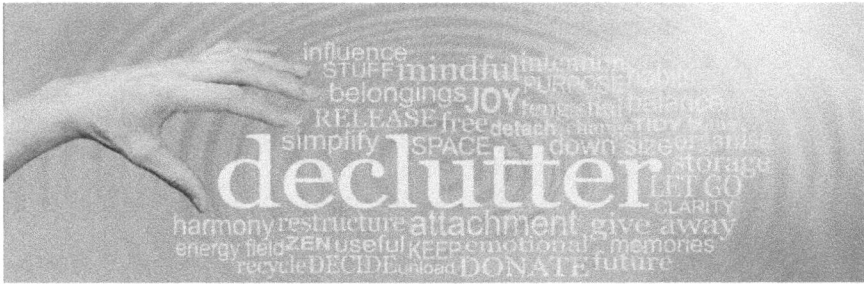

MODULE 10 – DECLUTTER

Your Opening Reflection

Invitation to Clear Space for Your Heart - As you enter this module, I invite you to see decluttering not just as the act of tidying your outer world, but as an offering of space to your inner one. Every object, thought, or emotion you release makes room for something more aligned, more nourishing, more true. This is your chance to breathe lighter, to shed what no longer serves, and to welcome in clarity and peace. Trust that in letting go, you are not losing, but creating space for your heart to expand.

- "What stories or old narratives are you still holding onto that no longer define who you are?"

- "Which habits or routines feel draining rather than nourishing for you, and how might you begin to gently let them go?"

- "What expectations, your own or those placed on you by others, can you release to make more room for your authenticity?"

- "If you cleared away one source of inner noise today, what deeper truth or peace within you might emerge?"

Let these questions open the doorway into presence. Every answer you give, whether in words, sensations, or silence, is a bridge between where you are and where you are going.

Learning Objectives

The learning objectives are included here to give you a clear focus for this module, ensuring that each practice you explore moves you closer to mastering the skills, insights, and heart-led awareness that will enrich your life well beyond the program. By the end of this module, you will:

- Understand the emotional and psychological impact of physical and mental clutter

- Recognise the connection between decluttering and emotional intelligence

- Learn practical strategies for decluttering both internal and external environments

- Cultivate habits of simplicity, mindfulness, and heartful decision-making

Core Emotional Domains

The core emotional intelligence domains covered here are essential because they form the foundation for lasting heart connection, guiding you to deepen self-awareness, regulate emotions, build resilience, and strengthen the mind-body bond throughout your *Unbound* journey.

- **Self-Awareness:** As you explore what clutter, physical, emotional, or mental, has accumulated in your life, you begin to recognise how certain attachments reflect deeper patterns and unmet needs. You learn to pause and reflect on what truly aligns with your heart.

- **Emotional Regulation:** Letting go is not just a practical act, it is an emotional one. By releasing what no longer serves you, you create space within your nervous system for calm, clarity, and grounded presence.

- **Self-Management:** Through mindful decision-making and courageous honesty, you build the inner discipline to say no to what distracts and yes to what nourishes. This develops a life guided by intention, not obligation.

- **Mindfulness & Intentionality:** Every choice to declutter becomes a practice of presence. You learn to be deliberate with your time, energy, and attention, living less by default and more by design.

- **Personal Growth:** As you create space externally, you make room internally for insight, growth, and transformation. Letting go becomes an act of renewal, an invitation to welcome what is next with an open heart.

"Declutter – Creating Space For What Matters"

Decluttering is often misunderstood as simply tidying your home or organising your belongings, but at its essence, it is so much more. It is a sacred practice of release, a deeply emotional and spiritual act of choosing to let go of what no longer aligns with who you are or who you are becoming. Every drawer you empty, every shelf you sort, every object you release can become a moment of self-inquiry. You might ask yourself: *Why did I hold onto this? What part of me once needed this? Am I ready now to release it and invite something new?* These questions help transform decluttering into a ritual of awareness, one where you meet not only your belongings but also the emotions and stories they carry. As you clear physical clutter, you may also find yourself face-to-face with emotional clutter, old narratives you have outgrown, unprocessed grief, patterns inherited from family, or silent obligations that weigh on your spirit. Letting go of these is not always easy; it can feel confronting, even tender. Yet with every release, you reclaim a piece of your energy. You return, gently but surely, to what truly matters. Decluttering is not about striving for minimalism or emptiness for its own sake. It is about creating space for meaning. When your surroundings are lighter, your inner world quiets. When your calendar is less burdened, your heart speaks more clearly. Life shifts from being lived out of habit to being lived out of intention. With each act of clearing, you open space, space for creativity to flow, for stillness to restore you, for joy to rise naturally, and for deeper connections with yourself and others. Decluttering is not deprivation; it is an invitation. An invitation to breathe more deeply, to move with greater freedom, and to make choices that align with your values. In a culture that glorifies accumulation, achievement, and busyness, the practice of decluttering becomes a radical act of love. It is a declaration: *I choose to create space for what truly serves me,* and in that space, your heart finally has room, to whisper, to expand, and to lead you home to yourself.

The Emotional Toll Of Clutter And The Illusion Of Attachment

Clutter in your life is never just about what is visible on the outside. It is not only the piles on your desk, the wardrobe stuffed with clothes you no longer wear, or the garage full of boxes you keep promising to sort through one day. Clutter is often a reflection of something much deeper, the emotional weight you have been carrying, sometimes for years, without realising it. Every object, every task you avoid, every commitment you can't quite release, holds a story. It may not just be about function or usefulness, but about the emotions, fears, and identities you have attached to them. When you look at the things you hold onto, ask yourself: *What part of me is this connected to? Why am I still carrying it?* That overstuffed drawer may not only contain old papers; it may contain the fear of failure, the belief that you must keep every detail *"just in case,"* or the perfectionism that says you can't let anything slip. The clothes hanging unworn in your closet might not just be fabric, but reminders of who you once were, or who you thought you had to be in order to be loved or respected. Even your packed schedule might not only represent busyness, but a shield, a way of avoiding silence, because stillness might feel too uncomfortable, too confronting, too real. You may often tell yourself things like: *"I might need this someday." "This reminds me of a better time." "If I let this go, it is like I am forgetting,"* but if you pause long enough to listen, you will notice that so often, these attachments are built not from love, but from fear. Fear of losing your identity. Fear of stepping into change. Fear of feeling emotions you have worked hard to keep buried.

The truth is: holding on does not protect you. In fact, it often traps you. It weighs you down, clouds your clarity, drains your energy, and makes it harder for you to hear the quiet, steady wisdom of your own heart, and so here is the deeper truth you need to remember:

- You are not what you own.

- You are not the memories that live in boxes.

- You are not defined by what you keep or release.

Letting go does not mean forgetting. It means finally choosing freedom. It means creating sacred space, in your environment, in your emotions, in your body, and in your spirit, and in that space, you will find something precious: clarity, peace, and the possibility of joy. Attachment is not the same as connection. When you release what no longer serves you, you reclaim the power to choose what truly does. You open the door for the new, the meaningful, the life-giving. Decluttering is not about living with less for the sake of less. It is about living with what matters most. You are allowed to live with less, but feel more. You are allowed to let go, and become more whole. You are allowed to release the old stories, and come home to yourself.

Reflection Prompts

As you sit with these truths, I invite you to take a few minutes to reflect and journal on the following:

1. What is one physical item in your space that feels heavy to hold onto? What does it represent emotionally?

---

2. Where in your life are you overcommitted, saying *"yes"* when your heart longs for a pause?

3. Which old identity, belief, or story are you still carrying that no longer reflects who you are becoming?

4. How would it feel to create space, in your environment or in your heart, for something new, something aligned, something true?

Historical And Cultural Perspectives: Feng Shui, Minimalism, Mindfulness

Decluttering has always carried a deeper meaning than simply cleaning a space or organising belongings. Across cultures and time, it has been seen as a spiritual act, a way to restore harmony, reconnect with truth, and align the inner and outer worlds.

Feng Shui – Flow of Life Energy

Feng Shui, born from ancient China, is a philosophy that teaches you to live in harmony with the natural currents of life energy, known as **qi**. It views your home not as a collection of walls and objects, but as a living organism, a mirror of your inner self. **Clutter in Feng Shui is not neutral.** It is stagnation, a sign that energy cannot move. A blocked pathway may reflect blocked opportunities. A room filled with unused items may echo unprocessed emotions or unresolved memories. By clearing clutter and arranging space with care, you invite the **five elements**, wood, fire, earth, metal, and water, to flow in balance, creating a sense of vitality and peace. For example, light and airflow are central in Feng Shui. A dark, crowded room can dampen your energy, while an open, light-filled space supports renewal, clarity, and emotional ease. To engage with Feng Shui principles is to treat your home as a **sacred partner** in your wellbeing. Every choice, where you place a chair, whether you keep an item, how you allow light to flow, becomes an act of aligning your outer environment with the life you long to live.

Minimalism – Returning to Essence

Minimalism, deeply influenced by Japanese Zen Buddhism, is more than a design trend. At its heart, it is a **spiritual discipline** of choosing essence over excess. In Zen temples, simplicity was intentional: uncluttered spaces allowed the mind to settle into stillness and the heart to open to the sacred. Minimalism asks you to strip away what is not essential so you can see clearly what truly matters. It is not about deprivation or starkness, but about **curating a life that reflects truth, meaning, and presence.** When you let go of unnecessary possessions, obligations, or noise, you are not reducing your life, you are **revealing it.** The treasures that remain, whether an object, a memory, or a relationship, shine more brightly when they are no longer buried in clutter. Minimalism offers a counter-narrative to the world's endless push for consumption. It whispers: *Less is not lack. Less is space for depth, for beauty, for authenticity.*

Mindfulness – Sacred Presence in Action

Mindfulness, based in ancient Buddhist practice and embraced around the world today, is the art of being fully present. When applied to decluttering, it shifts the act from task to **ritual**. With mindfulness, every object becomes a question: *Does this still belong in my life? Does it carry love, or does it carry weight?* As you pick up an item, you might notice the memories it stirs, the emotions it carries, the fears it triggers. Instead of rushing, you pause. You breathe. You decide not from habit or guilt, but from clarity and compassion. Even the physical act of decluttering becomes a practice in awareness. You notice the sound of items being placed away, the rhythm of your breath, the relief in your body as space opens. Mindfulness turns decluttering into a **mirror of the heart**. It helps you release not out of rejection, but out of reverence, making space for what is true, what is needed, what is life-giving.

The Mirror Between Inner and Outer Worlds

These cultural traditions, Feng Shui, Minimalism, Mindfulness, each carry the same timeless truth: **your outer environment reflects your inner state.** When your home is cluttered, your thoughts often feel scattered. When your calendar is overfull, your emotions often feel stretched thin. When your space is intentional, peaceful, and open, your heart rests more easily. Decluttering, then, is not about perfection or aesthetics. It is about **alignment**. It is about saying:

- I am ready to release what no longer serves me.

- I am ready to live not in survival, but in flow.

- I am ready to create space for my heart to speak, and for my life to expand.

To declutter is to remember that you are not here to be buried by things, but to be uplifted by life. It is a radical act of freedom, and a return to yourself.

Internal Clutter: Limiting Beliefs, Overthinking, And Emotional Residue

Not all clutter lives on shelves or in inboxes. Some of the most suffocating clutter is the kind you carry silently inside, unseen by others, but deeply felt by you. This is **internal clutter**: the tangle of old beliefs, anxious thoughts, and unresolved emotions that weigh down your mind, your spirit, and your sense of possibility. You may find yourself replaying the same thoughts, looping through *what ifs*, *should haves*, and *not enoughs*. This is the clutter of **overthinking,** a mental traffic jam that crowds out clarity and clouds your connection to the present moment. It is the voice that second-guesses your decisions, that fears judgment, that catastrophises the future. It is exhausting, and it is easy to mistake for truth. Then there are the **limiting beliefs** you have unknowingly absorbed over time: *I have to be perfect to be loved. Success means constant busyness. I am too old to change.* These beliefs form the emotional wallpaper of your inner world, so familiar you might not even realise they are there. Yet they shape your choices, dim your courage, and keep you tethered to stories that no longer serve your growth.

Also, beneath it all may live **emotional residue,** the unprocessed grief, anger, shame, or sadness you have tucked away in quiet corners of your heart. You may think you have moved on, but those emotions remain stored in your body, waiting for the safety and space to be felt and released. This internal clutter does not just live in your mind, it echoes in your relationships, your boundaries, your energy. It shows up as chronic fatigue, irritability, disconnection, or self-doubt. It is heavy, even if invisible. Decluttering internally begins with **gentle awareness**. Noticing the narratives that are running your life. Naming the feelings you have been avoiding, and most of all, creating space, through breath, stillness, writing, or silence, to ask yourself: *What am I still carrying that no longer belongs to me?* You do not have to untangle it all at once. *Start by listening. Start by softening. Start by letting go, one belief, one thought, one feeling at a time.* As you clear this inner space, you create room for something far more powerful: *Truth. Peace, and the voice of your heart, unburdened and finally heard.*

Decluttering As An Act Of Self-Respect And Emotional Clarity

Decluttering is not just a practical task, it is a powerful declaration. It says, *I matter. My space matters. My peace matters.* When you choose to clear out what no longer serves you, physically, mentally, emotionally, you are not simply getting rid of things. You are making a bold, heart-led statement: **I respect myself enough to live with intention.** Self-respect is not always loud. Sometimes it is found in the quiet decision to release the clothes you never wear, the commitments that deplete you, or the story you have been telling yourself for years. It is in the way you clean your space not just for guests, but for you. It is in choosing quality over quantity, clarity over chaos, presence over performance. When your environment is cluttered, your nervous system remains in a low-grade state of vigilance. You feel overstimulated, scattered, or emotionally *"full"* without knowing why, but when you clear your space, shelf by shelf, thought by thought, you begin to feel different inside. Lighter. Calmer. More whole. Decluttering is also a practice in **emotional clarity**. As you sift through the items, roles, and habits in your life, you begin to ask deeper questions:

1. Does this reflect who I am now?

2. Does this support the life I want to live?

3. What am I holding onto out of fear, guilt, or habit?

It takes courage to let go, because sometimes, the clutter is tied to memories, identities, or people, but what you begin to discover is this: letting go does not erase the past. It honours it, while giving you the space to step more fully into the present. The clearer your space, the more clearly you hear yourself. The less weighed down you feel, the more grounded you become, and in this clarity, something powerful happens:

• You remember who you are without all the noise.

• You reconnect with what truly matters.

• You create room not just in your home, but in your heart.

Decluttering becomes less about cleaning, and more about coming home to yourself.

How Space Impacts Energy, Decision-Making, And Emotional Equilibrium

The spaces you inhabit, your home, your workplace, even your car, hold more than furniture and belongings. They hold **energy**. They carry your emotions, your memories, your habits, and your intentions, and whether you realise it or not, the state of your environment directly affects your inner state, your clarity, your choices, and your ability to stay emotionally balanced. When your space is chaotic or cluttered, it sends a subtle but constant message to your nervous system: *You are not in control. There is too much. You are behind.* This activates stress hormones, drains your mental energy, and makes even small decisions feel harder. Just like a cluttered desk can make it difficult to find a pen, a cluttered mind makes it difficult to access calm, insight, and direction. In contrast, when your space is clean, intentional, and aligned with who you are, it becomes a **container for peace and possibility**. You breathe more deeply. You think more clearly. You feel more empowered. Your surroundings begin to support your nervous system, not challenge it. You are no longer fighting your environment, you are being held by it.

This shift impacts your **decision-making** in profound ways. When your external world is overstimulating or burdened with unprocessed emotional cues (like unfinished projects, reminders of past relationships, or *"someday"* piles), your mind becomes fatigued. You are more likely to react from stress, doubt, or fear, but when you create space, literally and emotionally, you give your brain room to pause, evaluate, and respond with wisdom and intention. You also restore **emotional equilibrium**. With less external noise, your inner voice becomes clearer. You are more attuned to what you need, what you feel, and what aligns with your heart. Decision-making stops being about urgency and starts being about truth. Creating space is not just about aesthetics. It is about **energy hygiene**. It is about protecting the sanctuary of your own attention and creating an environment where your best self can emerge, steady, clear, and grounded. When your space supports you, your energy stabilises. When your energy is stable, your emotions flow, and when your emotions are flowing, your life begins to move again, in the direction of your deepest values.

Decluttering with Intention

Decluttering is not only about clearing space in your outer world, it is also about clearing energy in your inner world. Every item you choose to keep or release carries a story, an emotion, or a belief. When you engage with decluttering intentionally, you are not just tidying up, you are choosing freedom, creating space for peace, and aligning your environment with your heart.

Step 1: Choose Your Space (Outer or Inner)

Over the next 24 hours, select one small area of your life to lovingly

---

163

declutter. This might be:

- A **physical space**: a drawer, your desk, a shelf, your bag, your phone, or your closet.

- A **mental space**: an outdated belief, a repeating thought, or a self-critical voice.

- An **emotional space**: resentment, guilt, or a story you have been holding onto.

Start small. One space is enough. The power of this practice comes from focus and intention, not size.

Step 2: Prepare Yourself

Before you begin, pause for a few moments of presence:

- Take 3 slow, balanced breaths.

- Place your hand on your heart, reminding yourself: *I am safe to release. I am safe to let go.*

- If you can, play soft background music or light a candle, marking this as a ritual, not a chore.

Step 3: Ask the Heart Question

As you hold or consider each item, memory, or thought, quietly ask yourself: **"What am I ready to let go of in this space, and in myself?"**

- If it feels heavy, outdated, or no longer aligned, honour it, thank it for the role it once played, and gently release it.

- If it feels alive, nourishing, or truly useful, allow it to stay with love and intention.

Remember: you are not discarding things out of anger or guilt, but releasing them with reverence, creating space for what is real and true.

Step 4: Visualise the Freedom

Once you finish, pause again. Close your eyes. Breathe. Visualise the **spaciousness** that has opened, not just on the shelf, desk, or phone, but within you. Ask yourself:

- *How does my body feel now that I have released this?*

- *What new energy or possibility might flow into this open space?*

- *What word or image symbolises the freedom I feel?*

Step 5: Anchor the Shift

To integrate the practice, write a short reflection in your journal. You might use one of these prompts:

- *Today I created space for…*

- *Letting go of ____ helped me realise…*

- *The freedom I feel now reminds me that I am…*

This anchoring step helps your inner self register the act not just as a task, but as a transformation.

Closing Reminder

Decluttering with intention is not about deprivation. It is about **liberation**. Every time you let go of something that no longer serves you, you reclaim energy, presence, and joy. When you clear your space with care, you make room for peace. When you clear your heart with compassion, you make room for love. *May this practice remind you that you are worthy of a life uncluttered, spacious, and true.*

Case Study Discussion: Yasmine's Journey

Yasmine had felt a heaviness in her life for as long as she could remember. By her own admission she would describe her physical spaces as being 'untidy' and filled with 'stuff'. Her physical spaces were not the only spaces in a bit of chaos, her heart was filled with worries and anxieties. She wanted a sense of lightness and joy, but it seemed out of reach. We discussed her lived life's appearance as being reflective of what was happening within her. One day, Yasmine made the choice to declutter her life, both inside and out. She started with her physical space, her home, her car, and her office, sorting through her belongings and letting go of items that no longer brought her joy or served a purpose. As Yasmine cleared out the excess, she felt a weight being lifted off her shoulders. Yasmine knew that decluttering was not just about physical possessions. She also knew she needed to declutter her heart, her mind, and her emotions. She began to practice balanced heart breathing, mindfulness, and meditation, allowing herself to let go of negative thoughts and worries. She focused on her present moment, embracing a sense of peace and gratitude. Over time (many months) Yasmine found her smile again. She felt herself smiling and the more she let go of physical and mental clutter, the more space she created for joy, positivity, and compassion to enter her life. Yasmine discovered that getting rid of things that did not serve her was not just about creating an organised space to live in, it was about creating space for happiness and joy to exist. Yasmine's decision to declutter her life transformed her in ways she never imagined. She found her smile again, and it radiated from within. She told me that she realised that by letting go of what no longer served her, she had created space for what truly mattered to her, and in that space, she found her authentic self, her passions, and a deep sense of contentment.

Reflective Exercise: Yasmine's Journey

Here are four profound and reflective questions inspired by Yasmine's story to help you engage with your own decluttering journey:

1. **What physical clutter in your environment might be mirroring an inner weight you have been carrying, and what would it feel like to gently begin letting go?** Reflect on a space in your life, your room, car, desk, that feels heavy or chaotic. What emotions rise when you enter that space? What would releasing just one item from that space symbolize for your emotional wellbeing?

2. **Are there thoughts, worries, or beliefs that you continue to hold onto out of habit, fear, or familiarity, even though they no longer support your growth?** Close your eyes and ask your heart, *What am I ready to release?* Then breathe gently into that space. Your freedom begins the moment you honour the truth of that answer.

3. **What does joy need space for in your life, and what might it be competing with right now?** Consider the ways in which clutter, both internal and external, may be blocking your access to joy, ease, or creativity. What could you release this week, physically or emotionally, to make room for something more life-giving?

4. **If you saw your life as a sacred space, what would you choose to keep, and what would you lovingly release?** Imagine walking through the rooms of your life, not just your home, but your heart. What stays because it aligns with who you truly are? What do you bless and let go of, to honour the person you are becoming?

Affirmations For You – (Heart Whispers)

Affirmations have the power to quiet the noise of doubt, open the doorway to self-trust, and draw you back into the wisdom of your heart. When practised daily, they nurture an inner dialogue based in love and truth, helping you live each day more aligned with who you truly are. I invite you to repeat silently or write:

- I release what no longer serves me, creating space for growth.

- I let go of clutter, inviting clarity and peace into my life.

- I connect with my heart as I declutter my physical space.

- I embrace simplicity, finding joy in the essentials of life.

- I honour my heart's desires by letting go of excess.

- I create a sanctuary within, reflecting the beauty of my heart.

Create Your Personal Decluttering Map

Decluttering is not only about clearing your outer environment, it is about creating space for your heart to breathe more freely. To guide this process, I invite you to create a simple yet powerful **Decluttering Map**, a tool that helps you see where release is needed and how you can take compassionate, intentional action.

Step 1: Physical Release

Reflection Prompt: *What no longer supports or reflects who I am today?* Look around your environment. Notice what feels heavy, outdated, or disconnected from who you are becoming. This may be clothing that no longer feels like you, objects tied to old identities, or items you have been keeping out of guilt or obligation.

Action Step: Choose one physical object (or small group of objects) to release with gratitude. As you let it go, affirm: *I am making space for who I am now and who I am becoming.*

Step 2: Mental Release

Reflection Prompt: *What thoughts and habits clutter my peace?* Turn inward. Notice the stories, habits, or loops of self-talk that leave you feeling drained rather than uplifted. This could be overthinking, perfectionism, procrastination, or comparing yourself to others.

Action Step: Write down one mental habit you are ready to soften. Replace it with a grounding practice, such as pausing to breathe, journaling, or repeating a calming affirmation. Each time the thought arises, gently remind yourself: *This no longer has power over me. I choose peace.*

Step 3: Emotional Release

Reflection Prompt: *What feelings or patterns am I ready to thank and release?* Sometimes we hold onto emotions or protective patterns long after they have served their purpose. You might notice resentment, guilt, fear of rejection, or the need to please others. These patterns once kept you safe, but now they may keep you small.

Action Step: Identify one emotional pattern you are ready to let go of. Write it down and add a phrase of gratitude, such as: *Thank you for protecting me when I needed it. I release you now with love.* Then breathe deeply and imagine sending it into the light.

Step 4: Integration – Your Intention Map

Now bring your reflections together into a **three-part map**:

- **Physical:** I release ___ → Action: ___
- **Mental:** I release ___ → Action: ___
- **Emotional:** I release ___ → Action: ___

Keep this map visible in your journal, on your desk, or somewhere you will see it daily. Each step is not just about letting go, it is about reclaiming your energy, your presence, and your truth.

Closing Reflection

As you create your Decluttering Map, remember: every release is a gift to your future self. You are not just removing clutter, you are creating spaciousness, clarity, and peace. *When you release what no longer reflects your heart, you return home to who you truly are.*

Closing Reflection

Letting go is never just about things. It is about honouring your **inner space as sacred**, recognising that the energy you carry, both seen and unseen, shapes the way you live, love, and connect. By choosing to declutter, you have done something incredibly brave: you have said *yes* to yourself. You have chosen to make space. **Space to breathe. Space to feel. Space to rest.**

Space to hear your heart more clearly. Each drawer emptied, each thought questioned, each memory released, each belief surrendered, every act of release has been more than tidying. It has been an act of courage, self-respect, and quiet devotion to the person you are becoming. With every step, you have begun to **unburden your physical world and lighten your emotional landscape**, and in each choice to release what no longer serves, you are making a deeper invitation, an opening for clarity, intention, freedom, and truth to move in. This practice has never been about perfection. It is about **alignment.** It is about living in a way that reflects who you truly are, rather than who you thought you had to be, or who others told you to become. It is about learning that your worth is not measured by how much you accumulate, but by how deeply you live,and now, in the space you have created, something profound happens: **Joy** can find you more easily. **Peace** can move in and stay a little longer. **Your heart** feels just a little more at home within you. As you carry this practice forward, let this part of the journey whisper to you each time you are tempted to hold on too tightly: *You are not defined by what you cling to. You are revealed by what you are willing to release.* May you remember that every release is not a loss but a return, a return to yourself, a return to freedom, a return to love.

The Unbound Journey Belongs to You

Where you go from here is your choice, but you do not walk alone. The rest of the Unbound Series is there to guide you, and the online programs are there to support you. Choose the next chapter of your becoming – www.timetotransform.world

MODULE 11 - FORGIVENESS

Your Opening Reflection

An Invitation to Forgive - As you enter this module, give yourself permission to soften and open. Forgiveness is not about excusing the past, but about freeing your heart in the present. With each breath, allow yourself to release a little of the weight you have been carrying. Let this be a moment to imagine what it feels like to live lighter, to choose compassion over resentment, and to offer yourself the healing gift of peace.

- "What is one hurt you have been holding onto, and what would it feel like to release it?"

- "How has holding onto resentment or pain affected your life, relationships, or health?"

- "If you forgave fully, how might your heart and spirit feel lighter?"

- "What beliefs do you have about forgiveness that might be keeping you from it?"

- "How might forgiveness be a gift you give yourself, not just to the other person?"

- "What is one small step you can take today toward forgiving someone or yourself?"

- "Is there someone you still need to forgive, including yourself?"

Let these questions open the doorway into presence. Every answer you give, whether in words, sensations, or silence, is a bridge between where you are and where you are going.

Learning Objectives

The learning objectives are included here to give you a clear focus for this module, ensuring that each practice you explore moves you closer to mastering the skills, insights, and heart-led awareness that will enrich your life well beyond the program. By the end of this module, you will:

- Define forgiveness and differentiate it from enabling or excusing behavior.

- Understand how forgiveness promotes emotional healing and inner peace.

- Reflect on personal barriers to self-forgiveness and forgiveness of others.

- Apply practical techniques to begin the process of releasing resentment.

- Recognise forgiveness as a path to deeper heart connection and emotional resilience.

Core Emotional Domains

The core emotional intelligence domains covered here are essential because they form the foundation for lasting heart connection, guiding you to deepen self-awareness, regulate emotions, build resilience, and strengthen the mind-body bond throughout your *Unbound* journey.

- **Self-Awareness:** You learn to recognise the emotions, memories, and narratives that keep resentment or pain alive.

- **Self-Regulation:** Forgiveness invites you to respond to hurt with intention rather than reactivity, creating space for peace.

- **Empathy:** You begin to understand the pain of others without excusing harm, building compassion while maintaining boundaries.

- **Social Skills:** Releasing blame creating healthier relationships, clearer communication, and deeper trust.

- **Motivation:** Forgiveness becomes a path to emotional freedom, inspiring you to grow beyond the wound and reclaim your energy.

"Forgiveness – Releasing The Past"

Forgiveness as Inner Liberation. Forgiveness is not a gift you give to someone who wronged you, it is a sacred act of release that you offer to yourself. It is not about excusing harm, forgetting pain, or pretending it did not happen. True forgiveness is an inner act of liberation, a conscious choice to unhook your heart from the weight of resentment, anger, and emotional toxicity. When you hold onto hurt, your body holds it too. Your breath tightens, your thoughts loop, your nervous system stays alert to an old danger. Over time, this pain calcifies, not just in your memory, but in your spirit. Forgiveness does not erase the wound, but it tends to it with compassion, allowing you to heal from the inside out. To forgive is to reclaim your peace. It is a declaration that your wellbeing matters more than your grudges. It is the courage to soften a hardened heart, not for their sake, but for your freedom. In forgiveness, you open a door to emotional clarity, spaciousness, and even gratitude for how far you have come. You stop letting the past define your present. You choose to grow. You choose to feel light again, and most powerfully, you realise: *Forgiveness is not something they have to earn, it is something you decide to live.*

The Psychology and Spirituality Of Forgiveness

Forgiveness sits at the crossroads of psychology and spirituality, bridging the science of healing with the soul's deep longing for peace. From a psychological perspective, forgiveness is a transformative emotional process, one that invites you to meet your pain with courage rather than avoidance. It begins by acknowledging the reality of what happened: the wound, the injustice, the betrayal. This is not about denial, suppression, or pretending it did not matter. It is about facing the truth with both clarity and self-compassion. In this space, you are not asked to condone, excuse, or forget harmful behavior. Instead, forgiveness becomes an intentional act of reclaiming your mental and emotional freedom. It is a conscious decision to stop letting the hurt dictate your inner world. Research consistently shows that practicing forgiveness can significantly lower cortisol levels, ease symptoms of depression and anxiety, improve cardiovascular health, and strengthen immune function. Psychologically, it disrupts cycles of rumination, anger, and resentment that keep you tethered to the past. Forgiveness replaces reactive survival responses with grounded emotional regulation, helping you think, feel, and respond from a place of clarity rather than pain. In choosing to forgive, you are not giving power back to the person who hurt you, you are reclaiming it for yourself. You shift from being defined by what happened to being empowered by how you respond. Far from being a sign of weakness, forgiveness reflects deep emotional intelligence: the capacity to sit with pain, understand your emotions, integrate the lessons, and still act from your highest self. Forgiveness is not the closing of a chapter; it is the opening of a lighter, freer one, one in which your past no longer dictates the limits of your joy.

The Spirituality of Forgiveness

Spiritually, forgiveness is a sacred and transformative act, a gentle unraveling of bitterness, fear, and the invisible threads that bind you to past pain. It is not a forgetting, but a remembering: that within your heart resides the vast capacity to hold both grief and grace, to honour the truth of your wounds while still choosing love. Across spiritual traditions, forgiveness is often more than a single act; it is a lifelong path, a pilgrimage back to wholeness. In Christianity, forgiveness reflects the essence of divine mercy, an invitation to mirror the compassion and unconditional love of God, even when it feels undeserved. In Buddhism, it is a practice of letting go of attachments to anger and resentment, releasing the suffering that binds both self and others. In Indigenous wisdom, forgiveness is woven into the fabric of community, restoring harmony and balance not only between people, but between the land, the ancestors, and the spirit world. In each of these traditions, forgiveness is not a transaction or an act of surrendering power, it is an act of transcendence. It lifts you above the smallness of the wound and returns you to the vastness of your true self. It is a declaration that your identity is not defined by the harm you have suffered, but by the love you choose to embody. To forgive is to say with conviction: *This story will not define me. My heart is larger than this wound.* It is a spiritual commitment to inner peace, a conscious decision to stop rehearsing and re-enacting the hurt, and a willingness to live open-hearted in a world that sometimes shatters hearts. In the end, forgiveness is not only about setting someone else free, it is about liberating your own soul so it can move without the weight of the past, ready to love again without fear.

The Effects Of Resentment On Physical And Emotional Health

Resentment may seem like an invisible weight, hidden beneath the surface, tucked behind a polite smile, or pushed down in the name of strength, but over time, it becomes one of the most corrosive emotions you carry, impacting both your physical health and emotional wellbeing in deep and far-reaching ways.

Emotional Toll: Living in a Loop of Pain

Resentment is not just a passing emotion, it is a sustained state of unresolved hurt entwined with a sense of injustice. It keeps you locked in mental replays, revisiting conversations, events, and missed opportunities for closure. The mind becomes a theatre of *"what ifs"* and *"should haves,"* looping the same scene over and over. This constant rumination activates the stress response repeatedly, leaving your nervous system in a perpetual state of low-grade tension. You might notice yourself feeling on edge for no clear reason, or withdrawing emotionally because the hurt feels too raw to face. Over time, resentment shrinks your emotional world; joy feels distant, trust feels risky, and even moments of peace are interrupted by a lingering ache. Without release, it quietly shapes how you see yourself, others, and life itself.

Physical Toll: The Body Remembers

The mind may replay the wound, but the body stores it. Science confirms that chronic emotional stress, like the kind resentment breeds, takes a measurable toll on physical health. Elevated cortisol can disrupt the delicate balance of your immune, digestive, and cardiovascular systems. Sleep becomes shallow, muscles tighten like armour, and your breath unconsciously shortens, signalling to your body that danger is still present. Over months or years, this state of guardedness increases inflammation, slows healing, and leaves you more vulnerable to illness. Resentment does not just live in your thoughts; it settles in your shoulders, your jaw, your gut. It can become an unseen weight you carry everywhere, one that erodes vitality and keeps the body in a constant state of readiness for a battle that never arrives.

What Makes Resentment So Draining?

Resentment drains you because it demands constant energy to sustain. It is like keeping a fire smoldering, you must continually add emotional fuel in the form of rumination, anger, or silent bitterness. This emotional maintenance prevents you from fully engaging with the present, because part of you is still anchored in the past, guarding the wound. The cost is high: hope dims, creativity dries up, and compassion, for yourself and others, becomes harder to access. Resentment consumes the very qualities that make life rich and meaningful. It convinces you that holding on protects you, when in truth, it only keeps you tethered to pain.

The Healing Choice: Letting Go Does Not Excuse, It Releases

Letting go of resentment is an act of courage, not concession. It is not about pretending the harm never happened or absolving someone of responsibility, it is about reclaiming your freedom from the grip of the past. Letting go means loosening your identity from the story of hurt, so you are no longer defined by it. It is choosing to end the cycle of self-punishment and allowing your energy to flow toward what restores and nourishes you. When you release resentment, you create space for peace to take root, for joy to return, and for your heart to open again, stronger, wiser, and unburdened. As you begin to release resentment, through self-reflection, compassion, and forgiveness, you reclaim your emotional vitality and physical wellbeing. You begin to return to yourself, because resentment does not protect your heart. It holds it hostage and healing begins when you set it free.

Forgiveness vs. Excusing Behavior

One of the greatest misunderstandings about forgiveness is the belief that to forgive someone is to excuse or justify what they did, but true forgiveness is not about erasing the past, it is about releasing *yourself* from being held hostage by it.

Excusing Behaviour Means Minimising Harm

When you excuse someone's behaviour, you downplay the impact of their actions. You might say *"It was not that bad,"* or *"They did not mean it."* Excusing can lead to bypassing accountability, suppressing your truth, or staying silent in the name of keeping the peace. It can invalidate your feelings, create confusion about your worth, and even enable unhealthy dynamics to continue. Excusing often arises from a desire to avoid conflict, or from internalised beliefs that your pain is not valid,but your hurt matters. Your boundaries matter. Healing begins when you name what was true.

Forgiveness, on the Other Hand, Is a Conscious Release

Forgiveness does not erase the wrong, it **honours that it happened** and still chooses to let go of the emotional grip it has over you. It does **not** mean you condone the behaviour or pretend it did not cause harm. It means you are no longer willing to carry the bitterness, anger, or resentment that weighs on your heart. Forgiveness says:

- "I am choosing peace over pain."

- "I no longer want to re-live what hurt me."

- "I will not allow this to define my future."

It may involve setting boundaries. It may mean walking away. It may mean holding someone accountable, with love and clarity, but without vengeance.

<u>Forgiveness Empowers, Excusing Disempowers</u>

Forgiveness is an act of reclamation, it hands you back the keys to your own heart. When you forgive, you release the hold the past has over your present, and in doing so, you restore your agency. Your emotional energy is no longer drained by replaying the wound; instead, it becomes available for creating the life you want. Forgiveness clears the fog of resentment, allowing you to see yourself and your future with greater clarity. It is the choice to stand in your own sovereignty, no longer defined by someone else's actions. Excusing, however, is different. When you excuse harmful behaviour without addressing its impact, you bypass your own truth. You may shrink yourself to avoid conflict, rationalise what is unacceptable, or bury your pain in the hope that it will disappear. This often leads to cycles of guilt, self-doubt, and disempowerment, because you have abandoned your own boundaries. Forgiveness does not say, *"What happened was fine."* It says, *"What happened hurt, but I am choosing to heal. I am no longer tethered to that hurt."* It is the conscious decision to honour your worth, hold your boundaries, and live free from the emotional weight of the past. That shift, from *"It is okay"* to *"I am okay now"*, is everything. It is the difference between silencing yourself and liberating yourself.

Effects Of Resentment On Physical And Emotional Health

Resentment is one of the most corrosive emotions we carry, quietly building in the background, often masked as strength or righteousness, while slowly depleting your emotional reserves and affecting your physical wellbeing.

<u>Emotionally: Resentment Traps You in the Past</u>

Resentment is unresolved hurt wrapped in anger and replayed over time. When you hold onto it, your mind stays tethered to the original wound, replaying the story again and again. You might relive the betrayal, reimagine the argument, or rehearse what you wish you had said. This mental looping fuels anxiety, irritability, sadness, and emotional exhaustion. Resentment also blocks empathy and connection. It can harden your heart, make trust difficult, and cause emotional distancing in relationships. Over time, it narrows your worldview and disconnects you from joy, creativity, and peace. It is not just the event that causes harm, it is the ongoing emotional investment in *what was*, rather than what could be.

<u>Physically: The Body Keeps the Score</u>

The stress of resentment does not just live in your thoughts, it settles in your body. Chronic resentment can:

- Raise cortisol (the body's primary stress hormone)
- Disrupt sleep patterns
- Weaken your immune system
- Increase inflammation, linked to diseases such as heart disease and arthritis
- Contribute to headaches, digestive issues, and chronic fatigue

Because your nervous system cannot tell the difference between a past event and a current threat, it reacts as if you are still under attack every time you ruminate.

- Your muscles tense.
- Your breath shortens.
- Your heart rate elevates.

The result? You live in a state of low-grade, persistent fight-or-flight, even when the original danger is long gone.

The Hidden Cost: It Steals Your Present

The price of holding onto resentment extends far beyond your physical health, it quietly robs you of the life you are living right now. Every moment spent replaying the past is a moment stolen from the present. Resentment narrows your emotional landscape, reducing your capacity for joy, compassion, creativity, and peace. It colours the way you see others, the way you interpret their actions, and even the way you speak to yourself. Over time, resentment can become strangely familiar, almost comfortable in its predictability. You may find yourself returning to it like a well-worn story, not because it serves you, but because it is known. Yet, in clinging to it, you limit your own growth and dim the light of your spirit. Resentment may feel like self-protection, but it is often self-imprisonment.

The Antidote: Forgiveness and Emotional Release

Letting go of resentment does not mean erasing what happened or excusing the harm. It means choosing freedom over fixation. Forgiveness in this sense is not an act of surrender to the person who hurt you, it is a profound act of allegiance to yourself. It is a conscious choice to stop allowing the wound to dictate your emotional climate. This release is a process, often unfolding in layers. Self-awareness helps you recognise where the pain still lives in you. Breathwork can help regulate your nervous system, allowing your body to begin loosening its grip on stored tension. Compassion, both for yourself and others, softens the sharp edges of hurt, and forgiveness, when it comes, is the opening of the heart's gate, letting peace and possibility flow back in. Here, forgiveness is not about making someone else feel better. It is about reclaiming your wellbeing, clarity, and wholeness. When you release resentment, you create space, space for health, for love, for deeper connection, and for the future you truly deserve. It is not about forgetting your story; it is about writing the next chapter with a freer, lighter hand.

How Self-Forgiveness Cultivates Compassion And Authenticity

Self-Forgiveness: The Courage to Be Whole

Self-forgiveness is one of the most profound and courageous acts of emotional intelligence because it requires you to face yourself fully, your actions, your intentions, your mistakes, without turning away. It is not about denying responsibility or avoiding accountability. Instead, it is about loosening the grip of the harsh, unrelenting judgment you hold against yourself. It is allowing your humanity to breathe again. When you forgive yourself, you are not only releasing the weight of what you did; you are dismantling the limiting story you have been carrying about who you are because of it. You create the space for a truer narrative to emerge, one grounded in growth, learning, and the ongoing possibility of change. This is how self-forgiveness becomes an act of liberation, setting you free from the chains of your own self-condemnation.

Self-Forgiveness Awakens Compassion

You cannot offer authentic compassion to others if you cannot extend it inward. Self-forgiveness is the softening of your inner landscape, it turns the voice of your inner critic into one of understanding, wisdom, and care. It is the gentle reminder that you are not defined solely by your worst moments, but also by your capacity to rise from them. Through self-forgiveness, you stop seeing yourself as broken, unworthy, or irredeemable. Instead, you begin to recognise that mistakes, regrets, and imperfections are not flaws that exile you from love, they are the very evidence of being human. You learn to hold yourself with the same patience, empathy, and grace you would offer to a dear friend who has stumbled but longs to walk again. As your self-compassion deepens, so too does your compassion for others. You become less reactive, less judgmental, and more present. You begin to see the shared vulnerability that binds us all, the truth that we are all imperfect, all learning, and all worthy of forgiveness, and in this shared humanity, connection becomes easier, relationships grow richer, and peace takes root within you.

Forgiveness Across Cultures And Faiths: From The Teachings Of Jesus To Buddhist Metta

Forgiveness is not just a personal or psychological act, it is a spiritual practice embedded in the wisdom of cultures and religions across the world. While the language may differ, the invitation is the same: release what binds you, and return to love. Across traditions, forgiveness is viewed not as weakness, but as a courageous path to peace, reconciliation, and transformation, both within oneself and in relationship with others.

Christianity: Forgiveness as Divine Mercy and Human Responsibility

In Christianity, forgiveness is not a suggestion, it is a sacred calling. Grounded in the life and teachings of Jesus, forgiveness lies at the very heart of spiritual practice. It is seen as both a divine gift freely given and a human responsibility freely chosen. Jesus taught his followers to pray, *"Forgive us our trespasses, as we forgive those who trespass against us."* (Matthew 6:12) In this prayer, forgiveness is presented as a reciprocal act: *as we are forgiven, we must forgive.* It is not conditional on someone deserving it, it is anchored in the deeper reality that we are all in need of grace. Jesus himself modelled radical forgiveness, even in the face of betrayal, injustice, and violence. As he hung on the cross, he prayed, *"Father, forgive them, for they do not know what they are doing."* (Luke 23:34) This moment is not just one of divine mercy, it is a powerful call for all people to extend compassion even when deeply wronged. In this tradition, forgiveness is an act of moral courage, not moral weakness. It means letting go of vengeance and the right to retaliate, and choosing instead the path of mercy, reconciliation, and peace. It is a way to break cycles of harm and open the door to transformation, not just for the offender, but for the one forgiving. Forgiveness in Christianity also reflects God's nature. It is how human beings are invited to mirror divine love:

- Love that restores rather than punishes.

- Love that redeems rather than rejects.

- Love that says, *"You are not the sum of your mistakes, you are the beloved."*

At its core, Christian forgiveness affirms that every soul is capable of redemption, and that healing, personal and communal, is made possible when you choose mercy over judgment, and grace over resentment. In this light, forgiveness is not simply a response to wrongdoing. It is a spiritual pathway to freedom, and the highest expression of love.

Buddhism: Forgiveness Through Metta and Non-Attachment

In the Buddhist tradition, forgiveness is not framed as a moral duty, but as a path to liberation from suffering. It is deeply grounded in the practice of *metta*, a Pali word often translated as loving-kindness or boundless friendliness. Metta is the intentional cultivation of unconditional goodwill toward all beings, yourself, your loved ones, strangers, and even those who have caused you harm. It arises not from obligation, but from the understanding that every sentient being seeks happiness and freedom from suffering. This includes those who act unskillfully due to their own ignorance, pain, or confusion. In Buddhism, forgiveness is not about forgetting, excusing, or denying harm. It is about releasing the grip of anger, hatred, or resentment from your own heart. Holding onto these emotions is understood to create more suffering, not just for others, but for you. The Buddha taught that clinging to anger is like "*grasping a hot coal with the intent of throwing it at someone else, you are the one who gets burned.*" Through mindfulness (*sati*) and compassion (*karuṇā*), practitioners are guided to see painful emotions clearly, without judgment. You learn to observe the story of hurt with spaciousness, not resistance. Over time, this awareness softens your inner experience, and with it, your reactivity. This is where non-attachment comes in, not as indifference, but as the ability to witness your pain without becoming it. By letting go of your identification with the wound, you begin to touch a deeper truth: you are not your suffering. You are the awareness beneath it.

Forgiveness, then, becomes a skillful means (upaya), a wise response that helps you let go of the inner burdens that keep you bound. It is not about changing the past. It is about freeing yourself from its emotional hold so you can return to equanimity, clarity, and compassion. In this tradition, forgiveness is not a one-time act but a practice, a gentle turning toward your own pain with the intention of healing. Buddhist monks and lay practitioners often use *metta* phrases such as:

- May I be safe.

- May I be happy.

- May I be free from suffering.

- May you be free from the suffering that causes harm.

By repeating these phrases, even toward those who have harmed you, you train your heart to let go, not to approve of harm, but to reclaim your peace and wisdom. Ultimately, in Buddhism, forgiveness is not an external transaction. It is an inner purification, a conscious path to liberation through compassion, non-attachment, and deep inner peace.

Forgiveness Letter Exercise

I invite you to create space, take a few deep breaths, and write two letters that hold the power to lighten your heart:

1. **To Yourself:** Write as though you are speaking to a dear friend who has walked through the same mistakes, regrets, or self-judgments you carry.

   - Express compassion: acknowledge the pain you have felt without judgment.

   - Offer understanding: recognise the circumstances, emotions, and humanity behind your actions or choices.

   - Extend release: let go of the weight of harsh self-criticism and affirm that you are worthy of love, acceptance, and peace.

2. **To Someone You Need to Forgive:** This letter is for your own healing, whether or not you ever share it.

   - Acknowledge what happened and how it impacted you.

   - Express what you are ready to let go of not to excuse the hurt, but to free yourself from carrying it.

   - State your choice to release the emotional hold the situation has had on you.

3. **Afterward, pause for reflection:** Place both letters in front of you. Notice your breath, your body, and your emotions. Ask yourself:

   - How do I feel now compared to before I began?

   - Did I uncover emotions I had not acknowledged?

   - Do I feel lighter, softer, more spacious inside?

You might choose to keep these letters as reminders, tear them up as a symbolic release, or burn them safely as an act of letting go.

Case Study Discussion: Alice's Journey

Alice had been struggling with love for as long as she could remember. She had been in and out of relationships but never found herself truly happy. At the age of 58, she finally realised that she needed to forgive herself before she could truly love herself and be in a genuine relationship. Alice had always struggled with self–esteem and self–worth, and this had reflected in all of her relationships. She would always put her partners first and often found herself being taken advantage of. It was not until we started journeying together that she realised the root cause of her struggles. Through our sessions together over many months Alice was able to confront the issues that were holding her back and started working on self–forgiveness. She realised that in order to move on and start living a heart–led life, she needed to forgive herself for all the mistakes she had made in the past. With self–forgiveness came self–love, and Alice started to see herself in a new light. She started doing things that made her happy and began to take care of herself. She also started to attract genuine and loving relationships into her life. Alice's journey towards forgiveness was not an easy one, but it was definitely worth it. She realised that forgiveness was not just about letting go of the past but also about accepting herself and loving herself unconditionally. Her heart was finally open to receive and give love, and she began living a more fulfilled life than ever before. Alice's story is a powerful reminder that self–forgiveness is an essential step in living a heart–led life. It is about releasing yourself from the burden of your past mistakes, accepting yourself for who you are, and loving yourself unconditionally.

Reflective Exercise: Alice's Journey

Here are four profound and reflective questions inspired by Alice's story to help you engage with your own journey to forgiveness:

1. What pain have you been carrying that no longer serves your healing?: *Alice held on to the hurt because she thought releasing it meant the other person won, but in truth, it only kept her stuck. Forgiveness does not erase your experience, it frees you from reliving it.*

2. If you no longer needed an apology, what could you begin to let

> **go of today?:** *Waiting for an apology kept Alice tied to the past. When she chose to forgive without conditions, she reclaimed her energy and inner peace. You do not need permission to begin healing.*
>
> **3. What would it feel like to forgive yourself for what you did not know then?:** *Alice's greatest act of forgiveness was turning compassion inward. When she stopped blaming herself for how she coped, she softened. Forgiveness opened the door to self-love and wholeness.*
>
> **4. What part of your heart is asking to be heard, not hardened?** *Anger protected Alice for a long time, but underneath it was grief, and beneath that, longing. When she finally listened to her own heart, forgiveness emerged, not as a demand, but as a gentle return to herself.*

Affirmations For Integration: (Heart Whispers)

Affirmations have the power to quiet the noise of doubt, open the doorway to self-trust, and draw you back into the wisdom of your heart. When practised daily, they nurture an inner dialogue based in love and truth, helping you live each day more aligned with who you truly are. I invite you to repeat silently or write:

- I am willing to let go of resentment and anger.
- I am open to forgiveness as a healing process.
- I choose to release negative emotions and embrace forgiveness.
- I accept responsibility for my actions and seek forgiveness.
- I am learning to forgive myself and others.
- I am grateful for the peace that comes with forgiveness.
- I am committed to releasing grudges and embracing forgiveness.

> **Reflective Exercise - Forgiveness Visualisation Walk**
>
> **Step 1 – Prepare:** Choose a quiet path, whether it is through a park, along the beach, or in your neighbourhood, somewhere you can walk without rushing. Before you begin, place your hand over your heart and set the intention: *"I walk to release, to heal, and to move forward."*

Step 2 - Begin with Breath: As you start walking, focus on your breathing. Inhale deeply through your nose, drawing in fresh, clean air. Exhale slowly through your mouth, imagining that each breath out carries away a small piece of the pain, resentment, or hurt you have been holding.

Step 3 - Visualise Release: With every step, picture your emotional burdens as stones you have been carrying. Feel them grow lighter as they drop, one by one, onto the earth behind you. You might imagine them dissolving into the ground, transformed into something neutral, no longer weighing you down.

Step 4 - Engage Your Senses: Notice the warmth or coolness of the air on your skin, the sound of your footsteps, the rustle of leaves, the scent of nature around you. Allow the world to remind you that life is happening now, in this present moment, not in the pain of the past.

Step 5 - Closing Ritual: When you reach the end of your walk, stand still. Place your feet firmly on the ground and take three slow, deep breaths. In your final exhale, whisper or say aloud: **"I release the past. I walk forward in peace."**

Take a moment to notice the shift inside you, a little more lightness, a little more space, a little more peace.

Closing Reflection

Forgiveness is not about forgetting. It is not about making what happened acceptable or pretending it did not hurt. Forgiveness is about **reclaiming your peace**, your energy, and your capacity to love, even in the aftermath of pain. You have travelled through the raw terrain of resentment, grief, anger, and regret. You have sat with truths that were difficult to name, and now, you stand at a threshold, not of erasure, but of release. To forgive is not to condone. It is to choose freedom over fixation. It is to untangle yourself from a story that no longer defines who you are. It is to soften your grip on the past, so your hands can be open to the present, and perhaps most courageously of all, it is to forgive **yourself,** for what you did not know, for how you survived, for being human. Let this be your beginning, not your ending:

A return to wholeness. A renewal of compassion.

A quiet unbinding of the heart.

You are not here to be perfect.

You are here to be free.

The Heart Leads the Way

Your heart knows the direction, even when the mind feels unsure. Another Unbound book or program will give you the tools to walk that direction with clarity and confidence – www.timetotransform.world

MODULE 12 – REFLECTION

Your Opening Reflection

Invitation to Pause and Honour Your Journey - As you arrive in this module, I invite you to pause and recognise the courage it took to walk this far. Reflection is not about measuring progress, but about listening to the quiet truths your heart has revealed along the way. Every moment of insight, every breath of stillness, every tear or smile has been a step home to yourself. Allow this space to become a mirror, showing you how far you have come and how deeply you have grown. Honour your journey, not for its perfection, but for its honesty, resilience, and love.

- "What has shifted in your heart over this journey?"

- "What is one moment that you will carry with you forever?"

- "Which practice, teaching, or moment felt most alive for you, and why?"

- "Where in your life do you now feel a greater sense of freedom, clarity, or belonging?"

- "What part of yourself have you reconnected with or rediscovered along the way?"

- "If your heart could speak one truth from this journey, what would it say?"

Let these questions open the doorway into presence. Every answer you give, whether in words, sensations, or silence, is a bridge between where you are and where you are going.

Learning Objectives

The learning objectives are included here to give you a clear focus for this module, ensuring that each practice you explore moves you closer to mastering the skills, insights, and heart-led awareness that will enrich your life well beyond the program. By the end of this module, you will:

- Develop emotional intelligence through structured self-reflection
- Honour personal growth, insights, and transformation from the 28-day journey
- Learn to integrate heart-centred practices into everyday life
- Set heart-led intentions for future emotional development and authentic living

Core Emotional Domains

The core emotional intelligence domains covered here are essential because they form the foundation for lasting heart connection, guiding you to deepen self-awareness, regulate emotions, build resilience, and strengthen the mind-body bond throughout your *Unbound* journey.

- **Self-Awareness:** Reflection begins with noticing what has shifted within you. You become more attuned to your thoughts, emotions, and patterns, gaining insight into how you have grown and where you still hold resistance. This self-awareness helps you recognise your journey with clarity and compassion, not judgment.

- **Self-Reflection:** Taking time to pause and look inward allows you to make sense of your experiences. You begin to connect the dots, between your past and present, your choices and values. Through reflection, you learn to hold space for both your breakthroughs and your imperfections with honesty and grace.

- **Emotional Integration:** Emotions are not meant to be isolated or buried, they are meant to be understood and integrated. Reflection helps you acknowledge the full spectrum of what you have felt and lived. By weaving these emotional threads together, you create coherence within yourself and grow into greater wholeness.

- **Empathy and Compassion:** As you reflect on your own journey, you naturally open to the experiences of others. You begin to see that everyone is carrying their own story, their own struggles and triumphs. This awareness cultivates empathy and deepens your ability to meet both yourself and others with kindness.

- **Purpose and Values Alignment:** Reflection brings you back to what matters most. It realigns you with your inner compass, your values, your purpose, your truth. From this place of alignment, you can move forward with greater intention, choosing a path that honours both who you are and who you are becoming.

"Reflection – Integrating, Honouring, And Continuing Your Heart Journey"

Reflection is the final chapter of any meaningful journey, and the first page of the next. It is the sacred pause that allows you to breathe, integrate, and truly see how far you have come. Without reflection, even the most powerful experiences can pass unnoticed. However, when you take the time to look inward with honesty and compassion, experience transforms into wisdom, and moments become milestones. Reflection strengthens your **emotional intelligence** by inviting you to move beyond reaction into conscious understanding. It helps you trace the emotional patterns that shaped your choices, the shifts in your self-awareness, and the quiet inner awakenings that have taken root along the way. Through this process, you begin to internalise the growth you have undergone, not just as something you *did*, but as something you have *become*. In reflection, you give your heart a voice. You listen not only to what happened, but to what it meant. You begin to see your resilience, your courage, your tenderness, and your truth. You allow yourself to feel gratitude, grieve what's been released, and honour the parts of you that stepped forward in new ways, and most importantly, you use that insight to set **aligned intentions,** intentions that do not come from pressure or fear, but from clarity and purpose. These are heart-led intentions that help you move forward in a way that feels true to who you are now, not who you used to be. Reflection is not just about looking back. It is about looking within, and from there, stepping into the next chapter with grounded wisdom, emotional depth, and an open heart. This is the moment where your journey becomes part of you, woven into your being, carried forward not as memory, but as transformation.

The Neuroscience Of Reflection: How Pausing Strengthens Neural Integration

In a world that urges you to keep moving, stay productive, and push forward, choosing to pause might feel uncomfortable, or even unnecessary. However, neuroscience, like your heart, knows the truth: **reflection is not a luxury, it**

is a biological and emotional necessity. When you pause to reflect, you are not just thinking about your experiences, you are changing your brain. You are helping it integrate the stories you have lived, the emotions you have felt, and the growth you have undergone. This process is called **neural integration**, and it is essential for lasting healing and transformation.

What is Happening in Your Brain When You Reflect?

When you pause to reflect, powerful processes unfold within your brain. You engage the **prefrontal cortex**, the region responsible for self-awareness, emotional regulation, empathy, and future planning. This is where you begin to step outside of autopilot, observing your thoughts and feelings instead of being ruled by them. Reflection strengthens your ability to choose how you respond, rather than being swept away by old patterns. At the same time, the **default mode network (DMN)** becomes active. This interconnected system allows you to revisit memories, explore meaning, and imagine new possibilities. It is here that your brain weaves together past experiences with present insight, helping you see connections that may have been hidden in the busyness of daily life. When you reflect, your brain is literally rewiring itself. Neural pathways associated with mindfulness, compassion, and perspective-taking grow stronger. Stress pathways begin to quiet, and your ability to regulate emotions improves. Over time, this repeated practice builds resilience, clarity, and wisdom. In essence, reflection allows your brain to integrate experience into understanding. You begin to link what you have felt with what you have learned, bridging the gap between who you once were and who you are becoming. This is not just a mental process, it is the deepening of your emotional intelligence. You are learning to respond with clarity, compassion, and intention, instead of reacting from fear or habit. Reflection is where growth takes root. It is where insight turns into transformation, and where the wisdom of your journey becomes part of the person you are choosing to be.

Creating Coherence: The Power of Neural Integration

Throughout this journey, you have lived many different moments, some filled with joy, some marked by pain, and others still unfolding in quiet ways. Left unexamined, these experiences can remain fragmented, scattered across your inner landscape like unconnected puzzle pieces. Reflection is the practice that gathers them together, weaving them into a meaningful whole. When you pause to reflect, you bring your **thoughts, feelings, memories, and**

insights into alignment. This process is known as **neural integration**, the harmonising of different parts of your brain so that your inner world becomes coherent rather than chaotic. Instead of being pulled in many directions by conflicting emotions or scattered memories, you begin to see the larger picture of your own growth. Neuroscience shows that integration strengthens the connections between your prefrontal cortex (awareness and regulation), your limbic system (emotions and memory), and your body's felt sense of experience. This creates a state of **coherence**, where your mind, heart, and body work in synergy rather than opposition. The result is not only greater clarity but also greater resilience, you can hold complexity without being overwhelmed. Through reflection, your story shifts from a collection of isolated events to a narrative infused with **meaning and wisdom**. You begin to see patterns, lessons, and truths that may have been hidden in the noise. This understanding deepens your self-trust: you recognise that even the painful moments have shaped you, and that every step has been part of your becoming. Coherence is not about perfection; it is about wholeness. It is about allowing all parts of your experience, light and shadow, triumph and struggle to belong, and to find their place within the larger mosaic of your life. When you practice reflection, you give yourself the gift of integration. From this grounded sense of wholeness, you can move forward with greater compassion, stability, and courage.

What Happens When You Pause?

When you pause, even for a few breaths, you create a profound shift within your body and mind. Instead of running on autopilot or being carried by stress and distraction, your nervous system gently transitions into its **parasympathetic state**, the *"rest-and-digest"* response. This is the physiological space of **calm, safety, and restoration**. In this state, your heart rate slows and steadies, your muscles release tension, and your breath naturally deepens. These simple yet powerful changes signal to your body that you are safe, allowing your mind to soften its grip on survival mode. As your inner world quiets, your brain becomes more receptive to insight, creativity, and self-awareness. Science shows that during a pause, the **coherence between your heart and brain increases**. Instead of operating in conflict, these two powerful centres of intelligence begin to synchronise. Your heart sends signals of steadiness to your brain, helping you regulate emotions, while your brain supports clear thinking and balanced perspective. You literally become more attuned, able to listen with compassion, feel with clarity, and think with presence. Pausing also allows your **default mode network**, the part of the brain responsible for reflection, self-understanding, and meaning-making, to gently awaken. This is why moments of silence often bring sudden clarity, creative ideas, or the memory of something important you had overlooked. On a deeper level, pausing is an act of alignment. It reconnects you to the present moment, where your body, mind, and spirit can finally work together rather than pulling in different directions. You become more grounded in your truth, more open to possibility, and more aligned with your heart's quiet wisdom. The pause does not need to be long, a single mindful breath can be enough to shift you from reactivity into awareness. Over time, the more you practice pausing, the more you train your nervous system to find safety, your mind to find clarity, and your heart to find presence.

You Are the Integration

Reflection is not just something you practice, it is something you embody. It is not an activity separate from your life, but the very process through which you become who you truly are. Reflection is the meeting point of your **emotional growth and neurological transformation**, where your experiences, insights, and feelings weave themselves into wisdom. When you pause and reflect, you create the conditions for integration. You are not merely collecting lessons, you are allowing them to sink deeper, to shape the way you see yourself and the way you show up in the world. Every insight, every tear, every moment of joy becomes a thread, woven into the fabric of your becoming. Reflection is how you turn experiences into meaning, challenges into resilience, and knowledge into embodied truth. So, the next time you feel the urge to keep pushing forward, chasing the next goal or rushing through the moment, remember this: **the pause is powerful**. Growth does not only happen in action; it blossoms in stillness. It is in the quiet spaces of reflection that your transformation takes root.

- **In the stillness, you are healing.** Your nervous system recalibrates, your emotions soften, and your body remembers safety.

- **In the reflection, you are rewiring.** Your brain forms new pathways of clarity, resilience, and compassion.

- **In the awareness, you are becoming whole.** You no longer split yourself between past and future, doubt and desire, you come home to the present, to yourself.

Integration is not a final destination but a way of living. It is the art of carrying your lessons into each breath, each choice, each connection. This is how your heart becomes unbound, not in grand gestures, but in simple, steady moments of return. One breath. One insight. One pause at a time.

Reflection As A Tool For Long-Term Emotional Growth And Heart-Led Decision-Making

Reflection is not simply a backward glance, it is a powerful tool that shapes your future. When you take time to pause and reflect, you do more than revisit your experiences, you activate your inner wisdom. You begin to see your journey through the lens of growth, not just memory, and that shift is what transforms reflection into a lifelong resource for emotional intelligence and heart-led living.

Emotional Growth Through Honest Reflection

Every emotional experience you have, joy, sorrow, fear, excitement, carries within it a lesson, a message, a whisper from your heart, but these insights often go unnoticed in the busyness of your life. Reflection gives you the space to return, to feel, to understand. It invites you to explore not just *what happened*, but *how it shaped you*. Through regular, compassionate reflection, you begin to identify your emotional patterns: how you respond under pressure, what triggers your inner critic, where your wounds still ache, and what opens your heart. This awareness does not come from judging yourself, it comes from witnessing yourself with honesty and care. This is how emotional maturity is born, not by avoiding your feelings, but by understanding them and choosing to grow from them. Over time, this process strengthens your emotional resilience, your capacity for empathy, and your ability to meet life with grace rather than reactivity. Your heart becomes wiser, your responses more intentional, and your self-trust more deeply grounded.

Heart-Led Decision-Making Begins with Inner Clarity

When you reflect with presence and purpose, you begin to align your decisions not with fear or habit, but with your **core values**, your **authentic self**, and the quiet knowing of your heart. This is the essence of heart-led decision-making: choosing based on what feels true, not just what seems expected. Reflection helps you ask the deeper questions:

- *Is this choice in alignment with who I am becoming?*

- *Am I acting from fear or from freedom?*

- *Will this decision bring me closer to the life I want to live?*

These questions guide you away from autopilot and toward **conscious, values-based action**. They help you make decisions that nourish your emotional wellbeing and deepen your integrity, not just in moments of ease, but in times of challenge and change. When you learn to trust the wisdom that arises in reflection, you begin to lead your life from within. Your choices become anchored, not just reactive. Your direction becomes heart-led, not externally driven.

Reflection Is the Bridge

Reflection is the bridge between your past and your potential. It is where healing becomes growth, where insight becomes action, and where experience becomes wisdom. The more you return to yourself through reflection, the more empowered and aligned your life becomes. Let reflection be your quiet superpower, the space where you meet yourself honestly, listen deeply, and choose your next step not from pressure, but from purpose. *This is how you become emotionally free. This is how your heart becomes your compass. This is how you live, not just wisely, but fully.*

Differentiating Rumination From Healthy Contemplation

Reflection is one of the most powerful tools you have for emotional healing and growth, but not all forms of looking inward are helpful. To truly free your heart, it is important to recognise the difference between **rumination** and **healthy contemplation**. While both involve thinking about your experiences, only one leads to peace, insight, and transformation.

What Happens When You Ruminate?

When you ruminate, your thoughts loop in circles. You replay events, question yourself endlessly, or fixate on what went wrong. Rumination tends to be:

- Harsh, self-critical, or full of regret

- Focused on the past without direction

- Driven by fear, guilt, or anxiety

- Emotionally draining and stuck

In this state, you are not learning from the past, you are reliving it. Rumination keeps you emotionally stuck, reinforcing patterns of self-doubt and often worsening your mental and physical wellbeing. It feels heavy, stagnant, and closed.

What Does Healthy Contemplation Look Like?

When you engage in healthy contemplation, you reflect with purpose and compassion. You ask gentle, curious questions like:

- *What am I learning about myself through this?*

- *How did this moment shape me?*

- *What do I need to release or forgive?*

Contemplation invites you to notice without judgment. You begin to understand, integrate, and honour your emotional truth. You give space to both pain and growth, and from that space, you create meaningful direction forward. Contemplation brings movement. It opens your heart, rather than closing it down.

Why This Matters on Your *Unbound* Journey

Throughout this program, you have touched many deep and tender parts of yourself. You have remembered, released, and awakened, but now, in reflection, you are invited to tread gently. How you look back matters as much as what you look back on. Reflection can be a doorway to wisdom or a trap of self-criticism. The difference lies in the posture of your heart. When you choose to look back with compassion instead of judgment, you begin to see your journey not as a series of flaws or mistakes, but as the sacred unfolding of becoming. Every choice, even the ones you wish had been different, carries a lesson that has shaped your growth. Every moment of vulnerability has been an initiation into greater strength and authenticity. Reflection, then, is not about perfecting your past but about honouring the wisdom it has given you. This is the heart's invitation: to release the loop of rumination and step into the clarity of contemplation. Rumination keeps you circling the same pain, replaying the same doubts. Contemplation, on the other hand, invites you to pause, listen, and ask, *What is this moment here to teach me?* In doing so, you transform memory into meaning and struggle into strength.

By reflecting in this way, you give yourself the gift of emotional freedom. The past no longer defines you, it informs you. You learn to carry its lessons lightly, with grace, allowing them to guide rather than weigh you down. In this process, trust in your inner wisdom deepens. You begin to see that your heart has always been whispering the way forward, and that whisper becomes your compass. This is why reflection matters. It anchors your transformation. It helps you embody your insights, integrate your healing, and align with the deepest truth of who you are. In choosing reflection over rumination, you step into the freedom of living from your heart, not your history.

A Gentle Check-In

The next time your thoughts pull you into the past, pause and ask yourself: *"Am I looping, or am I listening?"* If you are looping, soften. If you are listening, keep going, with kindness. Let your reflection be a safe space, not a battleground. This is how your heart becomes unbound, not by repeating the pain, but by meeting it with understanding and choosing to grow from it.

Integrating Past Lessons To Build Future Resilience

Resilience does not mean you have never been hurt. It means you have allowed your pain to teach you something, and you have chosen to grow from it. As you reach this final stage of the *Unbound* journey, you are invited to reflect not just on what you have been through, but on **how you have emerged**. The process of *integration* is what transforms experience into strength, and memory into wisdom.

You have faced emotions, truths, and turning points, some of them uncomfortable, all of them meaningful, but reflection is what allows you to hold these moments in your hands and ask, *"What did this teach me? Who have I become because of it?"* This is how you build resilience, not by forgetting the past, but by **weaving it into your foundation**.

Why Integration Matters

There have been moments when you felt heavy with uncertainty, weighed down by doubt, or caught in the tangle of old patterns, and there have also been moments when your heart lifted, when your breath deepened, when you touched a strength or softness within you that surprised you. Both are part of your journey. Both hold meaning. If you rush past these experiences, they scatter like fragments of a story left unfinished. They remain unanchored, unable to guide or sustain you, but when you pause to reflect, something powerful begins to happen: the fragments start to form a whole. You begin to notice the threads that connect your pain to your healing, your challenges to your growth, your fears to your courage. Integration is not about erasing the past or fixing every wound. It is about honouring what has been, reclaiming the lessons, and recognising that nothing was wasted. The heartbreaks, the breakthroughs, the struggles, and the joys all become woven into a tapestry that tells the truth of who you are becoming. To integrate is to gather your pieces and place them gently where they belong, not tucked away in shame or regret, but honoured as part of your strength. It is the process of seeing yourself clearly, of realising that your journey has shaped you in ways that are both tender and resilient. When you integrate, you no longer live in fragments. You stand whole. You carry your past not as a burden, but as a foundation. You live with greater clarity, steadiness, and compassion for yourself and others. Integration matters because it transforms experience into wisdom, wounds into gifts, and moments into meaning.

Resilience as a Heart-Led Practice

When you integrate your lessons, you do more than remember, you strengthen the foundation of your being. Each reflection becomes a brick laid with intention, building a steadiness that holds you even in life's storms. You begin to trust that no matter what unfolds, you have the capacity to move through it. Why? Because you already have. You have faced challenges, felt the ache of uncertainty, and still found a way forward. That memory lives in your heart as evidence of your strength. True resilience is not about armouring yourself or hardening against life. It is not the absence of pain, but the presence of trust. It is a soft, steady knowing that you are capable of meeting what comes with awareness, grace, and compassion. This heart-led resilience does not reject struggle, it recognises it as part of the path. Every challenge becomes an invitation to return to your breath, your truth, and your deeper self. With each cycle of falling and rising, reflecting and realigning, you expand your inner capacity. You begin to see your past not as a series of wounds that broke you, but as experiences that shaped and built you. What once felt heavy becomes a teacher. What once felt overwhelming becomes a reminder of how far you have come. Resilience, then, is not just survival, it is transformation. It is the gentle, powerful truth that you are not defined by what happened to you, but by how you continue to meet life with heart.

From Reflection to Future Readiness

When you pause to reflect, you are not only honouring your past, you are preparing your future. Each moment of awareness plants a seed for the life you are still creating. The insights you have gathered, the emotions you have navigated, and the truths you have reclaimed now become guiding lights for the path ahead. Reflection transforms what once felt heavy into wisdom you can carry with strength and grace. As you carry these lessons forward, you begin to make more grounded, heart-aligned choices. You recognise the difference between a reaction based in fear and a response anchored in clarity. Old patterns lose their hold because you have taken the time to understand their roots, and in that understanding, you free yourself from repeating them. Future readiness does not mean predicting or controlling what comes, it means cultivating the inner stability to meet whatever arises. You begin to live from trust: trust in yourself, trust in your resilience, trust in the wisdom of your journey. Decisions flow not from urgency or doubt, but from alignment with your deepest values. This is what long-term emotional resilience looks like: a life guided by reflection, not reaction. It is the quiet confidence that you can move through change without losing yourself. It is the freedom to create your future with intention rather than habit, and it is the courage to step forward knowing that your heart already carries everything you need.

<u>Your Journey Is Your Strength</u>

Everything you have experienced, every stumble, every breakthrough, every tender or painful moment, has shaped you into who you are today. Yet it is not the challenges alone that define you, but the way you have chosen to meet them. It is your willingness to reflect, to integrate, and to grow that transforms life's raw material into wisdom. This is where your true resilience is born. Your strength does not come from having an easy path. It comes from the moments when you were tested and still chose to rise. It comes from the courage to soften instead of harden, to seek understanding instead of shutting down, to open your heart even when fear told you to close it. These choices, repeated again and again, are what make you whole. Let this be your reminder: you are not defined by what you have gone through. You are defined by how you have carried those experiences, how you have learned from them, and how you have allowed them to shape a deeper compassion within you. The scars you carry are not signs of weakness but symbols of strength, evidence that you have endured, healed, and kept moving forward. This is how your heart becomes unbound: not because it has never broken, but because it has been pieced back together with wisdom, truth, and love. Every fracture has become a window for light. Every loss has made space for growth. Every moment of reflection has pulled you closer to your authentic self. Your journey is not just a story of survival, it is a story of transformation, and as you step forward, you carry within you the undeniable truth: **you are strong, not in spite of your journey, but because of it.**

Gratitude And Forward-Vision As Tools For Inner Alignment

Gratitude and forward-vision are more than feel-good practices, they are powerful tools for aligning with your heart's truth. Together, they help you close the chapter behind you with grace and open the one ahead with purpose. Gratitude anchors you in the present, while forward-vision calls you toward your next becoming. When used together, they create a bridge between where you have been and where you are ready to go. This is inner alignment: the state where your emotions, values, choices, and direction are all moving in the same rhythm, **the rhythm of your heart.**

Gratitude Grounds You in Truth

Gratitude is not about ignoring your pain or pretending everything has been easy. It is about choosing to acknowledge the gifts within the journey, *especially* the unexpected ones. When you pause to name what you are grateful for, even in the midst of uncertainty or challenge, you activate a shift in perspective. Gratitude reminds you of your growth. It reconnects you with the people, moments, lessons, and even struggles that shaped your becoming. It turns experience into meaning and scarcity into sufficiency. When you thank the path you have walked, you create the emotional space to move forward without resentment or regret.

Forward-Vision Awakens Possibility

Once you have honoured what has been, you are more open to imagining what could be. Forward-vision invites you to dream beyond your past limitations, to see with the eyes of your heart, not your fear. It is the act of asking, *"What kind of life do I want to live now? Who am I ready to become?"* This visioning is not about rigid goal-setting or chasing perfection. It is about clarity. It is about listening inward and aligning with the values that matter most to you. Forward-vision helps you make choices not out of obligation, but out of alignment, with your purpose, your healing, and your inner truth.

Your Journey Is Your Strength

Everything you have experienced, every stumble, every breakthrough, every tender moment, has shaped you, but it is your willingness to reflect, to integrate, and to *grow from it all* that unlocks your true resilience. Let this be your reminder: you are not defined by what you have gone through. You are defined by what you have *learned*, *integrated*, and *risen from*. This is how your heart becomes unbound, stronger not because it has never broken, but because it has been pieced back together with wisdom, truth, and love.

When Gratitude Meets Vision, You Realign With Your Heart

Gratitude without vision can keep you stuck in comfort. Vision without gratitude can leave you restless and unsatisfied, but when you bring the two together, you create powerful alignment: You recognise the sacredness of where you have been.

- You honour who you are now.

- And you choose where you are going, with intention, not reaction.

- This is what it means to live *from the heart*. You stop running from the past or racing toward the future. Instead, you *align*, step by step, with a life that reflects your wholeness.

Let Gratitude and Vision Guide You Forward

As you complete this stage of your *Unbound* journey, let gratitude be your foundation and vision your guide. Look back with tenderness. Look forward with trust, and in between, return to your breath, your truth, your heart. *You do not need to have all the answers. You just need to stay aligned with what matters. Let that be enough to take the next step.* This is how you walk forward, grateful for the past, open to the future, and fully alive in the now. This is how your heart stays unbound.

"Mirror of the Heart" Reflection Meditation (Guided Practice)

I invite you to listen to the Reflection meditation and as you listen to the meditation I would ask you to revisit one moment from this program where you felt the light, your heart felt most open, connected, or free.

Reflection After Meditation:

- What emotions arose as you revisited that moment of openness and freedom?

- How does your body respond when you hold that memory in your awareness right now?

- What gentle reminder can you carry with you to return to this feeling when life becomes heavy?

- What did that moment teach you?

- How will you protect and grow that light moving forward?

Integration Exercise – Heart Anchoring

After the meditation, place both hands over your heart. Take three slow breaths, and on each inhale, silently repeat: *"I welcome this light."* On each exhale, silently repeat: *"I release what dims it."*

Then, write down one word or phrase that captures the essence of that moment of light (e.g., *peace, belonging, joy, courage*).

Keep this word somewhere visible, on a card, a journal page, or your phone, as an anchor to return to when you need to remember your heart's freedom.

Case Study Discussion: Nathan's Journey

(The following is a transcript of a conversation I (Dr John McSwiney) had with Nathan.)

"Heart Unbound: The Ultimate 28–Day Heart Connection Challenge' is a significant chapter in my life's story. Prior to this journey, it is fair to say that I was a stranger to my own heart. The first day of the challenge, I was skeptical. Could connecting with my heart really change my life? The first day of the challenge was a revelation. I was guided to close my eyes, take a deep breath, and listen to the whispers of my heart. It was a simple act, but it felt like the start of an extraordinary voyage. Each day, I delved deeper into the program's practices, exploring the uncharted territories of my emotions. I committed to the daily practices and something remarkable started happening. Breathing exercises helped me relax, reducing stress and bringing peace. With every guided meditation, I felt more in tune with my emotions and began to understand the power of vulnerability. Days turned into weeks, and I found myself expressing empathy, forging deeper connections with friends and family. The newfound creativity I discovered astonished me. It was not just a program; it was a profound journey of self–discovery. I was a pragmatist, a workaholic who rarely paused to reflect on my inner self. Stress and deadlines ruled my existence, leaving little room for emotions or personal growth. Through the soothing meditations and introspective exercises, I learned to embrace my vulnerability and connect with my true self. I began to understand that strength lay not in suppressing my emotions but in acknowledging them. With time, I found myself extending this understanding to others, forging profound connections and nurturing empathy in my relationships. As the 28–day challenge drew to a close, I marveled at the person I was changing into. I had transformed from a stoic corporate machine into someone who embraced life's complexities, cherished relationships, and reveled in the beauty of the present moment. 'Heart Unbound' showed me how to unlock my heart's potential, making me a more authentic and fulfilled version of myself. I couldn't help but smile, knowing that this program had changed my life in ways I could never have imagined. The 28–day challenge concluded, but its impact endures. I wake each morning with a heart that beats in harmony with my deepest desires. I have unearthed a wellspring of creativity that colours my world with beauty and purpose. I have grown from a closed–off soul into an authentic, open–hearted individual who revels in life's intricacies. I have spent time with Dr John and have learned to go deeper into my heart and have realised that this is a lifestyle choice, and it is one that I have loved embracing. I would encourage anybody reading this to really embrace this journey because it will change your life.

Reflection Exercise: Nathan's Journey

Here are four profound and reflective questions inspired by Nathan's story to help you engage with your own journey of reflection:

1. **In what ways have you come home to yourself during this journey, and how has connecting with your heart shifted the way you see your life, relationships, or purpose?** Like Nathan, you may have begun this journey uncertain or guarded, how has your heart responded as you have opened it day by day?

2. **What past version of yourself do you now hold with greater understanding or compassion, and what strengths have emerged as you have embraced vulnerability and self-awareness?** Consider how your emotional landscape has evolved. Where have you softened? Where have you grown stronger?

3. **What moments during the journey surprised you, moments of insight, connection, or inner stillness that you did not expect?** Think about the days that felt like turning points. What happened, and how did they move you?

4. **As you look ahead, how will you carry this heart-centred way of living into your daily life, and what intentions will guide the next chapter of your journey?** Nathan discovered that this was more than a program, it was a way of being. What will your heart ask of you now?

Each of these questions is designed to help you, like Nathan, integrate the transformation you have experienced and move forward with intention, awareness, and an unbound heart.

Affirmations For You – (Heart Whispers)

Affirmations have the power to quiet the noise of doubt, open the doorway to self-trust, and draw you back into the wisdom of your heart. When practiced daily, they nurture an inner dialogue based in love and truth, helping you live each day more aligned with who you truly are. I invite you to repeat silently or write:

- I listen to my heart's whispers and follow its guidance.

- I embrace vulnerability and allow my heart to lead the way.

- I nurture my self–compassion and connect with my heart.

- I choose to align with my heart's deepest desires and values.

- I practice gratitude to open my heart to the abundance of life.

- I trust the wisdom of my heart to guide me towards a fulfilling and authentic life.

Integration Circle & Future Intentions

This practice is designed to help you anchor the wisdom of your journey and carry it into your daily life with clarity and intention. Integration is where transformation takes root, not just in your mind, but in your heart, relationships, and choices. Whether you are in a group or reflecting individually, take your time with this process:

1. **Identify Three Key Learnings**: Pause and consider the most powerful lessons you have received during this program. These may be insights about yourself, truths about how you connect with others, or practices that have shifted your perspective. Write them down clearly and concisely, as if you are creating guideposts to return to.

2. **Share Two Emotional Shifts**: Reflect on the inner changes you have felt along the way. Perhaps you moved from fear to trust, from tension to calm, from loneliness to connection, or from self-criticism to self-compassion. Sharing these shifts, with yourself in writing, or with others if in a circle, helps you honour your growth and embody the change.

3. **Set One Heartfelt Intention Moving Forward**: Ask your heart: *"What do I want to carry into my next chapter?"* This intention may be simple yet profound, such as *"I choose presence," "I honour my heart daily,"* or *"I live with openness and courage."* Anchor it in words that feel alive and real for you.

4. **Record and Revisit**: Write your reflections on a *"Heart Integration Commitment"* card or in your journal. Place this somewhere you will see it often, a reminder on your desk, a note in your wallet, or a page you return to weekly. As you revisit your reflections, allow them to evolve, deepening your sense of alignment and accountability.

Optional Closing Ritual: To seal the circle or personal reflection, place your hand over your heart, take three slow breaths, and silently repeat: *"I carry my learnings. I honour my shifts. I walk with intention."*

Closing Reflection

You have walked a sacred path, through breath, gratitude, stillness, courage, creativity, vulnerability, and now, reflection. This is not the end of your journey. It is a quiet threshold. A moment to pause, gather what you have learned, and honour the growth that has unfolded within you. Reflection invites you to hold your story with gentleness. To see not only what happened, but *how you have changed.* It is in this space that healing becomes wisdom, and experience becomes purpose. You are not who you were when you began. You carry more insight, more softness, more strength. Through reflection, you begin to integrate all the lessons, all the emotions, all the heartbeats of this journey, and you begin to see yourself more clearly. So take this moment to honour yourself. Not for being perfect, but for showing up. For feeling deeply. For choosing truth. For choosing your heart. As you step into whatever comes next, carry this with you: *Your story matters. Your heart knows the way, and every pause to reflect is a powerful step forward.* Let this final part not be a closing, but a deepening. Let reflection be the thread that ties your inner work to your outer world, and let your unbound heart continue to lead you, home to yourself, again and again.

Transformation Loves Momentum

Do not stop now. Momentum is a sacred energy, once it moves, let it carry you. Another Unbound chapter, book, or online experience will help you keep that energy alive – **www.timetotransform.world**

NEXT

A Final Word: Becoming an Unbound Organisation

This book began with a simple yet demanding proposition: that organisations do not thrive through systems, strategies, or structures alone, but through the quality of human experience that lives within them. While policies, processes, and performance metrics have their place, they are ultimately expressions of something deeper, the way people think, feel, relate, and respond under pressure. What you have explored across these pages is not a collection of discrete wellbeing tools, diversity initiatives, or organisational reset strategies to be selectively applied. Rather, this book offers an integrated way of reimagining how organisations function, lead, and endure in an era defined by complexity, rapid change, and increasing human strain. It invites a shift away from fragmented interventions and toward a coherent, human-centred operating philosophy. An unbound organisation is not defined by the absence of pressure, challenge, or uncertainty. Complexity is inevitable. Competing priorities, constrained resources, and heightened expectations are realities of modern organisational life. What distinguishes an unbound organisation is not what it avoids, but how it meets these conditions.

An unbound organisation meets pressure with presence rather than panic. It meets uncertainty with discernment rather than reactivity. It meets challenge with collective capacity rather than individual depletion. At its core, an unbound organisation understands that sustainable performance, genuine inclusion, and long-term contribution do not arise from relentless output or control-based leadership. They emerge when people are supported to function as whole human beings, physically regulated, emotionally aware, psychologically safe, and ethically grounded. People are not treated merely as roles to be filled, outputs to be maximised, or resources to be consumed, but as living systems whose wellbeing directly shapes organisational health. The journey through this book has therefore been intentionally structured across three interconnected domains: **Workplace Wellbeing Reset, Diversity and Inclusion Through the Heart**, and **The Corporate Reset**. These are not separate programs competing for attention, nor sequential initiatives to be implemented and completed. Together, they form a coherent and reinforcing pathway, one that moves organisations from regulation to relationship, and from clarity to contribution.

The **Workplace Wellbeing Reset** establishes the conditions for human functioning. It recognises that without physiological and emotional regulation, no amount of strategic intent can be sustained. The **Diversity and Inclusion Through the Heart** deepens this foundation by addressing how people relate to themselves and one another, recognising that inclusion is lived emotionally before it is enacted structurally. The **Corporate Reset** then creates space for renewal, reflection, and realignment, ensuring that organisations do not carry forward outdated practices, unresolved tensions, or misaligned priorities. Together, these three domains form a living system rather than a checklist. They reflect a progression from stabilising individuals, to strengthening relationships, to renewing organisational purpose and coherence. When integrated, they enable organisations not merely to function, but to evolve, responsively, ethically, and sustainably. This is the work of becoming unbound.

Part One Revisited: Workplace Wellbeing Reset

The first part of this book returned organisational attention to a truth that is frequently acknowledged in theory but rarely honoured in practice: wellbeing is not an optional addition to work, it is the operating system upon which all meaningful performance depends. Without it, even the most sophisticated strategies falter. With it, clarity, creativity, and resilience become possible. In many organisations, wellbeing is addressed only after strain has become visible, when absenteeism rises, engagement drops, or burnout can no longer be ignored. The Workplace Wellbeing Reset challenges this reactive mindset. It reframes wellbeing not as a remedial response, but as a foundational condition that must be intentionally designed and protected if organisations are to remain viable in the long term. Through the practices of breathing, nutrition, relaxation, and grounding, this section invited a return to the most basic requirements of human functioning. These modules were not concerned with optimisation or acceleration. They did not promise greater output through greater effort. Instead, they focused on restoring regulation, physiological, emotional, and attentional, so that people can meet the demands of work with steadiness rather than strain. Breathing reminds us that clarity begins in the body, not the calendar. Nutrition reframed energy as something to be sustained rather than extracted. Relaxation challenged the assumption that constant vigilance equates to commitment. Grounding reconnected individuals to presence, stability, and perspective in environments that often reward speed over awareness. Taken together, these practices revealed a quiet but profound insight: when people are dysregulated, organisations suffer. Stress accumulates silently, narrowing perception and compressing decision-making. Attention fragments, relationships strain, and small pressures begin to feel overwhelming. Over time, this erosion manifests as disengagement, conflict, burnout, and attrition, not because people lack capability, but because the system has exceeded their capacity.

An organisation that neglects wellbeing does not become more efficient. It becomes brittle. It may continue to function for a time, but its tolerance for uncertainty diminishes, and its ability to adapt weakens. In contrast, the Workplace Wellbeing Reset reframes calm not as complacency, but as a strategic asset. Calm creates space for reflection. Regulation supports discernment. Presence enables better judgment under pressure. What this part of the book ultimately asks of leaders and organisations is maturity. It calls for a shift away from extractive cultures that prize endurance at any cost, and toward environments that support sustainable energy, attentional clarity, and human dignity. This is not about reducing expectations or lowering standards. It is about recognising that sustained excellence cannot be built on exhaustion. When people are supported to breathe fully, nourish themselves appropriately, rest without guilt, and remain grounded amidst complexity, the organisation gains something invaluable. It gains people who can stay steady in uncertainty, think clearly in moments of challenge, and respond with intention rather than reflex. It gains resilience that is not forced, but inherent. This is where an unbound organisation begins, not with grand strategy statements or cultural slogans, but with regulated human systems capable of meeting complexity without collapse.

Part Two Revisited: Diversity and Inclusion Through the Heart

The second part of this book deepened the work by shifting attention from individual regulation to relational awareness. While wellbeing establishes the internal conditions for human functioning, inclusion determines how you experience one another within shared spaces. Diversity and inclusion, when approached through the heart, move beyond policy compliance, representation metrics, and formal statements of intent. They enter the realm of lived experience, how it feels to belong, to be seen, and to be respected in everyday organisational life. Many organisations invest considerable effort in diversity frameworks, training programs, and reporting structures, yet continue to struggle with inclusion at a cultural level. This section addresses why. The challenge is rarely a lack of policy. More often, it is the presence of unexamined assumptions, emotional defensiveness, and self-protective behaviours that operate beneath conscious awareness. These dynamics shape interactions long before formal processes are engaged. Through mirror work, self-love, kindness, and compassion, this part of the book explored the internal origins of inclusion. Mirror work invited you to confront your own self-perceptions, biases, and inherited narratives. Self-love challenged the belief that acceptance must be earned through conformity or performance. Kindness and compassion reframed interaction as an ethical choice rather than a personality trait. Together, these practices revealed an essential truth: inclusion begins internally before it can be expressed externally. People who have not learned to meet themselves with honesty and care often struggle to extend the same to others. In contrast, people who are grounded in self-acceptance are more capable of listening without defensiveness, engaging without threat, and remaining open in the presence of difference.

An unbound organisation understands that inclusion is not achieved by erasing difference or insisting on sameness. It is achieved by meeting difference with curiosity, dignity, and respect. This requires emotional literacy, the capacity to notice discomfort without rushing to justify or withdraw, to sit with unfamiliar perspectives without needing to dominate the conversation, and to engage in dialogue without diminishing yourself or others. The heart-led approach to inclusion recognises that people do not arrive at work as neutral entities. They bring with them histories, identities, experiences of belonging and exclusion, and varying degrees of safety and vulnerability. When these realities are denied or minimised, culture fractures. Silence replaces honesty. Compliance replaces trust. When they are acknowledged and held with care, cultures strengthen. Psychological safety grows not because it is mandated, but because it is felt. This section reframes leadership as a relational responsibility. It asks leaders to look beyond technical competence and consider the emotional climate they create.

Leaders who model self-acceptance make it possible for others to show up more fully. Leaders who respond to difference with curiosity rather than threat signal that belonging is not conditional. The invitation here is for organisations to move beyond tolerance toward genuine connection, and beyond surface-level diversity toward deep inclusion. It is the difference between being allowed to be present and being welcomed as one truly is. In an unbound organisation, people are not required to leave parts of themselves at the door in order to contribute. Difference is not managed as a risk to be mitigated, but recognised as a source of insight, creativity, and collective intelligence. When people feel seen and respected, collaboration deepens, trust strengthens, and the organisation gains access to a broader and more resilient range of human capability.

Part Three Revisited: The Corporate Reset

The final part of this book turned attention toward a moment that many organisations resist but ultimately cannot avoid: the point at which continuing as before is no longer sustainable. The Corporate Reset addressed what becomes possible when an organisation is willing to release what no longer serves it and make space for something more coherent to emerge. Reset, in this context, is not synonymous with upheaval. It is not about dramatic reinvention or discarding everything that has come before. Rather, it is about discernment, the capacity to pause, to look honestly at what is being carried forward, and to decide deliberately what belongs in the future and what does not. This requires courage, not because change is unfamiliar, but because stillness and honesty often are. Modern organisations accumulate weight over time. Practices persist long after their usefulness has faded. Decisions made under past constraints harden into assumptions. Unresolved conflicts linger beneath the surface, shaping behaviour and eroding trust. Grievances remain unspoken, not because they are insignificant, but because addressing them feels inconvenient or risky. Without deliberate reflection, these layers accumulate quietly, obscuring purpose and draining momentum. The Corporate Reset reframes this condition not as failure, but as an invitation. It recognises that organisations, like people, need periods of clearing and renewal if they are to remain alive and responsive. Reset is therefore not about disruption for its own sake. It is about creating space for coherence to return.

The practice of nothingness invited organisations to step out of constant motion and into stillness. In cultures that equate busyness with value, this can feel deeply uncomfortable. Yet without stillness, there is no perspective. Nothingness is not inactivity; it is the deliberate creation of space in which insight can arise and direction can be reassessed. Decluttering extended this principle into organisational structures and processes. It challenged the assumption that progress requires continual addition, more initiatives, more frameworks, more complexity. Instead, it asked what could be simplified, streamlined, or released in service of clarity and focus. Decluttering is an act of respect for attention, energy, and purpose. Forgiveness addressed a dimension of organisational life that is rarely named but widely felt: emotional residue. Past decisions, conflicts, and disappointments leave traces. When these are ignored, they harden into mistrust, cynicism, or quiet disengagement. Forgiveness, in this context, is not about excusing harm or avoiding accountability. It is about releasing the emotional weight that prevents people and systems from moving forward with openness and integrity. Reflection ensured that reset did not become repetition. It created a space for learning to be integrated rather than lost, for experience to be metabolised rather than merely endured. Reflection transforms activity into wisdom. Without it, organisations risk cycling through the same patterns under new labels. Together, these practices enable organisations to move forward without carrying unnecessary weight. They allow renewal to emerge in a grounded and deliberate way, rather than as a reaction to crisis. Reset becomes a strengthening process rather than a destabilising one. An unbound organisation understands that renewal is not a single event or a finite project. It is a cyclical process of pausing, learning, and realigning as conditions change. Leaders who embrace this rhythm cultivate organisations that can adapt without losing their centre, evolve without abandoning their values, and grow without becoming incoherent. This is where legacy begins. Not in slogans, branding, or short-term success, but in the capacity to evolve with integrity. An organisation that can pause, reflect, and reset deliberately leaves behind more than results. It leaves behind a way of working that remains humane, resilient, and meaningful long after specific leaders or strategies have passed.

From Framework to Practice

Across all three parts of this book, one principle has remained constant: meaningful transformation is not achieved through information alone. Insight may open the door, but it is practice that carries the work forward. Without presence, repetition, and sustained commitment, even the most compelling ideas remain abstract, understood intellectually but unrealised in lived experience. The frameworks offered throughout this book were never intended to function as prescriptions or checklists. They are not instructions to be followed mechanically, nor standards against which perfection is measured. Rather, the modules you have encountered are invitations, designed to be lived, revisited, and interpreted within the realities of your organisational context. Their value emerges not from strict adherence, but from thoughtful engagement.

An unbound organisation is not built in a moment, nor is it ever complete. It is shaped incrementally through daily choices that often appear small but carry cumulative weight. How meetings are opened and closed. Whether people are given space to speak without interruption. How conflict is approached, defensively or with curiosity. How leaders respond when pressure rises and expectations tighten. These moments, far more than formal initiatives, define culture. This work asks leaders to broaden their sense of responsibility. It is not enough to be accountable for outcomes alone. Leaders are also responsible for the conditions under which those outcomes are pursued. Conditions shape behaviour. They influence how people show up, how decisions are made, and how strain is absorbed or transferred. When conditions are misaligned, even the most capable people struggle to perform well.

To lead an unbound organisation is to pay attention to these conditions with intention. It means noticing when pace has replaced presence, when urgency has crowded out discernment, or when performance has begun to erode wellbeing and trust. It requires leaders to intervene not only at the level of tasks and targets, but at the level of environment, rhythm, and relational tone. This perspective challenges conventional measures of success. It asks organisations to consider not only what is delivered, but how people experience the process of delivering it. Outcomes achieved through depletion, fear, or disconnection carry hidden costs that eventually surface. In contrast, outcomes achieved through clarity, inclusion, and steadiness strengthen the organisation's capacity for future work. Frameworks provide direction. Practice gives them life.

Looking Forward

As you step beyond the pages of this book, the question is not whether the ideas resonate. Resonance, on its own, changes little. The more enduring question is how these principles will be embodied when conditions are less than ideal. Pressure will return. Competing demands will persist. Complexity will remain a defining feature of organisational life. What changes is not the absence of challenge, but your capacity to meet it differently. The practices explored here are not designed to remove difficulty, but to alter your relationship with it. An unbound organisation is one that remembers its humanity precisely in moments of stress. It does not abandon care in the name of accountability, nor does it avoid accountability in the name of care. It understands that the two are not opposites, but complements. Strength and softness, when held together, create resilience rather than fragility. This is not the end of a journey. It is the point at which responsibility shifts fully into lived practice. The ideas in this book find their meaning not in agreement, but in application. They are expressed in conversations that choose honesty over avoidance, in decisions that consider long-term impact over short-term gain, and in pauses that create space for reflection rather than reaction. The work continues quietly and persistently, in how leaders listen, in how teams recover from strain, in how organisations choose to respond when old patterns resurface. In those moments, the choice remains simple, though not always easy: to lead from habit, or to lead unbound. That choice, repeated over time, is what ultimately shapes an organisation capable of enduring with integrity.

Support

YOU ARE NOT ALONE

A Message for Every Leader, Colleague, and Human Being

As you move through *The Unbound Organisation*, there may be moments when the reflections invite you to pause, moments when the truths you uncover feel heavy, personal, or confronting. That is not failure. That is healing. Transformation, whether personal or organisational, often begins in discomfort. It asks us to face what has been avoided, to feel what has been numbed, and to restore what has been forgotten, but you are not meant to walk this journey alone. Support is not just available, it is your right. The organisations and services listed here exist for one reason: to remind you that help is close, that listening hearts are near, and that even in the hardest moments, you are held within a network of care. Reaching out does not make you weak. It is one of the most courageous acts of self-leadership, the moment you choose connection over isolation, hope over silence, and life over exhaustion. Whether you are a leader navigating pressure, a professional balancing responsibilities, or an individual simply trying to find steadiness in the storm, please know that there is help available. Day or night. Confidential. Free. Take these resources as companions on your journey, not as a sign that something is wrong, but as a reminder that you are human, and in the heart of every healthy organisation is precisely that: humanity. If ever you feel overwhelmed, anxious, or lost in the noise of modern work, please pause. Breathe. Reach out. You are not alone, not in this book, not in this moment, not in this world.

Australia

- **Lifeline Australia** – 13 11 14 (24/7 crisis support and suicide prevention)

- **Beyond Blue** – 1300 22 4636 (24/7 support for anxiety, depression, and mental health)

- **Kids Helpline** – 1800 55 1800 (24/7 for children and young people aged 5–25)

- **Suicide Call Back Service** – 1300 659 467 (24/7 counselling for people at risk of suicide and their carers)

New Zealand

- **Lifeline New Zealand** – 0800 543 354 or free text 4357 (24/7 support)

- **1737, Need to Talk?** – Call or text 1737 (24/7 to talk with a trained counsellor)

- **Youthline** – 0800 376 633 or free text 234 (support for young people)

United States

- **988 Suicide & Crisis Lifeline** – Call or text 988 (24/7 for anyone in crisis)

- **National Alliance on Mental Illness (NAMI) Helpline** – 1-800-950-NAMI (Mon–Fri, 10am–10pm ET)

- **Crisis Text Line** – Text HOME to 741741 (24/7 to connect with a crisis counsellor)

Canada

- **Talk Suicide Canada** – 1-833-456-4566 or text 45645 (24/7 support for suicide prevention)

- **Kids Help Phone** – 1-800-668-6868 or text CONNECT to 686868 (24/7 for young people)

- **Wellness Together Canada** – 1-866-585-0445 (mental health and substance use support, available 24/7)

United Kingdom

- **Samaritans** – 116 123 (24/7 support for anyone in emotional distress)

- **Mind Infoline** – 0300 123 3393 (mental health support and resources)

- **Shout Crisis Text Line** – Text SHOUT to 85258 (24/7 support via text)

Please keep this page close. Just as you turn to your breath, your journal, or your heart, you can also turn to these voices of compassion whenever you need them. Reaching out is a way of returning home to yourself.

A Final Word on Support

Reaching out for help is not a sign of weakness, it is one of the deepest expressions of strength. In workplaces that move fast and expect more, it takes courage to pause and say, *"I need support."* When you make that choice, you are not stepping away from leadership; you are embodying it. You are honouring your heart's call for care, reflection, and renewal.

Your journey through *The Unbound Organisation* is not meant to be travelled alone. Just as organisations thrive through connection, so do the people within them. The same compassion you extend to colleagues and teams must also be extended to yourself. These services and networks of support exist for that reason, to listen, to guide, and to remind you that your wellbeing matters as much as your work.

In moments of exhaustion or uncertainty, reaching out is not a retreat; it is a return, to balance, to humanity, to truth. Each time you take that step, you affirm that strength and vulnerability are not opposites, but partners in resilience.

By asking for help, you model a new kind of leadership, one that breathes, listens, and invites others to do the same. You remind your workplace, and yourself, that care is not a disruption to performance; it is its foundation.

So, if ever the weight feels too heavy, pause. Breathe. Reach out. You are not alone in this journey. You are part of a living, breathing community of people who are learning, like you, to lead Unbound, with courage, with compassion, and with the quiet knowing that no heart, and no organisation, ever truly heals in isolation.

To lead Unbound is to remember that strength is found not in holding everything together, but in knowing when to reach for another hand.

The Unbound Series

References

RESOURCES AND FURTHER READING

The following resources support the themes explored throughout *The Unbound Organisation* Each selection offers additional pathways for deepening self-awareness, compassion, and heart-centred transformation.

Breathing, Relaxation, and Grounding

Kabat-Zinn, J. (2013). *Full catastrophe living: Using the wisdom of your body and mind to face stress, pain, and illness* (Revised ed.). Bantam Books.

Nestor, J. (2020). *Breath: The new science of a lost art.* Riverhead Books.

Brown, R. P., & Gerbarg, P. L. (2012). *The healing power of the breath.* Shambhala Publications.

Gratitude, Kindness, and Compassion

Emmons, R. A. (2013). *Gratitude works: A 21-day program for creating emotional prosperity.* Jossey-Bass.

Gilbert, P. (2009). *The compassionate mind.* Constable & Robinson.

Brown, B. (2021). *Atlas of the heart: Mapping meaningful connection and the language of human experience.* Random House.

Self-Compassion, Identity, and "I Am…"

Neff, K. (2011). *Self-compassion: The proven power of being kind to yourself.* William Morrow.

Di Angelo, M. (Ed.). (2014). *The self-acceptance project: How to be kind and compassionate toward yourself in any situation.* Sounds True.

Meditation and Mindfulness

Harris, S. (2014). *Waking up: A guide to spirituality without religion.* Simon & Schuster.

Siegel, D. J. (2010). *Mindsight: The new science of personal transformation.* Bantam.

Mirror Work and Forgiveness

Enright, R. D. (2015). *8 keys to forgiveness.* W. W. Norton.

Hay, L. (2016). *Mirror work: 21 days to heal your life.* Hay House.

Embodiment, Dance, and Spontaneity

Levy, F. (2005). *Dance movement therapy: A healing art.* American Alliance for Health, Physical Education, Recreation and Dance.

Brown, B. (2019). *The call to courage* [Film]. Netflix.

Nutrition and Nourishment

Hyman, M. (2016). *Eat fat, get thin: Why the fat we eat is the key to lasting weight loss and vibrant health.* Little, Brown Spark.

Lipman, F. (2019). *How to be well: The 6 keys to a happy and healthy life.* Houghton Mifflin Harcourt.

Presence, Nothingness, and Reflection

Rohr, R. (2011). *Falling upward: A spirituality for the two halves of life.* Jossey-Bass.

Tolle, E. (2005). *A new earth: Awakening to your life's purpose.* Penguin.

Neurolinguistic Programming and Focus

Andreas, S., & Faulkner, C. (2008). *NLP: The new technology of achievement* (Revised ed.). HarperCollins.

Newport, C. (2016). *Deep work: Rules for focused success in a distracted world.* Grand Central Publishing.

Creativity: Photography, Drawing, Painting, and Happy Places

Cameron, J. (2016). *The artist's way: A spiritual path to higher creativity* (25th anniversary ed.). Penguin.

Peterson, K. C. (2013). *The mindful photographer.* Rocky Nook.

Nature, Sunrise, and Sunset

Williams, F. (2017). *The nature fix: Why nature makes us happier, healthier, and more creative.* W. W. Norton.

Listening and Heart Communication

Nhat Hanh, T. (2013). *The art of communicating.* HarperCollins.

Chödrön, P. (2019). *Welcoming the unwelcome: Wholehearted living in a brokenhearted world*. Shambhala.

Inner Child Healing and Homecoming

Bradshaw, J. (1990). *Homecoming: Reclaiming and healing your inner child*. Bantam.

Schwartz, R. C. (2021). *No bad parts: Healing trauma and restoring wholeness with the Internal Family Systems model*. Sounds True.

Decluttering and Simplicity

Jay, F. (2016). *The joy of less: A minimalist guide to declutter, organize, and simplify*. Chronicle Books.

Kondo, M. (2014). *The life-changing magic of tidying up: The Japanese art of decluttering and organizing*. Ten Speed Press.

Laughter and Lightness

Cousins, N. (2002). *Anatomy of an illness: As perceived by the patient*. W. W. Norton.

Fry, W. (2014). *Humor: The psychology of living buoyantly*. AuthorHouse.

Leadership, Purpose, and Living Invitations

Sinek, S. (2019). *The infinite game*. Portfolio.

Wheatley, M. (2017). *Who do we choose to be? Facing reality, reclaiming leadership, restoring sanity*. Berrett-Koehler.

Digital Tools and Practice Resources

- Insight Timer – Meditation and breathwork library
- HeartMath Institute – Heart-coherence practices and research
- Mindful.org – Secular mindfulness education and guidance

Recommended Readings for Continued Growth

Cooperrider, David & Whitney, Diana. *Appreciative Inquiry: A Positive Revolution in Change*. Berrett-Koehler, 2005.

Kegan, Robert & Lahey, Lisa. *Immunity to Change: How to Overcome It and Unlock Potential in Yourself and Your Organization*. Harvard Business Press, 2009.

Csikszentmihalyi, Mihaly. *Flow: The Psychology of Optimal Experience*. Harper & Row, 1990.

Siegel, Daniel J. *Aware: The Science and Practice of Presence*. TarcherPerigee, 2018.

Amabile, Teresa & Kramer, Steven. *The Progress Principle: Using Small Wins to*

Ignite Joy, Engagement, and Creativity at Work. Harvard Business Review Press, 2011.

YOUR UNBOUND JOURNEY SERIES

Completing *The Unbound Organisation* marks the beginning of a broader journey within the **Unbound Series**. Each book in the series has a distinct purpose, audience, and depth, while remaining grounded in the same heart-centred philosophy. You are encouraged to choose your next step based on **where you are now**, rather than where you think you should be.

THE UNBOUND SERIES – CORE BOOKS

Heart Unbound: The Ultimate 28 Day Heart Connection Challenge - The gentle, guided, and grounded introduction to the Unbound Series. This book establishes the foundations of presence, self-awareness, emotional regulation, compassion, and integration. It is designed as an accessible entry point for individuals beginning their Unbound journey.

Time to Transform: Living Unbound - The flagship *magnus opus* work of *Time to Transform*. This book forms the philosophical, practical, and conceptual foundation from which all Unbound Series books are drawn. It is a comprehensive handbook for life transformation, integrating heart-centred awareness into everyday living.

The Unbound Leader - Designed for leaders at all levels, this book explores heart-led leadership, emotional intelligence, ethical decision-making, and sustainable performance. It supports leaders seeking to align personal integrity with professional responsibility.

The Unbound Organisation - Focused on building cultures of connection, courage, and compassion, this book supports organisations navigating wellbeing, leadership development, and cultural renewal. It translates Unbound principles into organisational and systemic contexts.

The Unbound Student - Tailored for students and emerging leaders, this book supports self-awareness, resilience, identity formation, and purposeful learning. It provides a grounded framework for personal growth during formative educational and life stages.

Time to Transform: Evidence Companion - Provides the research, theory, and professional assurance that underpin the heart-centred practices of the Unbound Series.

CHOOSING YOUR NEXT STEP

There is no required order in which to read the Unbound Series. Each book stands alone while contributing to a unified body of work. You may choose to continue with deeper personal exploration, leadership development, organisational application, or long-term integration. What matters is **alignment, not progression**.

CONTINUING WITH TIME TO TRANSFORM

The Unbound Series is part of the broader *Time to Transform* ecosystem, which includes programs, facilitated experiences, and sector-specific applications across leadership, education, wellbeing, and organisational development. To explore the full range of books and programs, visit: **www.timetotransform.world**

Your journey does not end here. It continues with clarity, structure, and heart.

CONTINUE YOUR UNBOUND JOURNEY

Every Unbound book is part of a wider ecosystem of transformation:

- Online Courses
- Leadership Programs
- Heart-Connection Challenges
- Student Success Pathways
- Organisational Wellbeing Systems
- Celtic-Inspired Emotional Intelligence Journeys
- Live Events & Workshops
- Author Community & Resources

You are invited to take the next step - deeper, braver, wiser.

All paths begin here:

www.timetotransform.world

THE UNBOUND CALL

There is always a deeper breath to take, a truer story to live, and a wider life waiting for you. When you are ready to walk further, the Unbound Path will meet you there.

CLOSING NOTE

"The future of organisations will not be shaped by control, but by the courage to lead with presence, care, and clarity."

The Unbound Series

Author

ABOUT THE AUTHOR

Dr. John's mission is to guide people around the world to connect with their hearts and embark on a transformative journey of healing, learning, and growing. A pivotal moment in his life occurred shortly after his 22nd birthday when tragedy struck his beloved younger brother, Daniel, was killed by a drunk driver. This devastating loss led Dr. John to shut off his own emotions, inadvertently subjecting himself to many years' of merely existing and surviving without truly embracing life. Through his personal journey, Dr. John learned a profound truth: life's richness unfolds when lived from the heart. He ardently believes in a world where compassion, integrity, respect, and love prevail over fear, negativity, greed, and ego. His commitment is to empower people to envision a life where every day becomes an opportunity for self–transformation, love and growth by reconnecting with their heart.

Dr John is a transformational leader, practising lawyer, author, and Associate Professor of Law and Business. His life's work unites the disciplines of law, leadership, and emotional intelligence to help people and organisations live, lead, and work with authenticity and heart. As the Founder and Managing Director of **Time to Transform**, John has spent over twenty-five years guiding individuals, teams, and leaders across education, government, corporate, and community sectors. His programs and publications help organisations move beyond compliance and performance metrics toward cultures built on trust, wellbeing, and purpose. John's professional journey is distinguished by both executive and academic leadership. He has served as **Director of Technical Training for the Royal Australian Navy, CEO of Haileybury International Beijing**, and **Director of VCAA International**, leading large-scale transformation projects that bridged education, governance, and cultural renewal. Today, as a **practising lawyer and**

Associate Professor, he brings a unique interdisciplinary lens to leadership and organisational development, one grounded in ethics, evidence, and empathy. His *Unbound* framework has evolved into a family of books and programs that blend neuroscience, emotional intelligence, and organisational psychology with real-world application. Each publication is aligned with Australia's highest professional and educational standards, the **Australian Qualifications Framework (AQF)**, **ASQA**, **NSQHS**, and the **APS Capability Framework**, ensuring that transformation is both measurable and meaningful. His works include:

- *Heart Unbound: The Ultimate 28-Day Heart Connection Challenge* – a personal journey into emotional intelligence and connection.

- *Time to Transform: Living Unbound* – thirty chapters of heart-based growth and leadership practices.

- *The Unbound Leader* – a nationally aligned framework for conscious, evidence-based leadership.

- *The Unbound Student* – a resilience and emotional intelligence handbook for emerging leaders.

- *Time to Transform: Living Unbound: The Evidence Companion* – the evidence companion linking wellbeing with professional recognition.

- *The Unbound Organisation* – the next evolution, exploring how workplaces can become living systems that breathe, adapt, and thrive through connection, compassion, and care.

Across his teaching, consulting, and executive practice, John continues to bridge two worlds, the analytical precision of law and the transformative power of the heart. He believes that the future of leadership will belong to those who can hold both, intellect and intuition, structure and soul. Whether working with executives, students, or communities, his message remains consistent: transformation begins not with systems, but with self. When he isn't teaching or writing, you will find John in the ocean, surfing, surf-lifesaving, reflecting, or walking in the quiet stillness that continues to shape his work.

Dr John McSwiney reminds us that true leadership is not about control, but connection, and that the strongest organisations are those built upon trust, integrity, and the courage to lead with heart.

Time To Transform

EMPOWERING LIVES

www.ingramcontent.com/pod-product-compliance
Lightning Source LLC
Chambersburg PA
CBHW032104280326
41933CB00009B/752